Constellation Analysis

KOMPARATISTISCHE BIBLIOTHEK
Comparative Studies Series
Bibliothèque d'Etudes Comparatives

Herausgegeben von
edited by/dirigée par
Jürgen Schriewer

Band/Vol. 26

Zu Qualitätssicherung und Peer Review der vorliegenden Publikation

Die Qualität der in dieser Reihe erscheinenden Arbeiten wird vor der Publikation durch einen externen, von der Herausgeberschaft benannten Gutachter im Double Blind Verfahren geprüft. Dabei ist der Autor der Arbeit dem Gutachter während der Prüfung namentlich nicht bekannt; der Gutachter bleibt anonym.

Notes on the quality assurance and peer review of this publication

Prior to publication, the quality of the work published in this series is double blind reviewed by an external referee appointed by the editorship. The referee is not aware of the author's name when performing the review; the referee's name is not disclosed.

Jason Nicholls

Constellation Analysis

A Methodology for Comparing Syllabus Topics Across Educational Contexts

Edited by Bryan Cunningham

PETER LANG
EDITION

Bibliographic Information published by the Deutsche Nationalbibliothek
The Deutsche Nationalbibliothek lists this publication in
the Deutsche Nationalbibliografie; detailed bibliographic
data is available in the internet at http://dnb.d-nb.de.

Cover photograph: Atlas supporting the globe.
Statue surmounting Frankfurt main station (1883-1888).

Library of Congress Cataloging-in-Publication Data
Nicholls, Jason, 1968-
  Constellation analysis : a methodology for comparing syllabus topics across educational
contexts / Jason Nicholls ; edited by Bryan Cunningham.
    pages cm. – (Komparatistische Bibliothek / Comparative studies series / Bibliotheque
d'etudes comparatives, ISSN 0934-0858 ; Band/vol. 26)
  Summary: "Jason Nicholls' Constellation Analysis is an important contribution to studies in Comparative Education. From a deeply philosophical perspective (drawing in
particular on the work of Hegel, Gadamer and Foucault), the author explores the ways in
which topics in history education may be analysed and compared across international
contexts. Utilising the Second World War as an 'exemplar topic,' the depiction of this
crucial historical event in three countries, Japan, Sweden and England, is subjected to a
highly novel form of interrogation. The book provides the reader not only with important
insights into the nature of the books in use in classrooms across these contexts, but also
into the educational–and indeed broad socio-political–environments beyond the classrooms"–Provided by publisher.
  ISBN 978-3-631-65130-8 (print) – ISBN 978-3-653-04255-9 (ebook) 1. History–Study
and teaching. 2. Comparative education–Methodology. 3. Comparative education–
Philosophy. 4. History–Outlines, syllabi, etc.–Evaluation. 5. History–Textbooks–
Evaluation. 6. World War, 1939-1945–Study and teaching. I. Cunningham, Bryan, 1951-
II. Title.
  D16.25.N75 2014
  907.1–dc23   2014015386

ISSN 0934-0858
ISBN 978-3-631-65130-8 (Print)
E-ISBN 978-3-653-04255-9 (E-Book)
DOI 10.3726/ 978-3-653-04255-9
© Peter Lang GmbH
Internationaler Verlag der Wissenschaften
Frankfurt am Main 2014
All rights reserved.
Peter Lang Edition is an Imprint of Peter Lang GmbH.

Peter Lang – Frankfurt am Main · Bern · Bruxelles · New York ·
Oxford · Warszawa · Wien

This publication has been peer reviewed.

www.peterlang.com

For Lara

Foreword

Jason Nicholls had star quality.

I first met him when he came to Oxford to be interviewed as a D.Phil. applicant. We were immediately struck by the warmth of his personality, by his huge intellect, and by his infectious enthusiasm for the topic he was proposing: a study of representations of the Second World War in the school textbooks of a range of countries. I agreed without hesitation to supervise his research.

From our early discussions following his arrival in Oxford it was clear that the subject of his thesis would be problematic. There was first the question of which countries to include. Germany was conspicuously absent from his plan, but Jason felt that without knowledge of the German language he would not be able to do justice to German sources of all kinds. (He was a proficient linguist, able to cope with material in the languages of the other countries initially proposed in his study.) And there was the problem of the precise focus – comparing textbooks could too easily become a catalogue of descriptive, juxtaposed presentations of the content of the textbooks concerned at all levels of the school curriculum and analysis would be difficult.

I suggested to him that he should instead focus on the problems involved in comparing textbooks, and in particular, history textbooks dealing with the War, and especially in selected countries: in other words, on how to undertake such a comparison. The study would then be essentially a contribution to comparative methodology. Jason's reaction was typical of him: he could immediately see how to shift the focus in this way, and he launched into doing so with unabated enthusiasm. The new focus would clearly build on his proven competence in philosophy, and enable him to write theoretically, which was his undoubted strength.

At the same time as he was delving deeply into sources for his thesis, spending time abroad and making full use of the excellent facilities of the *Georg-Eckert-Institut für Internationale Schulbuchforschung* in Braunschweig, he was also writing for academic journals, and he saw in those publications developing themes and an inter-connectedness that underpinned his approach to comparative studies. He would invite me into his room, where the articles were spread out in grouped sequence, and explain to me how this paper fed into that one and how they both contributed to another. He would often become

9

quite emotional at the sheer elegance of the symbiosis of these studies; he had a strong need for coherence in everything he did, and this became evident in all his writings, and especially in his thesis. In addition to the individual articles he published, he produced for my series *Oxford Studies in Comparative Education* a fine edited collection of papers on textbook research which brought together the work of scholars from the United States, France, Russia, Germany, and the UK (*School History Textbooks Across Cultures; International Debates and Perspectives*, Symposium, 2006). He began too to present papers at international conferences.

Whenever we could, we involved Jason in teaching students on the MSc course in Comparative and International Education. He was a natural teacher, transmitting his enthusiasm through both personal charisma and the authority that came with mastery of his subject. The students loved him. I began to hope that he might one day become my successor in Oxford.

When it came to writing the thesis, Jason chose to interweave the text with observations and thoughts from his experience as a teacher, using material from the extensive diaries he had kept. This was a risky move, since it could have made the study appear perhaps a little too idiosyncratic for his examiners' taste. But, as with everything he did, Jason navigated the path he had decided to take magnificently well, so that the work he submitted was emphatically and unashamedly personal – effectively an account of a journey he had embarked upon long before coming to Oxford and one which led logically to the philosophical/ theoretical approach adopted to his research topic. He wrote elegantly about the way in which his interpretation of Hegel, Gadamer, and Foucault in particular informed his argument. His examiners were impressed, recognising Jason's important contribution to the business of comparison and describing the thesis as 'an exhausting but rewarding read'.

For reasons of space, the editor has removed the more personalised parts of the thesis in this published form, to make it a more compact and conventional study. Readers interested in the individualised tenor of the original can refer to the full text through the services of the Bodleian Library. The text we now have serves as a profound and stimulating contribution to textbook studies in comparative context. It demonstrates Jason's ability to synthesise a mass of complex material and to do so in a clear, accessible, and coherent way that brings out the intrinsic interest of the topic and makes obvious its importance for comparative studies.

Jason Nicholls was indeed a star. Those whom the gods love die young. With his premature passing comparative education lost a future inspirational leader and is much the poorer for it.

David Phillips
St. Edmund Hall, Oxford
September 2013

Editor's Introduction and Acknowledgements

I feel privileged to have been given the task of editing Jason's Nicholls' important contribution to Comparative Education. I see the resulting volume as being not only a highly significant addition to the literature of the field, but as a commemoration, and celebration, of the energy and work of a hugely promising scholar whose life was cut tragically short.[1]

The Oxford University DPhil thesis on which this book is based was completed in 2006; a copy of this is held by the university's Bodleian Library. For readers who wish to read the original work, it can of course be readily accessed by following the library's guidelines. It is a relatively lengthy thesis, of approximately 115000 words. Its title is: The possibilities for comparing a syllabus topic in history across cultures: a contribution to method in comparative enquiry in education.

At the time of his death, Jason had written a proposal for a publication based on his work and was just beginning to seek out an interested publisher. From his files, we know that the title he had in mind was the one I have adopted for the book: Constellation Analysis: A methodology for comparing syllabus topics across educational contexts.

Jason Nicholls was a highly reflective writer, who became almost totally immersed in his research; a dimension of this immersion was the way in which he wished to consistently make explicit his own personal perspectives on his scholarly endeavours, and to offer for the reader the minutiae of his practice as researcher. My work as editor has in large part entailed reducing the proportion of the original thesis that comprised such – often highly intimate – narratives, without in any way rendering the research processes invisible, or distorting the exposition of either his methodology or the ensuing discussion. The most significant reduction in word length is evident in Chapter 1, originally titled: 'Traveller's tales, textbook research and thesis development'. This comprised a lengthy, detailed, account of such important elements of Jason's academic and professional life during the 1990s, and into the early 2000s, as his travels (hence the prominence given to traveller in the above title), his teaching (especially in Hiroshima) and his quest for

---

1   I have included as an Annex the obituary that I was asked to write, and which appeared in the St. Cross College, Oxford University, *Record* (No.28) of 2011.

13

a 'researchable' and fulfilling project on which to base his long-planned doctoral endeavours. He contemplates the options open to him to purposefully weave together his commitment to History, to Comparative Education and – perhaps above all else – the perspectives of certain theorists whose work he had found increasingly stimulating. In his own words, from the Abstract to the original thesis, it eventually brought together

> many years of work and while rooted in the philosophy of Hegel draws on the ideas and concepts of a wide plurality of thinkers. Essentially the thesis is a 'synthesis', developing from my pre-doctoral experiences as an educator in the UK and overseas (thesis) and my critique of comparative textbook research (antithesis). Nicholls, 2006

The 'many years of work' referred to above were not only strongly alluded to in Chapter 1, but in Chapter 9, the conclusion to the original thesis. This is entitled Labour, consciousness and agency, and is again a highly personal and reflective extended statement, this time essentially concerning 'how the thesis came into being'. The labour of the chapter title speaks to the strenuous focused academic endeavour represented by the writing of the series of papers Jason Nicholls published before the award of his doctorate; the consciousness being his evolving understanding and theorisation of an effective approach to researching educational contexts and how the teaching of history takes place within them. It was, then, in connection with Chapter 9, as fascinating as the original version was, that I have also had to fairly substantially reduce its length.

Using the Second World War (which Jason emphatically observed 'continues to raise fundamental questions' (ibid)) as an 'exemplar topic' (ibid), the original thesis, and now this book which has been born out of it, offers not only scholars but also a far wider readership a hugely valuable range of insights – or the 'possibilities' of the thesis title. My overriding aim has been to retain all of these, notwithstanding the need for the editorial work required by the publisher. It is my hope that in this aim I have been successful.

I would like to express my gratitude to both Jason Nicholls' widow, Lara Cancian, and to his mother, Oygun Turner. They have been unfailingly supportive, and patient, over the period during which I have been attempting to complete the editorial work that has tried to shape this book. Lara's contributions to the refinement of this book have been particularly invaluable. Patience has also been much in evidence on the part of Juergen Schriewer, Series Editor, and the staff of Peter Lang, especially Kathrin Kummer and Anja Mueller.

Professors Bob Cowen and David Scott, both of the Institute of Education, University of London, were able to offer positive and motivational perspectives on the merits of seeing the thesis being given the broader readership that publication would allow. And, at a purely personal level, they also have a place amongst the academic colleagues or friends who have been able to sympathise with the deep sense of loss I experienced on Jason Nicholls' death.

A number of other individuals also provided me with moral support by endorsing the aim of seeing this book in print, and by offering assistance with the project should any be needed. Professor David Bloom, of the Harvard School of Public Health, is certainly amongst this group. Sarah Gardner of City University, London was extremely generous of her time in providing much appreciated editorial expertise. Being able to draw on Jens Schimmelpenning's knowledge of technical and presentational matters has also been invaluable.

My sincere thanks are, however, especially due to Professor David Phillips, Emeritus Fellow of St. Edmund Hall, Oxford University, who from the inception of this project has had faith that it would ultimately be concluded in a worthwhile, and interesting, way. The fact that an academic of his stature has felt able to contribute the Foreword is enormously valued – and is testament to the worth, and potential influence, of Jason Nicholls' work.

Bryan Cunningham
Institute of Education, University of London, February 2014

[D]octrine is, at first, a plausible description of the universe; the years go by and it is a mere chapter…

Jorge Luis Borges, *Pierre Menard, Author of the Quixote*, 1944

Contents

Chapter One: Traveller's Tales, Textbook Research and
Theory Development 25

Chapter Two: Possibilities and Choices: Reflections
on the Literature 39

Chapter Three: The Philosophical Basis of Comparisons I –
From the Modernist 'Thesis' to the Postmodern 'Antithesis' 69

Chapter Four: The Philosophical Basis of Comparisons II –
Towards a Hermeneutic 'Synthesis' 105

Chapter Five: Hermeneutic Readings of Past Masters I –
Re-interpreting Bereday's Emphasis on the Importance of
Language and Contextual Immersion Using Gadamer 147

Chapter Six: Hermeneutic Readings of Past Masters II –
Isolating and Approaching Educational Contexts through a
Re- interpretation of the Brian Holmes / Edmund King Dialectic 171

Chapter Seven: Charting a Syllabus Topic in History Education
across Cultures – The Descriptive Exercise of Constellation Mapping 199

Chapter Eight: Comparative Constellation Analysis as Method 265

Chapter Nine: Conclusion – Labour, Consciousness and Agency 285

Index 289

Acknowledgements

This research would not have been possible without the generous financial support of the UK's Economic and Social Research Council (ESRC) for which I am grateful. Likewise, the thesis would not have come into being without the advice and support of friends and colleagues over the years. I would especially like to acknowledge Sean Bulson in London; Frank Lyons, Mark Mitchell and Sandy Smith; Mark Greenaway and Peter Nesturuk; Steve Giles and Douglas Tallack; Bryan Cunningham; Andy Cowie and Charlotte Johanson in Sweden; Wesley Dennis in Hiroshima; Shirley Palfreman; Jorge Rocca and my philosophy students in Buenos Aires; Stephen J. Thornton; Stuart Foster, David Crook and Peter Lee; and R. J. B. Bosworth.

Particular thanks must go to Richard Pring, Colin Brock, David Johnson, and Anna Pendry, for their useful advice, and to the staff and students of the Department of Educational Studies and of St. Cross College, University of Oxford. My wife, Lara Cancian, deserves to be acknowledged universally for her spiritual contribution. It is many years since our first trip to Nanjing, but now the task is done. I would also like to acknowledge my family for their support. Finally, I would like to express my most sincere gratitude to my doctoral supervisor, Professor David Phillips, at the Centre for Comparative and International Education, Department of Educational Studies, University of Oxford. Above all else, he recognised the comparative methodologist in me.

Jason Nicholls
Groomsport, Co. Down, N. Ireland
20th December 2006

List of Figures

Fig. 1.1: Early diagram depicting Hegel as source 29
Fig. 3.1: Antinomy between modernity thinking and
           post-modernity thinking 103
Fig. 4.1: Hermeneutic re-configuration 121
Fig. 4.2: New configuration 129
Fig. 4.3: Constellation Dynamics 1 138
Fig. 4.4: Constellation Dynamics 2 139
Fig. 4.5: Constellation Dynamics 3 139
Fig. 4.6: Constellation Dynamics 4 140
Fig. 4.7: Constellation Dynamics 5 140
Fig. 4.8: Constellation Dynamics 6 141
Fig. 4.9: Constellation Dynamics 7 141
Fig. 4.10: 'Frozen' Constellation 143
Fig. 5.1: Preparation for study 158
Fig. 5.2: Research horizons as they recede with distance 161
Fig. 5.3: Research horizons: limits and possibilities 162
Fig. 6.1: Holmes's 'ideal typical' model re-formulated to gauge
           syllabus topic variations across contexts 186
Fig. 6.2: King's pseudo 'ideal typical' model re-formulated to
           gauge syllabus topic variations across contexts 194
Fig. 7.1: Isolating contexts on the research horizon 200
Fig. 7.2: Constellation Mapping 257
Fig. 7.3: Constellation Mapping: Japan 260
Fig. 7.4: Constellation Mapping: Sweden 261
Fig. 7.5: Constellation Mapping: England 262
Fig. 8.1: Isolating variables for comparison: Japan 270
Fig. 8.2: Isolating variables for comparison: Sweden 270
Fig. 8.3: Isolating variables for comparison: England 271
Fig. 8.4: 'Outer Circle' variable cluster (Japan) 278
Fig. 8.5: 'Outer Circle' variable cluster (Sweden) 279
Fig. 8.6: 'Outer Circle' variable cluster (England) 279
Fig. 8.7: Comparing variable clusters across cultures 280

Chapter One
Traveller's Tales, Textbook Research and Theory Development

> It is not the general idea that is implicated in opposition
> and combat, and that is exposed to danger. It remains in the
> background, untouched and uninjured. This may be called
> the cunning of reason...
>
> G. W. F. Hegel, *The Philosophy of History*, 1991, p.33

Limits define possibilities in comparative education. What contexts can we engage with and what contexts are for one reason or another too remote? All comparisons must begin from somewhere. But the question is where? By acknowledging our limits as subjects we come to understand our proximity to settings in the world. This is as good as locating oneself on a map.

When we compare the education of one country with that of another we are comparing contexts of great complexity. Each will be made up of a web of relationships, influencing factors, configured differently from one setting to the next. The type of comparisons that we undertake should depend, therefore, on our understanding of the internal dynamics of each context. On approaching the context we will need special tools to somehow 'get inside' and view the dynamics of the system from within. What is affecting what? Where are the major points of influence? What is the relationship between the various parts and the context as a whole? We may find that several contexts share similar parts. However, where a certain part may be highly influential in one context it may significantly lack influence in another.

To a significant degree curriculum knowledge is an affect. It is shaped, formed and moulded by a dynamic array of factors. This will be true of all curriculum subjects but none more than history. History curricula are permeated with contextual particularities: cultural, ideological and political. The same is true of the ways in which history is taught and examined. If we were to ask teachers and students from cultures around the world 'What is school history education?' we would no doubt receive an array of different answers.

In a given context, school history as a whole will be made up of a variety of parts. Each part will exert influence on the meaning of the whole and vice versa. In an abstract sense, this dialectical relationship is central to Hegel's thought: 'The parts are diverse from each other and they are what is independent. But they are parts only...

25

insofar as, taken together, they constitute the whole'.[1] Later this dynamic provides the basis for the hermeneutics of Gadamer.[2] But the message is straightforward: when comparing contexts it is essential to understand that the relationship between school history education as a whole and the constituent parts is dynamic and may differ from one context to the next. History may be taught and studied at schools in a selection of countries. In addition, the constituent parts that affect the meaning of school history education across the contexts may not always vary in type. However, where in one context a particular part may have enormous influence, in another context the same part may have very little influence. Parts that are the same in type can mean different things in different contexts. If a part has no influence on the meaning of the whole then it has no meaning as a part of that whole.

I would like to use school history education in Japan and England as exemplars. Here are two contexts that I know. I have lived in both of the countries and in addition to my native English I have studied Japanese. History is taught at schools in both countries. By definition this means that there is a curriculum for history in both contexts. But curriculum knowledge across contexts is always an affect. And in different contexts parts may affect the whole in different ways. In Japan, for example, school history is defined by the all-pervasive dictates of government-censored textbooks and preparation for the high school/university entrance examinations. These factors exert enormous influence on what counts as school history in Japan. But in England, it is the centralised National Curriculum and the external examination syllabuses that exert the most influence. There are no university entrance examinations as such and textbooks are seen to 'typify' little more than 'an undesirable transmission model… incompatible with progressive educational practice'.[3] Where, for example, textbooks exert enormous influence on the shape and form of knowledge in the history curriculum in Japan, they exert almost no influence in England. To use an analogy, schoolbooks resemble an engine or fuel in the Japanese educational context, while in England they are a kind of back seat headrest used for support at times of rare need. How meaningful is it to compare an engine made by Toyota with a back seat headrest made by Rover? Picture it.

In this book I develop and present methodological system to facilitate the comparison of syllabus topics across contexts using the Second World War as an

---

1   G. W. F. Hegel, *The Philosophy of History* (New York: Prometheus Books, 1991), p.204.
2   H. G. Gadamer, *Truth and Method* (London: Sheed & Ward, 1989).
3   W. E. Marsden, *The School Textbook: Geography, History and Social Studies* (London: Woburn Press, 2001), p.1.

exemplar topic. With the end of the Cold War the importance and significance of World War II has receded in political terms. Nevertheless it remains as a popular subject in history classes around the world and is likely to do so for some time. Morally, the war continues to raise fundamental questions. Nevertheless, to understand the location and effects of the war as a syllabus topic in educational terms we must first identify its shape and form as an object. The syllabus topic as a whole will be made up of a constellation of parts, influencing factors, push and pull variables. What is the relationship between whole and parts in particular contexts? How does a particular syllabus topic express this relationship? To make meaningful comparisons of syllabus topics we must therefore compare relationships. To understand the impact or the effect of a relationship on teachers and students we must first identify what the relationship is.

My methodological system is based in a 'hermeneutic' reading of the philosophy of Hegel. Other thinkers – philosophers, theorists and comparative methodologists – are interpreted in light of this reading. Essentially, I attempt to develop a position, a synthesis for comparative education, using Hegel beyond the modern and the postmodern. Ideas developed by Gadamer and Foucault are of great importance. Gadamer's thought – his theorisation of the ongoing relationship between whole and parts – is implicitly Hegelian. However, Gadamer places additional stress on the importance of language as well as developing his concept of horizons. Foucault's ideas are commonly identified with post-modernity thinking and can appear in diametrical opposition to Hegel. However, by revealing the proximity of Foucault's later 'hermeneutics' to those of Hegel I re-position him. This provides a re-evaluated understanding of Foucault's concept of the subject and of power. Hegel, Gadamer and Foucault are re-conceived, therefore, providing complementary understandings of the subject and knowledge that together form a foundation upon which to build a distinctive comparative approach.

The ideas of other thinkers are adapted and re-understood within this Hegelian framework for the purposes of the book. Weber's methodological concept of the 'ideal type' is incorporated. So too is Adorno's notion of 'constellations'. As for the comparative methodologists, Bereday's insistence on the importance of foreign language acquisition and cultural immersion is of crucial importance, as is the work on hypothesis generation by Brian Holmes and Edmund King.

In Hegelian terms this book is in fact a synthesis. The original thesis was developed between 1993 and 2001. After completing my MA in Critical Theory in 1992 I became an educator as well as travelling extensively. During this period I developed the core principles of a comparative thesis on the Second World War in school history education, regularly detailing my thoughts and ideas in a hand-written journal. This was followed by the development of an antithesis in which I argued, ultimately, that school history textbooks represented a relatively poor unit of comparison for understanding World War II in school history education across the countries in which I specialised. This, in turn, led to my doctoral research thesis: 'The Possibilities for Comparing a Syllabus Topic in School History across Cultures: A Contribution to Method in Comparative Inquiry in Education'.

1.1 The Development of a Thesis: 'Journalling', 1993–2001

Many of the ideas fundamental to this book made their first appearance in a journal I began in the early 1990s. My practice of journal writing was integral to the development of the thesis, and subsequently this book, representing the vital first stage in the development of my comparative methodology.

The entries in my journal illustrated my ideas developing hermeneutically over time. From this perspective consecutive journal entries may be understood as a kind of 'moving procession'. E. H. Carr claims that the use of this 'metaphor is fair enough, provided it does not tempt the historian to think of himself as an eagle surveying the scene from a lonely crag'.[4] This is because '[t]he historian is a part of history'.[5] But why not imagine oneself as the eagle? Surveying years of hand written journal entries, it may be possible to observe a 'parade' in its entirety, each entry representing a particular present, one after the next. Then we may see in the writing how each entry has a past, a background informed by past entries, and how the past may lead to a particular type of present as well as various futures. From a hermeneutic perspective, the horizons of the diarist can be observed changing from one entry to the next, with the accumulation of experiences. Likewise, each entry represents an example of the diarist attempting to give meaning to the present, the repetition of themes along the parade of entries speaking to the reader of a kind of circular motion between the writing subject and experiences over time. From a hermeneutic perspective, the development of knowledge is essential to understandings of knowledge. The ideas presented in the chapters that follow are only meaningful from a hermeneutic perspective when understood in relation to the experiences and ideas recorded in the journal and vice versa.

---

4   E. H. Carr, *What is History?* (London: Penguin Books, 1990), p.35.
5   Carr, *What is History?*, op. cit. (note 4), p.36.

From the autumn of 1993 I make frequent references in my journal to Adorno's concept of constellations, an important concept in this thesis. 'Constellations' are constructed 'around objects... by subjects' (Journal, 25th September 1993, London). And the following year I would conceptualise '[t]he object... surrounded by a glistening constellation'. We attempt to understand concepts and objects by way of constellations because 'things' are complex and multifaceted, 'contoured' by 'their own histories and relationships' (Journal, 16th November 1994, London). But constellations must be crafted with care if their methodological potential is to be realised to maximum effect. Constellations are neither absolute nor random. Like the constructing subject, 'the constellation is' both centred and de-centred, 'universal and particular, absolute and relative, certain and ambiguous'. It is perhaps for this reason that '[s]ome constellations tell us more than others as we form them around objects and concepts' (Journal, 26th November 1994, London). My thoughts and interests at this time were clearly philosophical, a fascination with the work of thinkers from France and Germany. At the root of this 'tradition of speculation', moreover, was a way of thinking first

apparent in Hegel. From Hegel we take the Nietzschean road to Weber – ... from a mediation of Marx – and move on to Adorno. This road – a trajectory – doesn't take us to Derrida... in early/mid stage – ... or Foucault... [French] thinkers seem to become this position in their late[r] stage[s] (Journal, 21st November 1994, London).

EARLY DIAGRAM DEPICTING HEGEL AS SOURCE

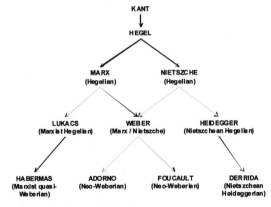

Fig. 1.1:   Early diagram depicting Hegel as source

During this period I sketched the above diagram (fig. 1.1) depicting Hegel as the source of a range of philosophical tributaries. Essentially, Kant is depicted leading to Hegel while Hegel leads to everything else. Although problematic in many ways the diagram provides overview of the philosophical direction in which I was heading at that time. An updated and more sophisticated version of the diagram appears in Chapter Four.

By 1997, having taught for some years, I had become interested in questions relating directly to education. 'How does history manifest itself in modern education?' I would ask. And 'what are the effects of globalization… its uneven waves of influence – on East Asian education…? Not simply the effects of modernization per se but … the effects of the current order of things… the influence of the balance of forces in the world today…?' (Journal, 8th December 1997, Hiroshima). Come 1998 and I comment increasingly on issues relating to comparative education with a particular emphasis on the countries in which I had lived. '[W]hat and how we are taught' I would now claim 'is to a significant extent, the manifestation of historically contested notions of truth, knowledge, freedom and justice… manifested here in the present'. This led me to consider going on to compare 'the modern identity of knowledge in Education' in 'America [meaning the United States], Sweden and Japan' (Journal, 16th April 1998, Hiroshima). Two days later and I would move the idea one step forward:

> Modern education is the embodiment of a particular set of values. Values are communicated through education. A particular education system or policy is the expression of a particular history. In different societies – across them – we find different educational values which are themselves the effects of different histories… Knowledge and Critique in Social Science Education: America, Sweden and Japan (Journal, 18th April 1998, Hiroshima).

The suggested thesis that concludes this entry is the first to sound at least something like the book that has since emerged. Three days later and I would suggest that 'Japan- Sweden- [and] America' represent 'three points of… [a] … triangle' due to their affiliations during the Second World War 'Axis-Neutral-Allies' (Journal, 21st April 1998, Hiroshima). One month on and I am commenting on the relationship between 'power and knowledge in education: America, Sweden, Japan'. In short, 'What are the implications of those rationalities and knowledge systems that are dominant against those that are not'? (Journal, 17th May 1998, Hiroshima).

Three events of significance occurred during my last six months in Hiroshima. The first of these related to a particular conservative victory on the level of government and society. Hiroshima had long been a seat of teacher radicalism. Almost all teachers in the prefecture are members of the leftist Japanese Teachers Union (JTU) and opposed to the conservative censorship of school history textbooks, the singing of the Japanese national anthem and the raising of the Japanese flag. But where the Hiroshima union had, in general, lost the battle over textbook censorship they had managed to hold their ground in the struggle against the anthem and the flag. In March 1999 they lost this battle. The following entry appeared in my journal:

> Graduation day today and for the first time in many years a directive from Monbusho [the Ministry of Education] for Hiroshima ken [prefecture] to fly the flag and play the national anthem during the [school opening] ceremony. Yesterday a principal killed himself. Japan's flag and national anthem symbolise the past in a distinctive and... [it could be said]...terrible way... [s]ymbolising the atrocities of Japan's militaristic past – fascism and the colonisation of East Asia (Journal, 1st March 1999, Hiroshima).

The 1990s would be a decade of intense ideological struggle in Japan, between right wing nationalists and radical leftists, over the question of Japan's history and particularly its role during World War II. Yet in a post-Cold War environment it was the right that appeared in the ascendant. A school principal had committed suicide as a result of this ever more 'sensationalised' battle. Debates over Japan's past – aggression in China in the 1930s, 'comfort women', controversies over the censorship of school history textbooks – repeatedly hit the headlines.

I would arrive in China at the beginning of September 1999, to begin my next teaching post. By the end of September I had become accustomed to my new surroundings. And from this point on I would make frequent references to World War II, history and social science education and the possibilities for comparative study. In China I began to construct a theoretical framework for understanding World War II across cultures. The conflict had been a pan-global event, a universal historical experience, but the role of different nations in the conflict had been highly specific. What can best be described as Hegelian imbibed logic is clearly present in the following journal entry:

> A universal reading of WW2 is nothing without the particulars that are its parts; the relative positions that different powers took in the war. At the same time, the particular roles of the different powers cannot be understood – defined – without a notion or concept of a universal understanding of the war (Journal, 26th September 1999, Nantong).

Nanjing was China's capital during the Japanese invasion in the 1930s. It was also the site of some of the Japanese army's most brutal war crimes. 'In December 1937', writes Bosworth,

> Japanese forces stormed the Chinese city of Nanjing and proceeded to sack it. In the next month, at least according to local accounts, some 200,000 died. So vicious was the rape, murder and pillage that a strict censorship on reporting the 'incident' was rapidly put in place. In post-war Japan, the brutality continued to be denied and only belatedly

became public knowledge although, even in the 1980s, nationalist writers disputed the death toll and rejected the view that the sacking was an exceptional event.[6]

Whether the massacre should be described in school history textbooks continues to be hotly debated in Japan to this day. I would make my first trip to Nanjing at the end of September 1999. I felt sombre on my arrival since it was 'Hiroshima and Japan' that had 'led me to this place... the sight of Japan's most brutal atrocities in WW2'. Visiting the Museum for the Victims of the Nanjing Massacre was an extremely powerful experience and I felt deeply affected. The museum displays the full brutality and cruelty of the occupying Japanese forces. In my journal that evening I wrote of how I could not 'think of anything more gruesome and horrific' (Journal, 1st October 1999, Nanjing). This visit caused me to reflect on the Japanese discourse on pacifism and peace. In Japan peace is officially championed and celebrated while, at the same time, the causes of war tend to be ignored. Visiting the Nanjing Museum would shed new light on the war waged and lost by Japan.

The trip to Nanjing vindicated my decision and determination to compare perspectives of 'WW2 in school history education' across contexts. Writing in Shanghai a few days later, with the idea for a project comparing 'Britain, Sweden and Japan' a series of new questions emerged, such as whether there is such a thing as a morally neutral 'interpretation of the war', a perspective that speaks to all peoples that is somehow above or beyond the 'national' – symbolically propounded by organisations like the United Nations? World War II is a universal event in one sense but did all nations that experienced the war do so in the same way? Once again we are back with Hegel and his conception of the dialectical relationship between universal and particular, the generic and the specific, the concept and the empirical deed. I continued to probe these issues through further questions:

'Is it possible to consider a thing universally – an act – when different actors played different roles in making the act what it is? [How] important [is it] to consider the war universally – on ethical/moral grounds? [How] important [is it] to understand the war from the viewpoints of the different particular actors?' (Journal, 25th October 1999, Nantong).

Understanding the war from the position of the universal is a reference to modernism. What is true about the war and how can the different actors in the war be judged accordingly? Understanding the war from the position of the particular, on the other hand, is a reference to postmodernism. Different actors from different

6   R. J. B. Bosworth, *Explaining Auschwitz and Hiroshima: History Writing and the Second World War 1945–1990* (London: Routledge, 1994), p.173.

nations experienced the war in different ways. But these positions in isolation present serious problems. By positioning themselves with the universal, modernists deny the reality of subjective experience. The truth is transnational, it applies to all situations and for all time. Similarly, by positioning themselves with the particular postmodernists deny ethics. It is very worrying indeed to consider the Holocaust as simply an interpretation. Is rabid nationalism OK? Surely the Second World War needed to be theorised in a way that was sensitive to subjective experience without denying ethics: beyond nationalism and transnationalism. In light of my interest in history education, this way of thinking would form the pulsating heart of my methodological pursuits on returning to the UK. Thus:

> Should history textbooks in schools be cleansed of their nationalism- their cultural baggage in favour of something more universal? A universal understanding of WW2 – this denies context. A particular understanding – denies ethics and morality – it relativises perceptions of the war to the actors in the particular. How should the war be understood – how should it be taught? Bring in Adorno – Foucault and the rest' (Journal, 25th October 1999, Nantong).

Here in essence was the idea that would form the core principle in much of my later work on perspectives of World War II in school history textbooks. At around this time, political reports in The Guardian Weekly did everything to confirm my belief that a 'WW2… thesis' was 'more urgent than ever'. It would be

> crucial. As Haider's far-right takes power in Austria; as Japan reviews the pacifism… in its constitution (under nationalist pressure); and as Sweden's Goran Persson denounces the Swedish government's actions/attitude during WW2 (Journal, 21st February 2000, Nantong).

1.2 The Emergence of Antitheses

Arriving at Oxford my proposed research would, however, change radically. Under the guidance of Professor David Phillips the research became philosophical and methodological in nature. How was it possible – on the level of theory and practice – to compare representations of the Second World War in school history textbooks from Sweden, Japan, and England? Could it be done from the perspective of comparative education? What were the alternatives? Essentially, I began to compare the Second World War in history education across contexts in order to identify the place of the textbook in that process. And I would discover that textbooks did not share the same educational value from context to context.

Perhaps more significantly, I discovered that the teaching of World War II continued across contexts with or without the textbook.

At Oxford, I would first attempt to develop a methodology for comparing the Second World War across samples of textbooks that I now recognised to be decentred However, the driving Neo-Hegelian principle would lead to my problematisation of comparative textbook research as a practice Essentially, I came to argue that where comparing textbooks as a means to understanding curriculum and instruction in history education may be useful across some contexts, this is not the case for all contexts. In some cultures the use of textbooks for the teaching and learning of history has long been in decline. And with the arrival of the Internet and new forms of educational media one can reasonably surmise that this trend will continue. Textbooks are at most dependent variables, de-centred objects; their educational meaning bound to the ways in which they are used in particular contexts. But in contexts where they are not used, or used only very infrequently, they lose their status as educationally significant variables.

1.3 The Doctoral Thesis as Synthesis

Fundamentally, the thesis came to be guided by the following research questions: 1. How is it possible to compare syllabus topics as objects in school history education across cultures? 2. How do the limits of the researching subject affect possibilities for meaningful comparisons? Thus the thesis would be concerned with the theorisation of limits and possibilities in comparative education. Since history education is saturated in cultural particularities, how are syllabus topics such as the Second World War located as concepts and objects? How are they positioned and shaped in relation to the constellation of influencing variables that surround them?

World War II as a syllabus topic is universal to many contexts. Yet the parts that influence the topic as a whole may be configured differently from one context to the next. To understand the nature of the whole as an object it is crucial to examine the influence exerted by the various parts. There is little to be gained from examining and comparing parts – e.g., textbooks, examinations, curriculum guidelines etc. – irrespective of their educational value across contexts. To understand the meaning and composition of a syllabus topic we need, therefore, to identify and examine those parts that exert the greatest influence. This requires the examination and comparison of relationships between whole and parts. Only then, when the syllabus topic has been mapped and located and positioned as an object – as the expression of particular relationships – can we begin to conceptualise the relationship of that object to subjects – i.e. students, teachers and parents, etc.

As concepts, limits, horizons, and constellations make their first appearance across the philosophy chapters, Three and Four. In Chapter Three we observe the opposition between the modernist thesis and the postmodern antithesis and the implications for making comparisons. For modernists the subject is potentially endowed with absolute liberty. In the beam of the bright light of truth, the knowing subject may experience a limitless horizon, and have access to all contexts. Here the whole is everything – truth, the scientific method, or consciousness – while the culturally specific parts appear reduced and insignificant. The postmodern subject, on the other hand, is limited to the point of being denied; anchored to the particularity of its own context, the liberty to compare across contexts vanishes into thin air. Here the culturally specific parts are everything, regardless of truth or method. There is no horizon, only provincialism and darkness.

But in Chapter Four we are presented with the Hegelian/hermeneutic synthesis beyond thesis and antithesis. Here the truth exists, within limits, enabling comparisons within specific grounds and parameters. Here the comparative researcher's horizon will depend on background factors and past experiences; the euphoric glow of spirit emanating from the subject, the expression of its creativity and resourcefulness, shining to illuminate particular contexts, with varying degrees of clarity. According to this synthesis, whole and parts are conceived in dialectical relationships; constellations of parts appearing dynamically configured around a given topic in a given context and vice versa. Importantly, different parts will exert different levels of influence on the shape and form of the topic. And from Foucault we come to recognise that the relationship between whole and parts is at the same time the expression of the dialectic between power and knowledge.

Where the modernist thesis offers a kind of pure light through science or consciousness, the postmodern antithesis, in its denial of these concepts, brings darkness. Both deny comparison, however, for 'in pure light nothing is seen, just as little as in pure darkness'.[7] Yet from the perspective of the synthesis objects appear contrasted, defined, distinguishable or not as the case may be – in the mixed and varied light of the surrounding constellation constructed by the researching subject. In some constellations particular stars will shine brightly, illuminating the shape and composition of the topic, in others they will not.

In Chapters Five and Six, limits, horizons, and constellations are conceptualised in a more practical light through hermeneutic re-interpretations of Past-Masters in

---

7   G. W. F. Hegel, *Philosophy of Nature* (Oxford: Clarendon Press, 2004), p.89.

comparative education. In Chapter Five, the ideas and concepts of Gadamer, conceived as an implicit extension of Hegelian thinking, are used to re-interpret the ideas of Bereday. Here the importance of language and inter-cultural experience are understood defining the limits and the horizons of the researching subject, comparative researchers qualified to investigate only those contexts where they have access to evidence – through a knowledge of languages and experiential background.

But where Chapter Five concentrates on limits and the breadth of the subject's research horizons, Chapter Six focuses on how we may approach complex educational contexts, using Holmes, King and Weber. First, the work of Holmes and King is considered to be dynamic and complementary rather than static and in opposition. Second, this spiralling dynamic is understood as a means for creating speculative hypotheses through which it becomes possible to introduce Weber's concept of ideal typical models. Ideal types comprise an array of variables or influencing factors: a constellation of parts. Essentially, it is argued, ideal typical models may be constructed to gauge syllabus topic variations across contexts.

Chapter Seven introduces the reader to the concept and practical exercise of 'constellation mapping'. Using the ideal typical models developed in Chapter Six we look in depth at the 'parts' that influence syllabus topics in history education across three exemplar nations: Japan, Sweden, and England. Where in Chapter Four the relationship between whole and parts is conceived in a highly abstract way, by Chapter Seven we 'get our hands dirty' so to speak, looking closely at the material reality of the various parts across contexts. How is a given part – e.g., the official curriculum, examinations, textbooks etc. – shaped and formed in a particular country? What kind of influence does the part have on the shape of the syllabus topic? What is the relationship between the various parts in a given context?

Having described each of the parts in each context, I then move on to demonstrate, in Chapter Eight, how it is possible to investigate the relationship between the parts and syllabus topics as a whole across contexts using 'comparative constellation analysis'.

This book is thus in fact a synthesis, which begins with Hegel. The work is composed of various elements and particularities, but the universal that underpins them all is Hegel's philosophy. Essentially, I attempt to construct a comparative education that 'draw[s] on a wide range of social theories and methodologies' to enable 'systematic explanations'.[8] Gadamer is understood as an extension of Hegel and is used

---

8   P. Broadfoot, 'Editorial: structure and agency in education: the role of comparative education', *Comparative Education* (2002) 38 1, p.5.

to reinterpret Bereday. Foucault, after reading Kant and the Frankfurt School, is conceived within the Hegelian orbit, the power/knowledge dialectic conceptualised in a new way in the context of a resurrected subject. Holmes and King, mighty opposites of the 1960s, appear as two halves of an integral Hegelian dynamic that leads the researcher to Weber's concept of ideal types. Using Hegel, syllabus topics are understood in terms of a fundamental relationship between whole and constituting parts that together in a given context form a constellation, Adorno's concept, to be mapped and analysed. Even the dynamic underpinning this researcher's intellectual development – from thesis, to antithesis, to synthesis – is interpreted according to the philosophy and method of Hegel.

Hegel is the philosopher of particularity as much as universality, the conceiver of a reality that rumbles and spirals through time, and 'the sphere of liberty', that space in time where the subjective and objective limits and possibilities of critique may be realised. Essentially, Hegel's conception of reason is both utilitarian and dynamic. By using reason we become immersed in the particularities of an initial endeavour. Piece by piece the specific idea grows. Motivated to discover new truths, and in the direction of a new vision, the thesis may take flight, like a glowing firebird, ascending, bold, a soaring thrust of concentrated reason. Yet conscious of the relationship between particularities, it is by using reason that contradictions and inconsistencies in the thesis become exposed. Reason may even cause us to abandon the former endeavour. But we should never abandon reason itself.

What is critique without reason? It is pure hostility, opposition for some personalised end, an isolated particularity accountable to nothing but itself; it is the rule of 'anything goes', the deliberate manipulation of evidence, condemnation without trial, without jury. It is destruction for its own sake, consent to the dominion of 'might over right', the negation of foundations, a specific means to a specific end; it denies the concept of knowledge and stops at nothing. It is the champion of antipathy and the enemy of spirit.

What is reasoned critique? It is to evaluate with the power of hindsight, to assess from the position of new standards, and to judge in light of the alternatives. It is to be accountable to the parameters of a particular rationality, to raise consciousness in the light of evidence, and to recognise limits. It is to revere understanding and awareness, knowledge for the sake of knowledge, to locate the present in relation to the past and to what might be, and to lay foundations from which to proceed. It is reason in action, alive, energised, spirit engaged, and at the height of its powers.

Chapter Two
Possibilities and Choices:
Reflections on the Literature

> [L]abour shapes and fashions the thing... [T]his activity
> giving shape and form, is at the same time... the pure self
> existence of that consciousness, which now in the work...
> is externalised and passes into the condition of permanence.
>
> G. W. F. Hegel, *Phenomenology*, 1966, p.238

A wide body of literature informs this book. Philosophical and methodological texts have played a major role, as have those on the Second World War, history education, and the .educational systems of Japan, Sweden and England. Essentially, the themes that emerge are the expression of a fundamentally hermeneutic dynamic. Patterns and meanings developed and consolidated themselves as this researcher engaged – increasingly and persistently – with texts. Over time it became possible to cluster texts around particular themes.

2.1 Personal Journals

In many respects the writings in my personal journals express the dialectical unfolding that characterises the entire book. In Volume III (1993–1995) the entries are philosophical in nature, written before I begin my period as an overseas educator. During this time I would live in London, frequently writing down my thoughts on Hegel, Foucault, Adorno, and Weber in my journal. In Volume IV (1995–1996) the content of the journal entries changes. Although continuing to be philosophical in nature, I had now qualified as an educator, and would look to find employment in Japan.

Volume V (1996–2000) covers the entire period of my stay in Japan and China. In this text I apply philosophical perspectives to concrete situations. Equally, I start to compare social systems, drawing on experiences in the countries in which I had now lived, studied and/or worked. Certain patterns and rationalisations now emerge. In Volume V I am clearly interested in comparative education and by 1999, the treatment of World War II in school history across former belligerent and non-belligerent states.

Volume VI (2000–2001) covers my one year stay in Argentina. Extremely busy with teaching, there are fewer entries in the journal than before. Nevertheless, I do make several observations, particularly in relation to the undergraduate philosophy course that I would teach at Universidad Argentina de la Empresa (UADE) in Buenos Aires. In many respects I tie up the loose ends of what had gone before. The philosophy course ended with Hegel, whose philosophy would underpin my doctoral research. I had my doctoral thesis planned – focusing on World War II in school history across a cluster of countries.

2.2 Philosophical Underpinnings

A particular understanding of Hegel and Hegelian philosophy propels the book forward. Thus, the dialectical concept of history, the dialectic between whole and parts, and the relationship of the present to the past and the future are essential to the work.[1] Equally, as a Hegelian thesis, the emergence of spirit in relation to reason, labour and consciousness, as described in the *Phenomenology* and in the *Philosophy of Mind* is of fundamental importance.[2] Hegel is understood in the same way that Merleau-Ponty understood him: casting a long shadow over the contemporary age.[3] Thus, I offer the essential features of a Hegelian philosophy of comparative education.

Yet the reading of Hegel I use is by no means a 'classical' or 'orthodox' reading. It is for this reason that I reject 'teleological' or 'modernist' understandings of Hegel, even though many scholars understand Hegel in this way.[4] In Singer's work, reason and alienation are perceived struggling through history, consciousness of alienation refining and solidifying the reasoning subject's identity of itself. With identity comes a sense of purpose, driving the subject through history towards the unfettered freedom of a 'modem' and 'rational' future.[5] This reading

---

1   G. W. F. Hegel, *The Philosophy of History* (New York: Prometheus Books, 1991). G. W. F. Hegel, *Science of Logic* (New York: The Macmillan Company, 1921). G. W. F. Hegel, *Philosophy of Nature* (Oxford: Clarendon Press, 2004). G. W. F. Hegel, *Philosophy of Right* (Oxford: Oxford University Press, 1967).

2   G. W. F. Hegel, *Phenomenology of Mind* (London: George Alien & Unwin, 1966). G. W. F. Hegel, *Philosophy of Mind* (Oxford: Clarendon Press, 1990).

3   M. Merleau-Ponty, *Sense and Non-Sense* (Chicago: Northwestern University Press, 1964).

4   S. B. Smith, *Hegel's Critique of Liberalism* (Chicago: University of Chicago Press, 1989). C. Taylor, *Hegel and Modern Society* (Cambridge: Cambridge University Press, 1989).

5   P. Singer, *Hegel* (Oxford: Oxford University Press, 1988).

of Hegel, which I identify with critical theory and modernity thinking, is shown to feature strongly in the work of 20th century intellectuals.[6] It also underpins the work of numerous scholars of critical theory, and can be identified in the work of the young Karl Marx as well as Marx and Engels.[7] But for me, modernity thinking is not identified solely with critical theory but also with its bourgeois predecessor: positivism. Thus positivism represents, according to Bilton et al, the first form of Enlightenment thinking.[8] Many authors detail the strong critique of positivism implicit in critical theory.[9]

According to the perspective developed here, positivism and critical theory embody the modernist 'thesis'. In contrast, based in the philosophy of Nietzsche, post-modernity thinking is posited as an 'antithesis'.[10] As pointed out in the work of Giddens, for postmodernists, knowledge is no longer conceived leading to power but rather as an effect of power.[11] Progress is questioned as myth, difference championed over unity, truth relativised and ultimately denied, the de-centred subject defended, modernist universals re-conceptualised as the expression of truth regimes that marginalise alternative forms of knowledge and silence the 'Other', as described by Dunn.[12] The works of thinkers such as Lyotard, Deleuze and Derrida are important here.[13] There are also a series of

6   G. Lukacs, *History and Class-Consciousness* (London: Merlin Press, 1983). H. Marcuse, *Reason and Revolution* (London: Routledge & Kegan Paul, 1986). J. Habermas, *Communication and the Evolution of Society* (London: Heinemann, 1979).

7   D. Held, *Introduction to Critical Theory: Horkheimer to Habermas* (Berkeley: University of California Press, 1980). T. Bottomore and M. Rubel (eds.) *Marx: Selected Writings in Sociology and Social Philosophy* (London: Pelican Books, 1983). J. G. Merquior, *Western Marxism* (London: Paladin Books, 1986). K. Marx, *Early Writings* (London: Penguin, 1992). K. Marx, *Capital*, Vol. 1 (London: Lawrence & Wisehart, 1983). K. Marx and F. Engels, *The Communist Manifesto* (London: Penguin, 1987).

8   T. Bilton et al, *Introductory Sociology* (Basingstoke: Macmillan, 1981).

9   D. Held, *Introduction to Critical Theory,* op. cit. (note 7). R. Usher, 'A critique of the neglected epistemological assumptions of educational research', in D. Scott, and R. Usher (eds.) *Understanding Educational Research* (London: Routledge, 1996). D. Scott and R. Usher, *Researching Education: Data, Methods and Theory in Educational Enquiry* (New York: Cassell, 1999).

10 F. Nietzsche, *A Nietzsche Reader*, R. J. Hollingdale (ed.) (London: Penguin, 1977).

11 A. Giddens, *Politics, Sociology and Social Theory* (Cambridge: Polity Press, 1995).

12 R. Dunn, 'Postmodernism: Populism, Mass Culture, and Avant-Garde', *Theory Culture & Society* (1991) 8 1, pp.111–135.

13 J. F. Lyotard, *The Postmodern Condition: A Report on Knowledge* (Manchester: Manchester University Press, 1984). G. Deleuze, *Foucault* (Minneapolis: University of

useful commentaries on postmodernism, both critical and sympathetic, provided by a range of scholars.[14]

Foucault's ideas during the 1960s and 1970s are central to the development of post-modernity thinking and to the location of 'the postmodern' in this thesis.[15] Most commentators on Foucault tend to identify his work with post-modernity thinking.[16] To a large extent, this is due to Foucault's appropriation of Nietzsche, through his use of the genealogical method and his development of the concept of power/knowledge. Essentially, this position is presented as the antithesis of the classical reading of Hegel discussed above.

Yet, in this work, I read Hegel in such a way as to be sensitive to the post-modern concern for difference and cultural sensitivity. My interpretation of Hegel appears, therefore, to be closer to the work of Rose in *The Broken Middle*.[17] But unlike Rose, my understanding owes much to the philosophy of Gadamer. Where Gadamer is understood as an implicitly Hegelian thinker, Hegel is re-positioned using Gadamer. *Truth and Method* represents Gadamer's most complete statement on the relationship between knowledge, language, meaning, and the concept of horizons.[18] Essentially, in the book Gadamer's philosophy plays a central role;

Minnesota Press, 1990). J. Derrida, *Of Grammatology* (Baltimore: The John Hopkins University Press, 1974).

14 S. Aronowitz, and H. A. Giroux, *Postmodern Education: Politics, Culture and Social Criticism* (Minneapolis: University of Minnesota Press, 1991). R. Dunn, 'Postmodernism: Populism, Mass Culture, and Avant-Garde', op. cit. (note 12). J. G. Merquior, *Foucault* (London: Fontana Press, 1991). R. Usher, 'A critique of the neglected epistemological assumptions of educational research', op. cit. (note 9). D. Scott, and R. Usher, *Researching Education: Data, Methods and Theory in Educational Enquiry*, op. cit. (note 9).

15 M. Foucault, *Power/Knowledge: Selected Interviews and Other Writings 1972–1977* (Brighton: The Harvester Press, 1980). M. Foucault, *The Order of Things: an Archaeology of the Human Sciences* (London: Routledge, 1991).

16 P. Rabinow (ed.) *The Foucault Reader* (London: Penguin, 1984). D. Couzens Hoy (ed.) *Foucault A Critical Reader* (Oxford: Basil Blackwell, 1989). J. Habermas, 'Taking Aim at the Heart of the Present', in D. Couzens Hoy (ed.) *Foucault A Critical Reader*, op. cit. R. Rorty, 'Foucault and Epistemology', in D. Couzens Hoy (ed.) *Foucault A Critical Reader* op. cit. B. Smart, 'The Politics of Truth and the Problem of Hegemony', in D. Couzens Hoy (ed.) *Foucault A Critical Reader*, op. cit. C. Taylor, 'Foucault on Freedom and Truth', in D. Couzens Hoy (ed.) *Foucault A Critical Reader*, op. cit.

17 G. Rose, *The Broken Middle* (Oxford: Blackwell, 1992).

18 H. G. Gadamer, *Truth and Method* (London: Sheed & Ward, 1989).

hermeneutics understood looking back to Hegel and forward towards a 'synthesis' beyond post-modernity. A succinct overview of the work of Gadamer is provided in Bleicher's *Contemporary Hermeneutics*.[19]

Yet Gadamer's philosophy should be understood as an interpretation and an extension of the hermeneutic tradition and, in particular, the writings of Dilthey. In his *Introduction to the Human Sciences*, Dilthey would identify the hermeneutic relationship between spirit and the material world in a manner not dissimilar to the reading of Hegel I propose. Essentially, he argues that the identity of each realm is separate and yet inter-dependent.[20]

Foucault in his third and final period is re-positioned by me according to the circular dynamics of hermeneutics. In Poster's *Critical Theory and Post-structuralism* Foucault's move away from post-modernity thinking is detailed in some depth.[21] Essentially, Foucault is shown to make what I would describe as an 'epistemological break' with the archaeology and genealogy periods. This change begins at the end of the 1970s, after the first volume of *The History of Sexuality*.[22]

In the collection of interviews with Duccio Trombadori, *Remarks on Marx*, Foucault has clearly engaged with the ideas of the Frankfurt School, particularly Adorno and Horkheimer's *Dialectic of Enlightenment*.[23] Moreover, by the 1980s, Foucault had begun to develop a close analysis of Kant's important essay 'What is Enlightenment?'[24] In his writings of the 1980s, Foucault takes a new position, post-Kantian, neither modern nor postmodern, in the synthesis beyond both, that pulls his last contributions into the orbit of the hermeneutic reading of Hegel I have offered here.[25]

19   J. Bleicher, *Contemporary Hermeneutics: Hermeneutics as Method, Philosophy and Critique* (London: Routledge & Kegan Paul, 1980).

20   W. Dilthey, *Introduction to the Human Sciences*, 1883. [Internet] Available from <http://www.marxists.org/reference/subject/philosophv/workd/ge/dilthey.htm> [Accessed 19 December 2006].

21   M. Poster, *Critical Theory and Poststructuralism: In Search of a Context* (Ithaca: Cornell University Press, 1989).

22   M. Foucault, *The History of Sexuality*, Vol. 1 (London: Penguin, 1976).

23   M. Foucault, *Politics Philosophy Culture: Interviews and Other Writings 1977–1984*, L. D. Kritzman (ed.) (New York: Routledge, 1988). T. W. Adorno, and M. Horkheimer, *Dialectic of Enlightenment* (London: Verso, 1992).

24   M. Foucault, *The Politics of Truth* (New York: Semiotext(e), 1997).

25   M. Foucault, 'The art of telling the truth' (1984), in M. Foucault, *Politics Philosophy Culture*, op. cit. (note 23).

The conceptualisation of education, especially comparative education, from the perspectives of modernity, post-modernity and beyond I view as central. Yet, as Scott and Usher argue in their work, philosophical concerns are all too often neglected in educational research.[26] Pring's *Philosophy of Educational Research* is an important text, providing an essential platform from which to proceed towards philosophically informed research practices.[27] Scholars such as Templeton reflect upon the theoretical dimension in comparative education.[28] However, as McLaughlin points out, a philosophy of 'comparative education' has yet to be consolidated due, in part, to the lack of co-operation between comparative educationists and philosophers of education.[29] Standish observes the importance of philosophy as a means to understanding limits in comparative educational research. In other words, it is philosophy that determines the parameters of 'what cannot be known' in our cross-cultural analyses and investigations.[30]

In *Toward a Science of Comparative Education*, Noah and Eckstein pioneer a positivist comparative education, offering an approach involving comparisons of those educational phenomena that can be measured using the scientific method.[31] Epstein, on the other hand, draws attention to the problems associated with positivist approaches to comparative educational research. This being said, he also points to the difficulties that arise when using anti-positivist, or phenomenological approaches. Epstein argues that positivist and anti-positivist methods are irreconcilable.[32] In Epstein's work, comparison means different things according to the philosophical as well as ideological orientation of the researching subject.[33]

---

26 D. Scott, and R. Usher, *Researching Education: Data, Methods and Theory in Educational Enquiry*, op. cit. (note 9).

27 R. Pring, *Philosophy of Educational Research* (London: Continuum, 2000).

28 R. G. Templeton, 'Some Reflections on the Theory of Comparative Education', *Comparative Education Review*, 2 2 (1958), pp.27–31.

29 T. H. McLaughlin, 'Education, philosophy and the comparative perspective', *Comparative Education*, 40 4 (2004), pp.471–483.

30 P. Standish, 'Europe, Continental philosophy and the philosophy of education', *Comparative Education*, 40 4 (2004), pp.485–501.

31 H. J. Noah, and M. A. Eckstein, *Toward a Science of Comparative Education* (New York: Macmillan, 1969).

32 E. H. Epstein, 'The Problematic Meaning of "Comparison" in Comparative Education', in J. Schriewer and B. Holmes (eds.) *Theories and Methods in Comparative Education* (Frankfurt am Main: Peter Lang, 1988).

33 E. H. Epstein, 'Currents Left and Right: Ideology in Comparative Education', in P. G. Altbach and G. P. Kelly, *New Approaches to Comparative Education* (Chicago: University of Chicago Press, 1986).

Although its popularity has waned, there has long been a critical theory tradition in educational research and in comparative education. Althusser conceptualises education as a form of ideological state apparatus.[34] Bowles and Gintis and Willis concentrate on the relationship between education, ideology, and the aspirations of working class youth. Others make considerable contributions.[35] Comparative educationists such as Carnoy attempt to develop an approach that exposed injustices and to analyse educational systems within their wider socio-economic contexts.[36] Likewise, Thanh Khoi offers a comparative education based around the ideas of the Frankfurt School that draws attention to the problematic use of critical concepts across cultural settings.[37]

In recent years postmodern perspectives have been used extensively in educational research.[38] Cowen argues that comparative education at universities has been very much a part of the modernity project and late to adopt postmodern perspectives.[39] Comparative educationists have been correspondingly late to theorise a perspective beyond post-modernity. In his work, Paulston 'maps' the positions and perspectives of various comparative educationists 'after post-modernity'.[40] Likewise, scholars

34   L. Althusser, 'Ideology and Ideological State Apparatuses', in *Lenin and Philosophy and Other Essays* (New York: Monthly Review Press, 1971).

35   S. Bowles, and H. Gintis, *Schooling in Capitalist America: Educational Reform and the Contradictions of Economic Life* (New York: Basic Books, 1976). P. Willis, *Learning to Labour* (Aldershot: Gower, 1977). B. Bernstein, *Class, Codes and Control* (London: Routledge & Kegan Paul, 1977). M. Apple, *Ideology and Curriculum* (London: Routledge & Kegan Paul, 1979). M. Apple, *Teachers and Texts: A Political Economy of Class and Gender Relations in Education* (New York: Routledge & Kegan Paul. 1986). M. Apple, 'Ideology, Reproduction, and Educational Reform', in Philip G. Altbach and Gail P. Kelly (eds., *New Approaches to Comparative Education* (Chicago: University of Chicago Press, 1986).

36   M. Carnoy, 'Education for Alternative Development', in P. G. Altbach and G. P. Kelly (eds.) *New Approaches to Comparative Education*, op. cit. (note 35).

37   L. Thanh Khoi, 'Conceptual problems in inter-cultural comparisons', in J. Schriewer and B. Holmes (eds.) *Theories and Methods in Comparative Education*, op. cit. (note 32).

38   S. Aronowitz, and H. A. Giroux, *Postmodern Education: Politics, Culture and Social Criticism*, op. cit. (note 14). R. Usher and R. Edwards, *Postmodernism and Education* (London: Routledge, 1994).

39   R. Cowen, 'Last Past the Post: Comparative Education, Modernity and Perhaps Post-Modernity', *Comparative Education*, 32 2 (1996), pp.151–170. R. Cowen, 'Performativity, Post-Modernity and the University', *Comparative Education*, 32 2 (1996), pp.245–258.

40   R. G. Paulston, 'Mapping Comparative Education after Postmodernity', *Comparative Education Review*, 43 4 (1999), pp.438–463.

such as Olssen and Marshall pioneer an approach to educational research based in a 'materialist' and, therefore, quasi-grounded reading of late Foucauldian ideas. Yet there appears to be something lacking in these works, a sense that the authors cannot break free from the shackles of post-modernity thinking. In the work of both Olssen and Marshall, Hegel and Foucault are positioned beyond reconciliation. As a consequence, there is no sense that, together, Hegel and Foucault provide the basis for a truly dynamic comparative education for the contemporary age.[41]

Where philosophical orientation underpins comparative approaches to educational research, it also affects understandings of the meaning of history. Bosworth provides a history of the historians in his *Explaining Auschwitz and Hiroshima*. The positivist history of Ranke is contrasted with the conservative orientation of Namier, the socialist perspective of Taylor, and the Marxism of E. P. Thompson.[42] In *The Order of Things* Foucault provides a postmodern theory of change that, in its denial of all things universal, appears to deny the concept of history.[43] Finally, Carr's orientation appears neither positivist nor Marxist, nor relativist, but hermeneutic. And it is this orientation that underpins my understanding of history. History is ongoing, a form of debate based around the interpretation of evidence.[44]

2.3 Past-masters in Comparative Education

I acknowledge the work of a wide range of comparative educationists.[45] However, it is the ideas of Bereday, Holmes and King that are located at the core of the book.

---

41 M. Olssen, *Michel Foucault: Materialism and Education* (London: Bergin & Garvey, 1999). M. Olssen, 'The School as the Microscope of Conduction: Doing Foucauldian Research in Education', in J. D. Marshall (ed.) *Post-structuralism, Philosophy, Pedagogy* (London: Kluwer Academic Publishers, 2004).

42 R. J. B. Bosworth, *Explaining Auschwitz and Hiroshima: History Writing and the Second World War 1945–1990* (London: Routledge, 1994).

43 M. Foucault, *The Order of Things: an Archaeology of the Human Sciences* (London: Routledge, 1991).

44 E. H. Carr, *What is History?* (London: Penguin Books, 1990).

45 M. Sadler, 'Study of Foreign Systems of Education', *Comparative Education Review*, 1 3 (1964), pp.307–314. I. L. Kandel, *Studies in Comparative Education* (London, Harrap, 1933). N. Hans, *Comparative Education* (London: Routledge & Kegan Paul, 1951). P. G. Altbach and G. P. Kelly (eds.) *New Approaches to Comparative Education* (Chicago: University of Chicago Press, 1986). V. Masemann, 'Critical Ethnography in the Study of Comparative Education', in P. G. Altbach and G. P. Kelly (eds.) *New Approaches to Comparative Education*, op. cit. R. Cowen, 'Last Past the Post:

Bereday is acknowledged as one of the great pioneers of method in comparative educational research.[46] In *Comparative Method in Education* Bereday argues that overseas experiences and a knowledge of foreign languages are essential prerequisites for comparative educational research.[47] Bereday emphasised these prerequisites as early as the 1950s, but in *Comparative Method in Education* and the works that followed he develops his ideas into a fully rationalised methodology.[48]

Syllabus topics in school history education are literally saturated in cultural particularities, historical knowledge encased within a language, and it is for this reason that Bereday's prerequisites for comparative research appear significant.

Comparative Education, Modernity and Perhaps Post-Modernity', op. cit. (note 39). R. Cowen, 'Performativity, Post-Modernity and the University', op. cit. (note 39). H. J. Noah and M. A. Eckstein, *Doing Comparative Education: Three Decades of Collaboration* (Hong Kong: University of Hong Kong Comparative Education Research Center, 1998). R. Alexander, P. Broadfoot, and D. Phillips (eds.) 'Learning from Comparing: New Directions', in *Comparative Educational Research*, Vol. 1: *Contexts, Classrooms and Outcomes* (Oxford: Symposium Books, 1999). P. Broadfoot, 'Editorial: Structure and Agency in Education: the Role of Comparative Education', *Comparative Education*, 38 1 (2002), pp.5–6. D. Phillips, 'Comparative Historical Studies in Education: Problems of Periodisation Reconsidered', *British Journal of Educational Studies*, 50 3 (2000), pp.363–377.

46   G. Z. F. Bereday, 'A Note on Textbooks in Comparative Education', *Comparative Education Review* , 1 1 (1957), pp.3–4. G. Z. F. Bereday, 'Some Methods of Teaching Comparative Education', *Comparative Education Review*, 1 3 (1958), pp.4–9. G. Z. F. Bereday and R. V. Rapacz, 'Kruschev's Proposals for Soviet Education', *Teachers College Record*, 60 3 (1958), pp.138–149. G. Z. F. Bereday and L. Volpicelli (eds.) *Public Education in America* (New York: Harper, 1959). G. Z. F. Bereday, 'Comparative Education at Columbia University', *Comparative Education Review*, 4 1 (1960), pp.15–17. G. Z. F. Bereday and J. Pennar (eds.) *The Politics of Soviet Education* (New York: Praeger, 1960). G. Z. F. Bereday, 'Sir Michael Sadler's "Study of Foreign Systems of Education"', *Comparative Education Review*, 1 3 (1964), pp.307–314. G. Z. F. Bereday, 'School Systems and Mass Demand: A Comparative Overview', in G. Z. F. Bereday (ed.) *Essays on World Education* (New York: Oxford University Press, 1969).

47   G. Z. F. Bereday, *Comparative Method in Education* (New York: Holt, Rinehart and Winston, 1964).

48   G. Z. F. Bereday, 'Some Discussion of Methods in Comparative Education', *Comparative Education Review*, 1 1 (1957), pp.13–15. G. Z. F. Bereday, *Comparative Method in Education*, op. cit. (note 47). G. Z. F. Bereday, 'Reflections on Comparative Methodology in Education, 1964–1966', *Comparative Education*, 3 3 (1967), pp.169–187.

In *Orientalism*, however, it is Said who reminds us that proximity to contexts is defined by cultural as well as linguistic and experiential parameters.[49]

The work of 'deductive' liberals such as Holmes and King appear in opposition to the work of the 'inductive' Bereday. And yet a hermeneutic reading of the work of all three, as utilised in this book, enables us to conceptualise a complementary approach – a synthesis. Holmes and King are the two most important methodologists of comparative education to have emerged from the UK in the 1960s. Where the writings of Bereday are useful in the way that they enable the conceptualisation of research horizons and proximity to contexts, the work of both Holmes and King provide the methodological tools necessary to approach contexts.[50]

Holmes provides a systematic and complex approach to comparative education – 'the problem approach'.[51] While strongly anti-positivist, Holmes nevertheless insists that his approach is scientific.[52] This is due in large part to his adherence to Popper.[53] In his work, Holmes charts a hermeneutic 'third way' between absolute determinism and chance, a position not dissimilar to either Popper or, his other major influence, Dewey. Research is regenerative and ongoing for Holmes, we test hypotheses through falsification rather than verification, and we investigate contexts on a piecemeal basis in order to solve problems as and when they arise. We cannot solve everything in one swoop, but we cannot leave problems to chance either.[54] In *Comparative Education: Some Considerations of Method*, Holmes draws attention to the importance of Weber in his

---

49 E. Said, *Orientalism* (New York: Pantheon, 1978).

50 B. Holmes, *Problems in Education: A Comparative Approach* (London: Routledge & Kegan Paul, 1965). E. King, *Comparative Studies and Educational Decision* (London: Methuen, 1968).

51 B. Holmes, 'The Problem Approach in Comparative Education: Some Methodological Considerations', *Comparative Education Review*, 2 1 (1958), pp.3–8. B. Holmes, *Problems in Education: A Comparative Approach,* op. cit. (note 50).

52 B. Holmes, 'Comparative Education as a Scientific Study', *British Journal of Educational Studies*, 20 2 (1972), pp.205–219.

53 B. Holmes, 'The Positivist Debate in Comparative Education: An Anglo-Saxon Perspective', *Comparative Education* , 13 2 (1977), pp.115–132. B. Holmes, 'Paradigm Shifts in Comparative Education', *Comparative Education Review*, 28 4 (1984), pp.584–604.

54 B. Holmes, 'Causality, Determinism, and Comparative Education as a Social Science', in J. Schreiwer (ed.) *Theories and Methods in Comparative Education,* op. cit. (note 32).

methodology. Through the use of ideal types we are provided with a means to gauge variations across educational contexts.[55]

The work of King may be said to complement the work of Holmes.[56] Where King's approach is similarly anti-positivist and liberal he draws significant attention to the importance of languages and cultural awareness, elements lacking in the work of Holmes.[57] Yet King's culturalism is not 'exclusive' or 'elitist' like Bereday's.

According to King, where the ability to speak particular languages is lacking, the researcher must work in teams with others who possess the necessary linguistic prowess.[58] Implicit in King's work is an approach conducive to hermeneutic interpretations and the use of Weber, to gauge variations across educational contexts.[59]

The work of Popper is important. Holmes describes his adherence to Popper contra critical theory in his largely critical assessment of the symposium that took place between Popper and the Frankfurt School during the 1960s.[60] Yet Dahrendorf's response to the symposium suggests that the debate was, in fact, not

---

55   B. Holmes, *Comparative Education: Some Considerations of Method* (London: George Alien & Unwin, 1981).

56   J. Nicholls, 'From Antithesis to Synthesis: re-interpreting the Brian Holmes/Edmund King dialectic', *Research in Comparative and International Education*, 1 4 (2006), pp.320–334.

57   E. King, 'Analytical Frameworks in Comparative Education', *Comparative Education*, 11 1 (1975), pp.85–103. E. King, 'Students, Teachers and Researchers in Comparative Education', *Comparative Education Review*, 3 1 (1959), pp.33–36. E. King, *World Perspectives in Education* (London: Methuen, 1962). E. King, *Education and Social Change* (Oxford: Pergamon, 1966). E. King, *Comparative Studies and Educational Decision* (London: Methuen, 1968). E. King, *Other Schools and Ours: Comparative Studies for Today* (London: Holt, Rinehart & Winston, 1979).

58   E. King, 'Book review, Comparative Method in Education by G. W. Z. Bereday', *Comparative Education*, 1 1 (1964), pp.37–38.

59   E. King, *Comparative Studies and Educational Decision*, op. cit. (note 50). E. King, 'Analytical Frameworks in Comparative Education', *Comparative Education*, 11 1 (1975), pp.85–103. E. King, 'Comparative Studies: An Evolving Commitment, a Fresh Realism', *Comparative Education*, 13 2 (1975), pp.101–108. E. King, 'Education, Individuality and Community: International Comparisons', in: *British Journal of Educational Studies*, 28 2 (1980), pp.112–123.

60   K. R. Popper, *The Open Society and its Enemies* (London: Routledge & Kegan Paul, 1945). K. R. Popper, 'Reason or Revolution?' in T. W. Adorno (ed.) *The Positivist Dispute in German Sociology* (London: Heinemann, 1976). B. Holmes, 'The Positivist Debate in Comparative Education: An Anglo-Saxon Perspective', *Comparative Education* (1977) 13 2, pp.115–132.

a debate: Popper and Adorno are understood by Dahrendorf to be essentially in agreement on many issues.[61]

The combined work of Holmes and King leads the researcher to Weber and, in particular, to the use of ideal types as a means to gauging variations across educational contexts. MacRae and Whimster provide useful introductions to the ideas of Weber.[62] In *The Methodology of the Social Sciences*, Weber himself details the key aspects of his interpretative approach and, in particular, his investigative tool: the 'ideal type'. According to Weber, ideal types act as a guiding point against which to assess variations. They allow us to construct hypotheses based on what is 'typical' rather than desirable. Where they are not a description they help to clarify descriptions. As tools, ideal types provide the necessary fixed moment in time and space against which it becomes possible to describe and make assessments, a provisional gauge against which comparisons become possible.[63]

Like Weber, Adorno inhabits a location that comes after Hegel, and exists between the opposition of Marx and Nietzsche. But in Adorno's hands the warmth of Gadamer, and the euphoria to be found in late Foucault is lost. Instead he offers a 'melancholy science', the expression of 'damaged life', a Negative Dialectics that leads the subject downwards towards political resignation. However, in Adorno's *Negative Dialectics* we are introduced to the useful concept of 'constellations' – the configuration of perspectives around the object that together enable us to understand the meaning of the object as a concept.[64] Constellations may be conceived as a sophisticated methodological device akin to Weber's concept of 'ideal types'.

Paulston provides the means to re-conceptualise 'social' relations and discourses using the concept of mapping. However, in his 'Mapping Comparative Education after Postmodemity', Paulston occupies a position between rather than 'beyond' the oppositions of modernity and post-modernity thinking. Trying to make sense of heterogeneity 'after postmodernity' he fails to detach himself from the concept of the de-centred subject.[65]

61 R. Dahrendorf, 'Remarks on the discussion of the papers by Karl R. Popper and Theodore W. Adorno' in T. W. Adorno, *The Positivist Dispute in German Sociology*, op. cit. (note 60).

62 D. MacRae, *Max Weber* (London: Fontana Modern Masters, 1987). S. Whimster (ed.) *The Essential Weber* (London: Routledge, 2004).

63 M. Weber, *The Methodology of the Social Sciences* (Illinois: The Free Press, 1949).

64 T. W. Adorno, *Negative Dialectics* (London: Routledge, 1973). M. Jay, *Adorno* (London: Fontana, 1984).

65 R. G. Paulston, 'Mapping Comparative Education after Postmodernity', *Comparative Education Review*, 43 4 (1999), pp.438–463.

2.4 Comparative Textbook Research

The methodology I propose for comparing syllabus topics across cultures develops, in part, from the problems identified with school textbook research. In my earlier published work, the application of Hegelian, late Foucauldian and hermeneutic ideas leads to the fundamental questioning of textbook research as a practice. By combining the work of Hegel, Gadamer, Weber, Adorno, Foucault, Bereday, Holmes and King, former endeavours appear flawed.

In my early papers, textbooks are conceived as centred objects, and as a means to understanding World War II as a syllabus topic in school history.[66] This perspective is implicit in the work of several authors involved in school textbook research.[67] But in my own work, in the attempt to apply Hegelian thinking, textbooks come to be understood as de-centred objects, meaning different things in different places.[68] Following the Hegelian dynamic through to its conclusions the

---

66   J. Nicholls, 'Methods in School Textbook Research', *International Journal of Historical Learning, Teaching and Research*, 3 2 (2003), pp.11–26. J. Nicholls, 'The portrayal of the atomic bombing of Nagasaki in US and English school history textbooks', *International Textbook Research*, 25 1 (2003), pp.63–84. S. J. Foster and J. Nicholls, 'Portrayal of America's Role in World War II: An Analysis of School History Textbooks from England, Japan, Sweden and the USA', paper presented at the American Educational Research Association (AERA) Annual Meeting, Chicago, USA, 21st–25th April 2003. J. Nicholls and S. J. Foster, 'Portrayal of the Soviet Role in World War II: An Analysis of School History Textbooks from England and the USA', paper presented at the International School Textbook and Educational Media Conference, Edge Hill College of Higher Education, Ormskirk, Lancashire, UK, 23rd–24th June 2003. J. Nicholls, 'Comparing the portrayal of World War II in School History Textbooks Beyond Describing: Epistemological and Methodological Issues in Comparative Textbook Research', paper presented at the Comparative Education Society of Hong Kong (CESHK) Annual Conference, University of Hong Kong, China, 7th February 2004.

67   V. R. Berghahn and H. Schissler, *Perceptions of History: International Textbook Research on Britain, Germany and the United States* (Oxford: Berg Press, 1987). F. Pingel, *UNESCO Guidebook on Textbook Research and Textbook Revision* (Hannover: Verlag Hahnsche Buchhandlung, 1999). J. Mikk, *Textbook: Research and Writing* (Frankfurt am Main: Peter Lang, 2000).

68   J. Nicholls, 'Beyond the National and the Transnational: Representations of WWII in the School History Textbooks of Five Countries', paper presented at the Comparative and International Education Society (CIES) 48th Annual Conference, Salt Lake City, Utah, USA, 9th–12th March 2004. J. Nicholls, 'Beyond the National and the Transnational: Perspectives of WWII in the School history Textbooks of Three European

---

final wave of my own publications calls fundamentally into question the school history textbook as a universal equivalent worthy of comparison.[69] The philosophical underpinning I now adopt propels 'reason' through and beyond textbook research, toward the methodology proposed here.

2.5 School History across Cultures: Japan, Sweden & England

Using a combination of thinkers and concepts the researcher is able to position a given syllabus topic in school history amidst configurations of power and knowledge in a given setting. Yet to understand school history in a setting will require in depth research into the context in question. In this book, Japan, Sweden and England have been identified and located on this subject's research horizon.

Education in Japan has long been a source of intrigue for scholars around the globe. Many point to Japan's distinctive traditions as a means of understanding the contemporary system.[70] Some focus on problems in the system and the need for reform while others investigate the successes or failures of particular reforms at particular points in time or the difficulties of reform.[71] White points to how

Countries', paper presented at the Comparative Education Society in Europe (CESE) 2004 Conference, Copenhagen, Denmark, 27th June–1st July 2004. J. Nicholls, 'The Philosophical Underpinnings of School Textbook Research', *Paradigm*, 3 1 (2005), pp.24–35.

69 J. Nicholls, 'Are Students Expected to Critically Engage with Textbook Perspectives of the Second World War? A Comparative and International study', *Research in Comparative and International Education*, 1 1 (2006), pp.40–55. J. Nicholls, 'Beyond the National and the Transnational: Perspectives of World War II in U.S.A, Italian, Swedish, Japanese, and English School History Textbooks', in S. J. Foster and K. A. Crawford (eds.) *What Shall We Tell the Children? International Perspectives on School History Textbooks* (Connecticut: Information Age, 2006).

70 E. R. Beauchamp, 'The Development of Japanese Educational Policy, 1945–1985', *History of Education Quarterly*, 27 3 (1987), pp.299–324. M. Stephens, *Japan and Education* (London: Macmillan, 1991).

71 Duke, 'The liberalisation of Japanese Education', op. cit. (note 1). T. Horio, 'Towards Reform in Japanese Education: a Critique of Privatisation and Proposals for the Re-creation of Public Education', *Comparative Education* (1986) 22 1, pp.2I–36. T. Horio, *Educational Thought and Ideology in Modern Japan* (Tokyo: University of Tokyo Press, 1988). G. Tsuchimochi, *Education Reform in Post war Japan: The 1946*

Western scholars look to Japan as an example of good practice due to the perception that a strong economy is the product of an efficient education system.[72]
School history education in Japan frequently receives scholarly attention.[73] Many authors focus on Japanese actions during World War II and the way that this past has been dealt with in schools.[74] According to Barnard, school history education in Japan is essentially conservative in terms of content and teaching methodology. In Japan, rote learning involving traditional teaching styles, heavy reliance on school textbooks and the memorisation of 'facts' continues to prevail.[75]

Kanaya points out that, unlike England and Wales, there is no centralised 'National Curriculum' in Japan, but rather a set of curriculum guidelines. The guidelines are relatively general in nature and open to interpretation, and nowhere near as influential as the high school and university entrance examinations.[76] In his important work, *The Japanese*, Reischauer traces the roots of the examination system in Japan back to ancient China and the Confucian bureaucratic selection process.[77]

According to Barnard, school history examinations in Japan do not test a student's ability to reason but rather their ability to memorise factual information.

U.S. Education Mission (Tokyo: University of Tokyo Press, 1993). L. Schoppa, *Education Reform in Japan: A Case of Immobilist Politics* (London: Routledge, 1993).

72   White, *The Japanese Educational Challenge*, op. cit. (note 2).

73   R. J. B. Bosworth, Explaining *Auschwitz and Hiroshima: History Writing and the Second World War 1945–1990*, op. cit. (note 42). L. Hein and M. Seldon (eds.) *Censoring History: Citizenship and Memory in Japan, Germany, and the United States* (Armonk: East Gate, 2000). Barnard, *Language, Ideology and Japanese History Textbooks*, op. cit. (note 6).

74   M. Yamazumi, 'State Control and the Evolution of Ultranationalistic Textbooks' in J. Shields (ed.) *Japanese Schooling: Patterns of Socialization, Equality and Political Control* (Pennsylvania: Pennsylvania State University Press, 1989). A. Gerow, 'Consuming Asia, Consuming Japan: The New Neonationalist Revisionism in Japan' in L. Hein and M. Seldon (eds.) *Censoring History*, op. cit. (note 73). V. J. Mayer, 'World War II in Social Studies and Science Curricula', *Phi Delta Kappan*, May 2000, pp.705–711. G. McCormack, 'The Japanese movement to "correct" history', in L. Hein and M. Selden (eds.) *Censoring History*, op. cit. (note 73). Y. Noguchi, and H. Inokuchi, 'Japanese Education, Nationalism, and Ienaga Subaro's Textbook Lawsuits', in L. Hein and M. Selden (eds.) *Censoring History*, op. cit. (note 73) M. Ogawa, and S. Field, 'Causation, Controversy and Contrition', op. cit. (note 7).

75   Barnard, *Language, Ideology and Japanese History Textbooks*, op. cit. (note 6).

76   Kanaya, 'Japan', op. cit. (note 10).

77   E. O. Reischauer, *The Japanese* (Cambridge: Massachusetts, 1977).

Successful students are those that possess the ability to memorise 'the facts' most effectively. With increasing competition, Barnard tells us, students are required to memorise greater amounts of factual information in order to enter the most prestigious high schools.[78] Others have made similar observations, arguing that the system is in desperate need of reform.[79]

According to Clark, the use of the Internet and other forms of digital media is a rarity in Japanese schoolrooms. Likewise, with relatively few students able to speak English, access to the huge range of on-line resources in the English language is likely to be lower than in many other developed countries.[80] As a form of classroom media, Nicholls observes how the school textbook continues to dominate history lessons in Japan.[81] Other authors point out that Japanese history syllabuses are dominated by the content of textbooks, with teachers teaching from the textbook to prepare their students for examinations.[82] As discussed by Larsson, Booth and Mathews, students in Japan are expected to learn history 'by heart' to guarantee examination success.[83]

Horio, Yamazumi and others point to the conservative treatment of events in school textbooks, particularly Japan's controversial role during the Second World War. This, they argue, is not simply a case of the conservative authorship of texts, but the Japanese government's controlling and illiberal censorship policies.[84]

---

78 Barnard, *Language, Ideology and Japanese History Textbooks*, op. cit. (note 6).
79 Duke, 'The Liberalisation of Japanese Education', op. cit. (note 1). White, *The Japanese Educational Challenge*, op. cit. (note 2).
80 T. Clark, 'Japan's Generation of Computer Refuseniks', 2003. [Internet] *Japan Media Review*. Available from <http://www.iapanmediareview.com/iapan/wireless/1047257047.php> [Accessed 2nd December 2005].
81 J. Nicholls, 'Are Students Expected to Critically Engage with Textbook Perspectives of the Second World War? A Comparative and International study', *Research in Comparative and International Education* (2006) 1 1, pp.40–55.
82 R. J. B. Bosworth, *Explaining Auschwitz and Hiroshima: History Writing and the Second World War 1945–1990* (London: Routledge, 1994). T. Yoshida, 'History Textbooks: For Whom and For What Purpose?', *Asian Studies Newsletter* (2000) 45 4, pp.13–14. M. Ogawa and S. Field, 'Causation, Controversy and Contrition', op. cit. (note 7).
83 Y. Larsson, M. Booth, and R. Mathews, R., 'Attitudes to the Teaching of History and the Use of Creative Skills in Japan and England: a comparative study', *Compare* (1988) 28 3, pp.305–314.
84 T. Horio, *Educational Thought and Ideology in Modern Japan* (Tokyo: University of Tokyo Press, 1988). M. Yamazumi, 'State Control and the Evolution of Ultranationalistic Textbooks' in J. Shields (ed.) *Japanese Schooling: Patterns of Socialization,*

In *Censoring History*, Hein and Seldon detail how, from the late 1980s, Japan's mass media played an important role with regard to raising national consciousness about the wartime past. Many of the 'liberal' perspectives encountered by students in the press and on TV called the treatment of events in school history textbooks into question.[85] Lichtenberg points out that Japan's press is liberal with a wide circulation.[86] Others suggest that the television media is more controlled, particularly with regard to the screening of programmes touching on Japan's role during World War II.[87] McCormack observes the nationalist backlash of the late 1990s as a counter reaction to the 'liberal press' from Japan's right wing media.[88]

Some commentators observe parallel patterns in Japanese politics. Several scholars detail the defeat of the long ruling conservative government in the national elections of 1993, and the brief ascendancy of 'reform' oriented coalition governments.[89] Other authors write about the ideological shift that led to an official apology to neighbouring Asian countries for atrocities committed by Japanese wartime forces.[90] Nevertheless, as pointed out by Fukui and Fukai, this period of liberal reform would be brief, the conservatives returning to power in 1996.[91]

Equality and Political Control (Pennsylvania: Pennsylvania State University Press, 1989). Y. Noguchi and H. Inokuchi, 'Japanese Education, Nationalism, and Ienaga Subaro's Textbook Lawsuits', in L. Hein and M. Selden (eds.) *Censoring History: Citizenship and Memory in Japan, Germany, and the United States* (Armonk: M. E. Sharpe, 2000). Barnard, *Language, Ideology and Japanese History Textbooks*, op. cit. (note 6).

85 L. Hein and M. Seldon (eds.) *Censoring History: Citizenship and Memory in Japan, Germany, and the United States* (Armonk: East Gate, 2000).

86 H. H. Lichtenberg, 'Japan's 6 Major Daily Newspapers', 2005. [Internet] *Japan Media Review*. Available at: <http://www.japanmediareview.com/japan/wiki/Shimbunwiki> [Accessed November–December 2005].

87 M. Fukayama, 'Japan's 6 Premier Television Broadcasters', 2005. [Internet] *Japan Media Review*. Available from: <http://www.japanmediareview.com/iapan/wiki/tvwi ki/> [Accessed December 2005].

88 McCormack, 'The Japanese movement to "correct" history', op. cit. (note 42).

89 G. W. Noble, 'Japan in 1993: Humpty Dumpty had a Great Fall', Asian Survey (1994) 34 1, pp.19–29. M. Blaker, 'Japan in 1994: Out with the Old, in with the New?', *Asian Survey* (1995) 35 1, pp.1–12. M. Blaker, M. 'Japan in 1995: A Year of Natural and Other Disasters', in: *Asian Survey* (1996) 361, pp.41–52.

90 P. C. Jain, 'A New Political Era in Japan the 1993 Election', *Asian Survey* (1993) 33 11, pp.1071–1082. R. Mukae, 'Japan's Diet Resolution on World War Two: Keeping History at Bay', *Asian Survey* (1996) 36 10, pp.1011–1030.

91 H. Fukui, and S. N. Fukai, 'Japan in 1996: Between Hope and Uncertainty', *Asian Survey* (1997) 37 1, pp.20–28.

With the end of the Cold War Japan has become uncertain with regard to its role and place in the world, write Ogawa and Field.[92] In such a climate, nationalism has become increasingly appealing on the popular level, to which conservative governments have responded. In the work of contemporary authors we see how the Ministry has made demands on schools. The singing of the national anthem and the raising of the national flag, for example, are now compulsory at school graduation ceremonies.[93]

Swedish education has long attracted the attention of scholars[94]. Due to its pioneering egalitarian ethos and efficient delivery, Ball and Larson argue that Swedish education offers an effective model to be followed.[95] Nicholls observes how, as a politically neutral country, Sweden would occupy a unique position between the ideological oppositions, both in the Second World War and in the Cold War.[96]

For Pontusson, the economic recession of the 1990s brought the welfare policies of the post-war 'golden age' to a distressing close.[97] And, as Nicholls points out, the end of the Cold War brought Sweden's neutrality policy into question in several respects. Without communism and the Soviet Union, what did neutrality now mean?[98] In the work of Salin and Waterman, the contemporary education scene, must be understood against the changes affecting Sweden during the 1990s.[99]

Salin and Waterman describe how school subjects in Sweden are taught following 'very loose' curriculum guidelines. Where education during the post-war era would be highly centralised, this feature would be radically reversed during the

---

92 Ogawa and Field, 'Causation, Controversy and Contrition', op. cit. (note 7).

93 Ogawa and Field, 'Causation, Controversy and Contrition', op. cit. (note 7).

94 S. Marklund, 'Sweden', in N. Postlethwaite (ed.) *International Encyclopaedia of National Systems of Education* (Oxford: Pergamon, 1995).

95 S. Ball and S. Larson, 'Education, Politics and Society in Sweden: an Introduction', in S. Ball and S. Larson (eds.) *The Struggle for Democratic Education, Equality and Participation in Sweden* (New York: Palmer Press, 1989).

96 J. Nicholls, 'Are Students Expected to Critically Engage with Textbook Perspectives of the Second World War? A Comparative and International study', *Research in Comparative and International Education*, 2006, 1 1, pp.40–55.

97 J. Pontusson, 'Sweden: After the Golden Age', in P. Anderson and P. Camiller (eds.) *Mapping the West European Left* (New York: Verso, 1994).

98 J. Nicholls, 'Are Students Expected to Critically Engage with Textbook Perspectives of the Second World War? A Comparative and International study', *Research in Comparative and International Education* (2006) 1 1, pp.40–55.

99 S. Salin, and C. Waterman, 'Sweden', in C. Brock and W. Tulusiewicz (eds.) *Education in a Single Europe* (London: Routledge, 2006).

1990s.[100] According to MacGregor-Thunell, it is now the local schools and their teachers who decide on the history that is taught at the compulsory *grundskola*. If a teacher can cover all the requirements stipulated by the curriculum guidelines by teaching only a single topic, then they are free to do so.[101] Examination procedures are equally liberal in Sweden. As Marklund points out, this has long been a feature of the system.[102] Salin and Waterman detail how, since the 1990s, national tests have been set for Swedish, mathematics and English, but not for other curriculum subjects such as history.[103]

As argued by Walker, the precise role of the teacher in the history classroom in Sweden is difficult to ascertain. This is because history teachers experience higher levels of freedom and autonomy to decide on what and how they teach than in almost any other country.[104] Teachers of history in Sweden may be usefully understood as important 'gatekeepers', using the concept developed by Thornton.[105]

Nicholls argues that due to the radically decentralised nature of compulsory education in Sweden, it is extremely difficult to identify the type of media commonly used to assist the teaching and learning of school history. Teachers are free to use textbooks, if and when they see fit. To teach classes without textbooks is equally permissible.[106] MacGregor-Thunell writes that textbook publishing has become an unprofitable business in Sweden, due to falling demand.[107] Yet, according to Groth, Sweden was quick to adapt to 'alternative' electronic forms

100 S. Salin, and C. Waterman, 'Sweden', op. cit. (note 99).
101 A. MacGregor-Thunell, *Teaching History in Sweden*, 2003 [Internet]. Available from: <http://www.schoolhistory.co.uk/forum/index.php?showtopic=2218> [Accessed December 2005].
102 S. Marklund, 'Sweden', in N. Postlethwaite (ed.) *International Encyclopaedia of National Systems of Education* (Oxford: Pergamon, 1995).
103 S. Salin, and C. Waterman, 'Sweden', in C. Brock and W. Tulusiewicz (eds.) *Education in a Single Europe* (London: Routledge, 2006).
104 A. Walker, *Teaching History in Sweden*, 2003 [Internet]. Available from: <http://www.schoolhistory.co.uk/forum/index.php?showtopic=2218> [Accessed December 2005].
105 S. Thornton, 'What is History in US History Textbooks?' in J. Nicholls (ed.) *School History Textbooks across Cultures: International Debates and Perspectives*, op. cit.
106 J. Nicholls, 'Are Students Expected to Critically Engage with Textbook Perspectives of the Second World War? A Comparative and International study', in: *Research in Comparative and International Education* (2006) 1 1, pp.40–55
107 A. MacGregor-Thunell, *Teaching History in Sweden*, 2003 [Internet]. Available from: <http://www.schoolhistory.co.uk/forum/index.php?showtopic=2218> [Accessed December 2005].

of classroom media. With its high average living standards and high levels of equity, most families residing in Sweden will possess a computer and be online. In addition to this, practically all schools will be connected.[108] The Swedish National Agency for Education provides popular Internet links, multilingual learning opportunities, and online interactive sources for students and teachers of school history.[109]

Educational media is not censored in Sweden but produced, bought and sold in an open and liberal market. In contrast to nations like Japan, writes Henry, the actions of the Swedish government have tended to support initiatives for increased openness and transparency.[110] According to Freedom House, the Swedish press and television media is liberal and open in Sweden, containing a wide variety of perspectives on past events.[111]

Sweden has not been to war for 200 years. Levine points to the profound effect that this has had on Swedish politics, consciousness and national identity[112]. Writing in the 1960s, Sandier speaks of an almost 'natural' connection between Sweden and political neutrality[113]. Yet, according to Nicholls, the collapse of the Soviet Union called Swedish neutrality into question in a most profound way. Essentially, it is argued, the Swedish political agenda has changed since the end of the Cold War.[114]

108 J. Groth, 'Physical or Virtual Networks? Connecting Swedish Schools to the Internet', paper presented at the 1998 Internet Summit, Geneva Switzerland 21st–24th July 1998.
109 Swedish National Agency for Education website [Internet]. Available from: <http://www.skolutveckling.se/skolnet/english/index.html> [Accessed June 2006].
110 J. Henry, 'Europe declares war on history books', *The Times Educational Supplement*, 2nd November 2001, p.3.
111 *Freedom of the Press 2005: Table of Global Press Freedom Rankings* (2005) [Internet]. Freedom House. Available from: <http://www.freedomhouse.org/research/pres survey.htm> [Accessed October–December 2005].
112 P. Levine, 'Swedish Neutrality during the Second World War: Tactical Success or Moral Compromise?' in N. Wylie (ed.), *European Neutrals and Non-Belligerents During the Second World War* (Cambridge: Cambridge University Press, 2002).
113 A. Sandier, 'Sweden's Postwar Diplomacy: Some Problems, Views, and Issues', *The Western Political Quarterly* (1960) 13 4, pp.924–933.
114 J. Nicholls, 'Are Students Expected to Critically Engage with Textbook Perspectives of the Second World War? A Comparative and International study', *Research in Comparative and International Education* (2006) 1 1, pp.40–55.

Puntasson describes how, since the 1930s, Swedish politics has been dominated by the Social Democrats, with few periods in opposition.[115] Moreover, as outlined by Jacob, Social Democratic Prime Minister Goran Persson would be the first to publicly denounce Sweden's wartime role.[116] The Persson government would go on to support the Living History Forum with, according to Henry, initiatives to change aspects of the curriculum for school history in an attempt to forge a new consensus.[117]

Convey and Merrit provide a useful overview of education in England. Where curriculum issues have been debated for many decades it was in 1988 that a prescriptive 'national curriculum' was introduced.[118] As detailed by Nicholls, history education in England has followed a distinctive path since the end of World War II. Prior to 1988, the tripartite and comprehensive systems offered forms of 'nonprescribed' curricula, content determined by the requirements set by the external examination syllabuses.[119]

The strongly prescriptive and centralised nature of the National Curriculum for history cannot be underestimated. Commentators such as Bolton draw attention to the importance of Callaghan's Ruskin speech on the need for a national curriculum.[120] Others such as Ross describe how the National Curriculum became the subject of intense debates.[121] Implemented during the years of conservative rule, writers such as Goodson and Hill remind us of the strong criticism pointed at the National Curriculum from commentators on the left.[122] In her diaries, Prime Minister Margaret Thatcher made it clear that she desired nothing less of National

115 J. Pontusson, 'Sweden: After the Golden Age', in P. Anderson and P. Camiller (eds.) *Mapping the West European Left* (New York: Verso, 1994).

116 G. Persson, G., quoted by A. Jacob, 'Persson turns spotlight on Sweden's dealings with Hitler', *The Guardian Weekly*, 27th January 2000.

117 J. Henry, 'Europe declares war on history books', *The Times Educational Supplement*, 2nd November 2001, p.3.

118 A. Convey and A. Merritt, 'The United Kingdom' in C. Brock and W. Tulusiewicz (eds.), *Education in a Single Europe* (London: Routledge, 2000).

119 J. Nicholls, 'Compulsory Schooling, Curricular Developments and History Education in England', *Journal of the Young Historians of Moldova* (2005) 6, pp.289–295.

120 E. Bolton, 'Perspectives on the National Curriculum', in P. O' Hear and J. White (eds.) *Assessing the National Curriculum* (London: Paul Chapman, 1993).

121 A. Ross, *Curriculum: Construction and Critique* (New York: Palmer Press, 2000).

122 I. F. Goodson, '"Nations at Risk" and "National Curriculum": Ideology and Identity', in I. F. Goodson, C. J. Anstead, and J. M. Mangan (eds.) *Subject Knowledge: Readings for the Study of School Subjects* (London: Palmer, 1998). D. Hill, 'The Third Way in Britain: New Labour's Neo-liberal Education Policy', paper presented

Curriculum history than a return to 'the facts', and a linear chronological story of the glories of Britain's past.[123] But, over the years, the National Curriculum has been re-adapted and transformed, in response to pressure from teachers, as outlined by Goodson.[124] This would culminate in the important Bearing Review.[125] Radicals such as Hill suggest that the National Curriculum was only superficially different under Blair and New Labour, and continued to exert an enormous as well as negative influence on what is taught and studied at schools.[126] At the official curriculum web site 'National Curriculum online' it is possible to ascertain the enormous popularity of World War II related topics.

Nicholls describes how the reforms of 1988 had a major impact on the examination and assessment of history in schools. Students would now be internally assessed by teachers throughout their entire school life, through the Key Stages.[127] As noted by the Qualifications and Curriculum Authority (QCA) history would be different to the core curriculum subjects of English, mathematics and science in terms of assessment.[128] As discussed by Nicholls, students must sit for GCSE examinations at the end of Key Stage 4 across all National Curriculum subjects, including history. GCSE level work has tended to involve both continuous assessment as well as preparation for externally examined 'closed' written papers, prepared by the powerful examination boards.[129] In recent years, the amount of

at Congress Marx International III, Universite de Paris-X Nanterre-Sorbonne, 29th September 2001.

123   M. Thatcher, *The Downing Street Years* (New York: Harper Collins, 1993).

124   I. F. Goodson, '"Nations at Risk" and "National Curriculum": Ideology and Identity', in I. F. Goodson, C. J. Anstead and J. M. Mangan (eds.), *Subject Knowledge: Readings for the Study of School Subjects*, op. cit. (note 137).

125   *Government Document, National Curriculum*, Department for Education (London: HMSO, 1995).

126   D. Hill, 'The Third Way in Britain: New Labour's Neo-liberal Education Policy', paper presented at Congress Marx International III, Universite de Paris-X Nanterre-Sorbonne, 29th September 2001.

127   J. Nicholls, 'Compulsory Schooling, Curricular Developments and History Education in England', *Journal of the Young Historians of Moldova*, 6, 2005, pp.289–295.

128   'Innovating with history' (2004) [Internet]. Qualifications and Curriculum Authority website. Available from: http://www.qca.org.uk/historv/innovating/key3/assessment [Accessed November 2005].

129   J. Nicholls, 'Compulsory Schooling, Curricular Developments and History Education in England', *Journal of the Young Historians of Moldova*, 6, 2005, pp.289–295.

continually assessed work involved in GCSE assessment has been debated, with calls from some to remove it completely.[130]

According to Nicholls, the school history textbook is in decline as a form of classroom media in England, in part due to the rise of alternative forms of media, educational software and the Internet.[131] Entrepreneurs like Bill Gates are now predicting the imminent demise of the textbook.[132] According to the E-Learning Foundation for England and the UK, computer access is increasingly taken for granted by young people attending schools.[133]

Moreover, this has mirrored reports from writers from other countries, such as Murray in the United States.[134] Yet, as argued by Liddle, large socio-economic inequities continue to divide UK society, having a direct impact on those with or without access to computers and the Internet.[135]

History textbooks once represented a central source of information in classes, as pointed out by Chancellor.[136] Yet according to Marsden, textbooks tend now to be looked down upon as teaching tools in England, conceived to be at odds with interactive and progressive forms of learning.[137] In the investigations of this author, if textbooks are to be used in history classes in England, it is as a single source among others.[138]

---

130 S. Bostock, 'Simplistic solution to plagiarism crisis', *Education Guardian*, 24th October 2006.

131 J. Nicholls, 'School History Textbooks across Cultures from the Perspective of Comparative Education', in J. Nicholls (ed.), *School History Textbooks across Cultures: International Debates and Perspectives* (Oxford, Symposium, 2006).

132 B. Gates, quoted by O. Gibson, 'Gates unveils his vision of a future made of silicon', *The Guardian*, 28th October 2005, p.1.

133 E-Learning Foundation web site [Internet]. Available from: <http://www.e-learning foundation.com> [Accessed November 2005].

134 C. Murray, 'Textbooks dumped in favour of laptops', 2004. [Internet] eSCHOOL NEWS. Available from: <http://www.eschoolnews.com/news/showStory.cfm> [Accessed October 2005].

135 R. Liddle, 'Secondary pupils struggle with the internet', 2003. [Internet] *Guardian Unlimited*, 29th July 2003. Available from: http://education.guardian.co.uk.

136 V. Chancellor, *History for their Masters: Opinion in the 18th Century History Textbook 1800–1914* (New York: Augustus Kelly, 1970).

137 W. E. Marsden, *The School Textbook: Geography, History and Social Studies* (London: Woburn Press, 2001).

138 J. Nicholls 'Beyond the National and the Transnational: Representations of WWII in the School History Textbooks of Five Countries', paper presented at the Comparative and International Education Society (CIES) 48th Annual Conference, Salt Lake City,

As pointed out by this author in two previous publications, even though student-centred approaches to teaching and learning history have been pioneered in Britain, the National Curriculum and the external examination boards tend to determine the syllabus in history classes in England.[139] This being said, authors such as Larsson, Booth and Mathews contrast the critical approach to engaging with historical evidence expected of students in England against the emphasis on rote learning and memorisation in schools in Japan. In England, teachers are expected to be facilitators, students to 'learn by doing'.[140] Nevertheless, there are limits to the freedoms experienced by teachers in England. For radicals like Hill, Ofsted represents one of several areas of knowledge surveillance by the state, implemented by the Conservatives and subsequently maintained by New Labour.[141]

Authors like Hedetoft make strong connections between the politics of Thatcherism and a new kind of nationalism in Britain. The New Right's mix of conservatism and the market gave rise to an aggressive platform on domestic and international issues in which the government appeared constantly at war.[142] For Coman, anti-European and especially anti-German attitudes are supported by the

Utah, USA, 9th–12th March 2004. J. Nicholls, 'Beyond the National and the Transnational: Perspectives of WWII in the school history textbooks of three European countries', paper presented at the Comparative Education Society in Europe (CESE) 2004 Conference, Copenhagen, Denmark, 27th June–1st July 2004. J. Nicholls, 'Student Engagement with Textbook Perspectives of World War II: Summary of an International and Comparative Study', *Research at Oxford by Students of Education (ROSE)* (2005) 1 3, pp.39–48. J. Nicholls, 'Are Students Expected to Critically Engage with Textbook Perspectives of the Second World War? A Comparative and International study', *Research in Comparative and International Education* (2006) 1 1, pp.40–55.

139 J. Nicholls, 'Compulsory Schooling, Curricular Developments and History Education in England', *Journal of the Young Historians of Moldova*, 6, 2005, pp.289–295. J. Nicholls, 'Are Students Expected to Critically Engage with Textbook Perspectives of the Second World War? A Comparative and International study', Research in Comparative and International Education, (2006) 1 1, pp.40–55.

140 Y. Larsson, M. Booth and R. Mathews, 'Attitudes to the Teaching of History and the Use of Creative Skills in Japan and England: A Comparative Study', *Compare* (1988) 28 3, pp.305–314.

141 D. Hill, 'The Third Way in Britain: New Labour's Neo-liberal Education Policy', paper presented at Congress Marx International III, Universite de Paris-X Nanterre-Sorbonne, 29th September 2001. The government referred to here lost office in May 2010, when a Coalition formed by the Conservative and Liberal parties came to power (Britain's first coalition government since World War 11). BC

142 U. Hedetoft, 'National Identities and Mentalities of War in Three EC Countries', *Journal of Peace Research* (1993) 30 3, pp.281–300.

'free' yet largely right-wing British tabloid press.[143] According to Hill, the legacy of the New Right revolution in education and society in England remains very much at large with the politics of New Labour.[144]

2.6 History Writing on World War II: Japan, Sweden & England

In this book I have used World War II as an exemplar topic. Next to variables such as the curriculum, examinations and censorship, historiography is understood as potentially affecting the content of a syllabus topic in a given context. In addition to this, knowledge of history writing on a given theme or issue will assist the researcher's assessment of content. In the three countries identified within this subject's research horizon, the meaning of World War II in history writing has seen major changes over the years.

In *Explaining Auschwitz and Hiroshima*, Bosworth provides a comprehensive overview of writings by Japanese historians on Japan and World War II. With the Cold War and US support for conservative political administrations in Japan, school history education would become the platform for the official version of the past. The voice of historians in the academy, like the radical teachers' unions, pushed to the sidelines and effectively silenced.[145]

As pointed out by Barshay, however, historians such as Murayama Masao would distinguish themselves during the 1950s and 1960s by emphasising the failures of the Japanese emperor system and Japanese fascism. While their influence outside of the academy would be marginal, the so-called 'modernist' school would dedicate itself to scrutinising the anti-democratic forces that controlled Japan during the 1930s and the 1940s.[146]

---

143 P. Coman, 'Reading about the Enemy: School textbook representation of Germany's role in the war with Britain during the period from April 1940 to May 1941', *British Journal of the Sociology of Education* (1996) 173, pp.327–340.

144 D. Hill, 'The Third Way in Britain: New Labour's neo-liberal education policy', paper presented at Congress Marx International III, Universite de Paris-X Nanterre- Sorbonne, 29th September 2001.

145 R. J. B. Bosworth, *Explaining Auschwitz and Hiroshima: History Writing and the Second World War 1945–1990* (London: Routledge, 1994).

146 A. E. Barshay, 'Imagining Democracy in Postwar Japan: Reflections on Maruyama Masao and Modernism', *Journal of Japanese Studies* (1992) 18 2, pp.365–406.

Olson details the work of other radicals of the post-war period such as Yoshimoto Takaaki and Takeuchi Yoshimi.[147] Yoshimoto would be concerned with what went wrong during the 1930s and the 1940s. Takeuchi would focus on the legacy of failure, of how Japan's war destroyed Japan's future. Japan had become a nation that should no longer be trusted, until it had atoned for its past. But atonement was not possible, it was argued, while the Japanese understood their future to be tied to the United States rather than Asia.[148]

Historians such as Tsurami challenge conventional perceptions of the past in light of the ever more vocal condemnations of Japan's wartime role by neighbouring countries. In Tsurumi's work, Japan is understood as having propagated a fifteen-year war, beginning in 1931. Accordingly, the war against the United States is interpreted as occupying the final four years of a much longer conflict.[149] But one particularly famous debate over Japan's wartime past begins in the 1960s. Noguchi and Inokuchi provide a summary of Ienaga Saburo's three-decade court battle with the Japanese Ministry of Education over the censorship of school history textbooks.[150] As early as the 1960s Caiger describes Saburo as an intellectual watchdog 'for the community'.[151] In *Censoring History*, Hein and Selden observe how Saburo was only the most famous of a host of intellectuals fighting the Japanese government over the censorship of the wartime past.[152]

The economic and political uncertainty characteristic of Japan in the 1990s is exhibited in history writing in the form of the rise of nationalist perspectives. For authors such as Fujioka, Nishio and Hata, Japan liberated neighbouring countries

---

147 L. Olson, 'Intellectuals and "The People"; On Yoshimoto Takaaki', *Journal of Japanese Studies* (1978) 4 2, pp.327–357. L. Olson, 'Takeuchi Yoshimi and the Vision of a Protest Society in Japan', *Journal of Japanese Studies* (1981) 1 2, pp.319–348.

148 L. Olson, 'Takeuchi Yoshimi and the Vision of a Protest Society in Japan', *Journal of Japanese Studies*, 1981, 1 2, pp.319–348.

149 S. Tsurumi, *An Intellectual History of Wartime Japan 1931–1945* (London: KPI, 1986).

150 Y. Noguchi, and H. Inokuchi, 'Japanese Education, Nationalism, and Ienaga Suba-ro's Textbook Lawsuits', in L. Hein and M. Selden (eds.) *Censoring History: Citizenship and Memory in Japan, Germany and the United States* (Armonk, M. E. Sharpe, 2000).

151 J. Caiger, 'Ienaga Saburo and the First Postwar Japanese History Textbook', in: *Modern Asian Studies*, 1969, 3 1, pp.1–16.

152 L. Hein and M. Selden (eds.) *Censoring History: Citizenship and Memory in Japan, Germany and the United States* (Armonk: M. E. Sharpe, 2000).

from Western Imperialism during the 1930s. The rise of nationalist history in Japan during the late 1990s is approached in detail by several authors.[153]

Swedish historians during the Cold War period take the same position on Sweden's role during World War II as the Swedish government. The story is one of 'neutrality put to the test' involving a righteous and virtuously pacifist Sweden and a world at war.[154] Hagloff points out that Sweden was one of numerous small states that desired to remain neutral at the beginning of the Second World War. Moreover, Swedish neutrality during the conflict was Germany's decision much more than it was Sweden's.[155] For writers like Sandier, Sweden's neutrality policy is conceived very much as the correct policy – a success for Sweden and an example to the rest of the world.[156] In the 1970s and the 1980s historians such as Carlgren and Johansson would continue to interpret Sweden's wartime actions as a form of justified pragmatism.[157]

For Nicholls, the economic and political uncertainties of the 1990s, led to identity crisis and re-alignment in Sweden. At the same time, a new consciousness emerged on the wartime past.[158] In *Honour and conscience – Sweden and the Second World War*, Boethius calls Swedish neutrality radically into question.[159]

---

153 A. Gerow, 'Consuming Asia, Consuming Japan: The New Neonationalist Revisionism in Japan' in L. Hein and M. Seldon (eds.) *Censoring History: Citizenship and Memory in Japan, Germany, and the United States* (Armonk, East Gate, 2000). G. McCormack, 'The Japanese movement to "correct" history', in L. Hein and M. Selden (eds.) *Censoring History: Citizenship and memory in Japan, Germany, and the United States* (Armonk, M. E. Sharpe, 2000). M. Ogawa and S. Field, 'Causation, Controversy and Contrition', op. cit. (note 7).

154 H. Wigforss, 'Sweden and the Atlantic Pact', *International Organization* (1949) 3 3, 1949, pp.434–443. W. I. Zartman, 'Neutralism and Neutrality in Scandinavia', *The Western Political Quarterly* (1954) 7 2, pp.125–160. G. M. Hagloff, 'A Test of Neutrality: Sweden in the Second World War', *International Affairs* (1960) 36 2, pp.153–167. D. J. Edwards, 'Process of economic Adaption in a World War II Neutral: A Case Study of Sweden', *The Journal of Finance* (1961) 6 3, pp.437–438.

155 G. M. Hagloff, 'A Test of Neutrality: Sweden in the Second World War', *International Affairs*, 36 2, 1960, pp.153–167.

156 A. Sandier, 'Sweden's Postwar Diplomacy: Some Problems, Views, and Issues', *The Western Political Quarterly*, 1960, 13 4, pp.924–933.

157 W. Carlgren, *Swedish Foreign Policy during the Second World War* (New York, St. Martin's Press, 1977). A. W. Johansson, *Per Albin och Kriget* (Stockholm, Tiden, 1984).

158 J. Nicholls, 'Are Students Expected to Critically Engage with Textbook Perspectives of the Second World War? A Comparative and International study', *Research in Comparative and International Education*, 1 1, 2006, pp.40–55.

159 M. P. Boethius, *Heder och Samvete – Sverige och Andra Vdrldskriget* (Stockholm, Nordstedts, 1992).

Essentially, the righteous pragmatism of the post-war era is turned on its head. How could a peace-loving nation like Sweden not fight Nazism to protect peace? Johansson notes how interpretations of Boethius's book differ among different generations of scholars.[160] According to Levine, it is especially the younger generation of Swedes that have come to question wartime neutrality.[161] The work of scholars like Ekman appears strongly influenced by the debates raised by Boethius. Swedish relations with Nazi Germany were unjustifiably flexible during World War II. But for Ekman this is not surprising. Important sections of Swedish society, the military, for example, were pro-German.[162]

Scholars in Sweden in the 2000s have come to be involved in an official reassessment of the wartime past. In the work of these scholars the pendulum appears to have swung back to an intermediate position. Supported by the Swedish government and through the Living History Forum, Sweden is portrayed needing to atone for the past while continuing to play a part in the building of a peaceful world.[163]

World War II has been an enormously popular topic of research for English authors and historians. In the early post-war years English commentators tended to write about the conflict from the perspective of victors. Churchill published the first volume of his six-volume, *The Second World War*, in 1948, and provides an overview of the war in its entirety from the perspective of statesman.[164] Scholars such as Bullock focus on Hitler and leadership.[165] Others, the conservative Trevor Roper, for example, argue that Nazism was an essentially collective phenomenon,

---

160 A. W. Johansson, 'Neutrality and Modernity: The Second World War and Sweden's National Identity', in S. Ekman and N. Edling (eds.) *War Experience, Self Image and National Identity: The Second World War as Myth and History* (Sodertalje, The Bank of Sweden Tercentenary Foundation and Gidlunds Forlag, 1997).

161 P. Levine, 'Swedish neutrality during the Second World War: tactical success or moral compromise?' in N. Wylie (ed.) *European Neutrals and Non-Belligerents during the Second World War* (Cambridge, Cambridge University Press, 2002).

162 S. Ekman, 'Skilful Realpolitik or Unprincipled Opportunism? The Swedish Coalition Government's Foreign Policy in Debate and Research' in S. Ekman and N. Edling (eds.) *War Experience, Self Image and National Identity: The Second World War as Myth and History* (Sodertalje: The Bank of Sweden Tercentenary Foundation and Gidlunds Forlag, 1997).

163 D. Gaunt, P. A. Levine and L. Palosuo (eds.) *Collaboration and Resistance during the Holocaust: Belarus, Estonia, Latvia, Lithuania* (Bern: Verlag Peter Lang, 2004). H. R. Huttenbach, *The Universality of Genocide* (Uppsala: The Uppsala Programme for Holocaust and Genocide Studies, 2004).

164 W. Churchill, *The Second World War*, Vol. 1, (London: Cassell & Co, 1948).

165 A. Bullock, *Hitler A Study in Tyranny* (London: Odhams, 1952).

rooted in the 'nature' of the German people.[166] The socialist historian, A. J. P. Taylor, agrees with Trevor Roper and Bullock on several issues in that Hitler is seen to have arisen from a series of essentially German elements.[167] In a different work, Taylor observes that Britain may claim the 'moral victory' for the Second World War, even if outright victory would have been impossible without the assistance of the Soviets and the Americans.[168] From the 1970s onwards, Britain's economic and political decline would become the theme of work by several authors.[169] Robbins connects changing perceptions of Britain's role during World War II with Britain's decline as a nation and imperial power.[170] In the work of revisionist historians of the 1980s, such as Barnet, the Second World War is perceived effectively exhausting Britain's future prospects as an international power.[171] Others like Charmley argue that entry into the war was a mistake for Britain from the very beginning. The approach taken by Churchill during World War II led only to American and Soviet supremacy in the post-war world and Britain's decline. Charmley argues, ultimately, that Britain's pre-war appeasement policy should be re-evaluated.[172]

In the post-Cold War reality of the present, writers on World War II in England occupy a wide plurality of positions and perspectives. The opening of war archives in Russia and other countries of the former Soviet Union lead to works that offer a re-evaluation of the Soviet contribution to the war effort.[173] In *Among*

166 H. T. Roper, Hitler's Table Talk: His Private Conversations 1941–4 (London, Weidenfeld & Nicholson, 2002).

167 A. J. P. Taylor, *The Course of German History: A Survey of the Development of German History Since 1815* (London: Routledge, 2001).

168 A. J. P. Taylor, *The Origins of the Second World War* (London, Penguin, 1963).

169 F. S. Northedge, 'Britain As a Second-Rank Power', *International Affairs* (1970) 46 1, pp.37–47. D. Reynolds, 'Rethinking Anglo-American Relations', *International Affairs* (1989) 65 1, pp.89–111.

170 K. Robbins, "This Grubby Wreck of Old Glories": The United Kingdom and the End of the British Empire', *Journal of Contemporary History* (1980) 15 1, pp.81–95. B. Collins and K. Robbins, *British Culture and Economic Decline* (London, Weidenfeld & Nicolson, 1990). K. Robbins, 'Commemorating the Second World War in Britain: Problems of Definition', *The History Teacher* (1996) 29 2, pp.155–162.

171 C. Barnet, *The Audit of War: The Illusion and Reality of Britain as a Great Power* (London: Macmillan, 1986).

172 J. Charmley, *Churchill: the End of Glory. A Political Biography* (London: Hodder & Stoughton, 1993).

173 R. Overy, *Russia's War* (London: Penguin, 1999). A. Beevor, *Stalingrad* (London: Penguin, 2000).

the Dead Cities, Grayling argues that the Allied bombing campaign of German cities towards the end of World War II was morally indefensible.[174] Some German writers, Matussek, for example, claim that English people continue to associate Germany with Nazism while David Irving, a British right-wing historian, underplays the horrors of the Holocaust to the point of denial.[175]

---

174 A. C. Grayling, *Among the Dead Cities: The History and Moral Legacy of the WWH Bombing of Civilians in Germany and Japan* (New York: Walker & Company, 2006).
175 M. Matussek 'Beethoven, Claudia Schiffer, Willy Brandt? No, the British are only interested in Germany when it involves Nazis'. [Internet] *The Guardian Unlimited,* 23rd May 2006. Available at: http://www.guardian.co.uk. D. Irving, *Hitler's War and the War Path* (New York: Basic Books, 2002).

Chapter Three
The Philosophical Basis of Comparisons I –
From the Modernist 'Thesis' to the
Postmodern 'Antithesis'

> The kind of freedom Hegel believes to be genuine is to be
> found...in rational choice. Reason is the essential nature of
> the intellect. A free mind, unimpeded by coercion of any
> sort, will follow reason as easily as a river unimpeded by
> mountains or hills would flow directly to the sea.
>
> Peter Singer, *Hegel*, 1988, p.67

> In the end, the final basis of Foucault's refusal of 'truth' and
> 'liberation' seems to be a Nietzschean one... Foucault sees
> truth as subordinated to power.
>
> Charles Taylor, *Foucault on Freedom and Truth*, 1989, p.93

Upon what grounds is it possible to make comparisons? What is the relationship between those making the comparisons and the contexts being compared? How can it be justifiable to evaluate differences across contexts, if at all? Answers to these questions are a matter of philosophical perspective. In other words, the practice of making comparisons will always be based in epistemological assumptions concerning the nature of knowledge and of what it is possible to know, and in ontological conceptions of what it means to exist in the world. Indeed, these assumptions will define the limits and the possibilities of any comparative methodology.

In a special issue of *Comparative Education* dedicated to Philosophy, Education and Comparative Education, Terence McLaughlin makes the case that 'a comparative approach to education needs a philosophical dimension'.[1] However, he goes on to argue that philosophical questions in comparative educational research have yet to be systematically expanded upon. Thus, 'although philosophy is, in one way and another, implicated in much of the work of comparative education, and comparative educationists themselves have not been inattentive to philosophical considerations, the role of philosophy in comparative education has not been brought into clear

---

1 T. H. McLaughlin, 'Education, philosophy and the comparative perspective', *Comparative Education* (2004) 40 4, pp.471–483.

focus'.[2] McLaughlin goes on to suggest that this is due, in part, to the fact that 're-lationships between the disciplines of "philosophy of education" and "comparative education" are relatively undeveloped' and 'afflicted by "compartmentalization"'.[3]

There are several theorists and methodologists in the field whose work is openly connected with the kinds of philosophical concerns that McLaughlin suggests: the work of Brian Holmes, for example, or of Robert Cowen or Holland Paulston.[4] Erwin Epstein has written in depth on epistemology and comparative education.[5] In an essay published in 1958, Robert Templeton spoke of the need for a theoretical dimension in comparative educational research:

> The general failure of serious studies to be genuinely comparative – to define and apply a *tertium comparationis* – is also closely related to the tendency in education to separate theory and practice and to emphasize the practical at the expense of the theoretical. This separation is to some degree a manifestation of that exaggerated concern in modern culture for the particular, the practical, the utilitarian. It reflects a kind of scientism in education linked with a desire to get quick results that threatens to become the bane of the social sciences. At best it is "scientific" in its passion for facts. At worst it is neither science nor art, for it lacks the discipline of a body of tested theory, the rigorousness of method, and the dynamic of clear purpose so essential to both.[6]

Yet to this day, there have been few if any 'philosophers' as such, at least not philosophers of comparative educational research. Like Templeton, more recent commentators have pointed out that the neglect of philosophical questions is a common feature of educational research in general.

In their important work, *Researching Education*, David Scott and Robin Usher draw attention to the disregard for philosophical issues in educational research

---

2   T. H. McLaughlin, 'Education, philosophy and the comparative perspective', op. cit. (note 1).
3   T. H. McLaughlin, 'Education, philosophy and the comparative perspective', op. cit. (note 1).
4   B. Holmes, *Comparative Education: Some Considerations of Method* (London: George Alien & Unwin, 1981). R. Cowen, 'Last Past the Post: Comparative Education, Modernity and Perhaps Post-Modernity', *Comparative Education* (1996) 32 2, pp.151–170. R. Cowen, 'Performativity, Post-Modernity and the University', *Comparative Education* (1996) 32 2, pp.245–258. R. G. Paulston, 'Mapping Comparative Education after Postmodernity', *Comparative Education Review* (1999) 43 4, pp.438–463.
5   E. H. Epstein, 'The Problematic Meaning of "Comparison" in Comparative Education', in Jurgen Schriewer and Brian Holmes (eds.) *Theories and Methods in Comparative Education* (Frankfurt am Main: Peter Lang, 1988).
6   R. G. Templeton, 'Some Reflections on the Theory of Comparative Education', *Comparative Education Review*, (1958) 2 2, pp.27–31.

generally. In their opening chapters, the authors argue strongly that in the majority of cases, researchers of education think 'it unnecessary to surface those ontological and epistemological relations which underpin the collection of data about activities, institutions and systems'.[7] For this reason the 'values, preconceptions and epistemological frameworks of the researcher' are all too often abandoned, considered 'irrelevant to the design of the research'.[8] For Scott and Usher this represents a major problem, since 'philosophical issues are integral to the research process and cannot be ignored until after the event'.[9]

Scholars such as Richard Pring have pioneered philosophy of educational research.[10] However, the need to engage with the philosophical dimension is perhaps even more crucial in comparative education. Making comparisons, the identification of similarities and differences, not to mention the making of judgements, evaluations, assessments and recommendations, is an intrinsically philosophical enterprise. Moreover, the making of cross-cultural comparisons is a highly complex affair requiring sophistication on several levels: philosophical, methodical and practical. Yet if we take out the philosophical element in the equation, how and upon what grounds are researchers arriving at their assumptions, their assessments and their evaluations? An awareness of philosophical issues implicit in comparative educational research is therefore empowering because it defines the limits, and hence the possibilities, of making comparisons.

Terence McLaughlin argues the case for developing the 'philosophical dimension' in comparative educational research based around four interconnected factors. First, to discern 'what is being compared with what (e.g. teachers, schools, teaching methods and educational systems in differing cultural, national and regional contexts)'. Second, to establish 'the evaluative basis of comparison (e.g. the norms and principles being invoked in making comparisons)'. Third, to define 'the reasons and motives underlying the comparisons being made (e.g. disinterested scholarly enquiry, a search for insights, etc., to be applied from one context to another)'. And finally, to provide grounding for 'the methods used in making comparisons (e.g. methods based on natural science, social science, hermeneutic traditions, etc.)'.[11] Based around these 'factors' we see that developing

---

7   D. Scott, and R. Usher, *Researching Education: Data, Methods and Theory in Educational Enquiry* (New York: Cassell, 1999), p.3.

8   D. Scott, and R. Usher, *Researching Education*, op. cit. (note 7), p.2.

9   D. Scott, and R. Usher, *Researching Education*, op. cit. (note 7), p.10.

10   R. Pring, *Philosophy of Educational Research* (London: Continuum, 2000).

11   T. H. McLaughlin, 'Education, philosophy and the comparative perspective', op. cit. (note 1).

the philosophical dimension in comparative research is not a journey into abstraction and obscurity. On the contrary, McLaughlin shows how philosophical issues underpin the most fundamentally practical concerns of the comparative educationist. What is being compared? How can we assess what is being compared? Why compare? Using which methods?

My position is that the comparison of politically sensitive topics in history education requires especially high levels of methodological refinement, sophistication, and skill on the part of researchers. This means, in part, that researchers need to realise the philosophical underpinnings of their work and the fundamental grounds upon which it is possible to comprehend objects and to make comparisons and claims. Understanding the philosophical basis for making comparisons is therefore deemed to be an essential prerequisite.

From researching the construction of methodologies for comparing the topic of World War II in school history education across contexts, three questions of a philosophical nature stand out from the rest. First, how is knowledge in history education defined as an object in epistemological terms? This question is important since competing definitions over what constitutes history are necessarily grounded in competing claims over what constitutes knowledge and about what it is possible to know. Researchers utilising comparative methodologies grounded in positivist epistemology, for example, will arrive at different results and conclusions compared with those using critical theory, postmodern, or hermeneutic approaches.

As recognised by Robin Usher, however, 'research involves imposing a closure that is not purely epistemological'.[12] This brings us to the second question: How is knowledge located in relation to power across educational contexts? This question is important since it draws attention to the politics of knowledge. Yes, historical knowledge will be defined according to epistemological perspective. However, what constitutes 'legitimate' historical knowledge at a given time and in a given place will also be a matter of politics and power. Different philosophical perspectives define power and the relationship between power and knowledge in different ways.

Finally, having defined knowledge in epistemological and political terms, there is the question of agency. How and to what extent can researchers construct comparative methodologies as agents? This question concerns conceptions of subjectivity and ontological understandings of what it means to exist in the world.

---

12 R. Usher, 'A critique of the neglected epistemological assumptions of educational research', in D. Scott and R. Usher (eds.) *Understanding Educational Research* (London: Routledge, 1996), p.16.

Definitions of how we are constituted as subjects will be central to any philosophical perspective and, therefore, to any research methodology. This is because arriving at any definition of the subject is simultaneously to define the parameters and limits of knowledge and action. In other words, positioned within a particular location in time and space, what is it possible to know and what are the possibilities for action in relation to what is known?

In comparative education the researching subject is confronted with an array of highly complex objects – both physical and conceptual – across educational contexts. Moreover, educational objects will be configured differently from context to context and across cultures. How and to what extent can subjects describe, measure and even assess the objects being compared? Fundamentally, the answers to these questions will be a matter of perspective, different positions underpinned by different assumptions concerning the nature of knowledge and the possibilities for action; as much a question of ontology, of being and existing in the world, as about epistemology and power.[13] To reiterate, whenever comparative educational researchers undertake the task of describing, comparing, assessing, and evaluating educational contexts, their practices will be underpinned by a series of philosophical assumptions. However, although implicit to all comparisons, the argument here is that these philosophical dimensions need to be made explicit within the research process. In other words, the philosophical dimension in comparative educational research cannot be ignored or neglected but, rather, needs to be actively and openly engaged with by researchers.

In the following two chapters I provide an outline of key philosophical positions in order to assess their implications in and for the practice of comparative educational research. What is the meaning of comparison according to the major philosophical perspectives? Here in Chapter Three I focus specifically on modernist perspectives, positivism and critical theory, as well as on postmodernism. This will provide the foundation for the discussion in Chapter Four on hermeneutic perspectives that, I argue, provide the basis not only for new readings of key comparative educationists but also for the development of the approach to comparative history education that I am proposing. Using Hegel, modernism is understood as a thesis, with postmodernism as its antithesis.

Likewise, hermeneutics is understood as a synthesis. By identifying the positions in relation to each other these two chapters will provide the essential platform from which to proceed.

---

13 R. Usher, 'A critique of the neglected epistemological assumptions of educational research', op. cit., p.16.

Making Comparisons According to Philosophical Perspective

Positivism

Emerging as a creative philosophical current during the 18th century Enlightenment, positivism embraces a particular understanding of reality and of what it is possible to know. Grounded in empiricism and in the use of the scientific method, positivist philosophies provided a critical alternative to conceptions of the physical and social worlds based around church and monarch, the prevailing ideologies up to and during the 1700s. Positivist approaches were extremely radical at the time of their inception, concerned with 'that which really exists and can be observed, as opposed to the dubious fancies of theology and metaphysics'.[14]

During the 19th century, Auguste Comte pioneered positivist sociology, convinced that society could only truly be understood using methods and procedures identical to those used in the natural sciences. For Comte, writes Roger Scruton, '[a]ll genuine human knowledge is scientific and methodical, and no question that cannot be answered by science has an answer.' As the basis of a factual and active science of society it thus became essential 'to strip away the veil of illusion from human things, and to reveal them, and to act on them as they really are'.[15]

The influence of Comte's positivism on the development of ideas in the social sciences is undeniable. Durkheim's conception of 'social facts' for example; 'thing[s] that can be identified as external to individual consciousness' and yet are integral to the wider empirical reality in which individuals exist, represents an important feature of his 'broad positivist methodology'.[16] Likewise, positivist ideas have been enormously influential in the United States during the 20th century. The ideas of Talcott Parsons, the structural functionalist, are a case in point.[17]

For positivists the world is filled with a finite and measurable quantity of objects, 'existing independently of knowers', that subjects must experience, register, record and validate according to scientific procedure.[18] Ultimately, the true

---

14 R. Scruton, *A Dictionary of Political Thought* (New York: Harper & Row, 1982), p.364.

15 R. Scruton, A *Dictionary of Political Thought*, op. cit. (note 16), p.84.

16 T. Bilton et al, *Introductory Sociology* (London: Macmillan, 1981), p.643.

17 Bilton, *Introductory Sociology*, op. cit. (note 16), pp.642–643

18 D. Scott, and R. Usher, *Researching Education: Data, Methods and Theory in Educational Enquiry* (New York: Cassell, 1999), p.25.

relationship between subjects and objects is considered to be neutral and passive, with no inter-dependence, dynamic interaction, connection or tension between them. In contrast to the irrational and non-verifiable dictates of religious belief, science is seen to provide the key to understanding truths about objects and to knowing in an 'unbiased' and factual way. Indeed, using the scientific method – considered wholly objective – it becomes possible for subjects to proceed neutrally, empowered to discover and validate patterns and categories among objects, and to establish facts about the physical and social worlds. As Anthony Giddens points out, 'the idea that the natural and the social sciences share a common logical and perhaps even methodological foundation' is essential for positivists.[19] Moreover, by recording more and more facts about the finite world researchers come to know more of what is true about the world, providing the grounds upon which to make practical decisions.[20]

Up to the 1960s, positivism dominated social science in English-speaking countries and, to this day, although 'subjected to a great deal of hard critique… remains a dominant approach in practice'.[21] This is especially the case with quantitative social and educational research that is, more often than not, heavily imbued with positivist assumptions concerning the nature of truth, knowledge and subject neutrality.

Making Comparisons from a Positivist Perspective

Comparisons from a positivist perspective are driven by specific epistemological assumptions concerning the empirical nature of knowledge as well as by procedural concerns over how to verify facts. In this way educational objects are conceived as finite measurable 'things' existing in the world – independent variables identified across contexts – to be objectively measured, compared, and assessed. International statistical data provided by UNESCO and the OECD, as well as the TIMSS and PISA studies, spring directly to mind here. Faced with a sample of test scores from across cultural settings the positivist researcher evaluates the data accordingly, higher test scores being assumed to be the effect of a culturally specific cause. Comparing curricular content the positivist researcher is likely to champion the centrality of factual information across settings, in contrast with the mystifying effects of ideological bias and prejudice.

---

19   A. Giddens, *Politics, Sociology and Social Theory* (Cambridge: Polity Press, 1995), p.137.
20   D. Held, *Introduction to Critical Theory: Horkheimer to Habermas* (Berkeley: University of California Press, 1980), pp.161–162.
21   D. Scott and R. Usher, *Researching Education*, op. cit. (note 7), p.13.

The parameters of objects being compared, their 'validity', will be defined in terms of what can be measured using empirically based scientific procedures. Let us not forget that for positivists science is the great equaliser – neutral and objective – allowing the researcher to 'see the wood for the trees' across settings. According to positivists, science is neither culturally or nationally specific but universal, possessing the power to cut through contextual biases to reveal truths.

As for the subject, the fact that the researcher is part of a distinctive cultural community, holding certain values, conducting research in a particular language, will be understood as relatively unimportant, as long as scientific procedures are strictly adhered to. If anything, the contexts in which subjects and objects are located, socio-economic, political, cultural, and spatial, become little more than contaminating variables, important only in the sense that they need to be isolated from the research at hand. Armed with the scientific method the comparative researcher is thus perceived as a 'centred' subject, essentially free to discover the facts about cross-cultural educational objects – and understood to have no impact on the meaning or identity of objects and vice versa.

Positivist perspectives have played an important if not central role in the development of the field of comparative education. The work of Marc-Antoine Jullien in the early 19th century, for example, draws from the same intellectual currents as the work of Comte. As Erwin H. Epstein, writing in the 1980s, points out,

> Jullien set the stage 170 years ago for positivism as the field's mainstream tradition. Among all comparativists none have staked out a more unambiguous position for comparative education than those who have displayed an epistemological affinity with his perspective. Indeed, some modern positivists have gone so far as to claim that only through comparison can human behaviour be studied truly scientifically.[22]

Jullien's approach would be grounded in Enlightenment thinking, both rational and empiricist, a platform from which, according to Epstein,

> nothing could be clearer than the meaning of comparison... In his now famous *Esquisse*, Jullien went so far as to specify concretely an appropriate methodology for comparison, involving the use of standard questionnaires to collect information and arranging findings into comprehensive tables so that differences in education among countries could be appreciated at a glance.[23]

---

22 E. H. Epstein, 'The Problematic Meaning of "Comparison" in Comparative Education', in J. Schriewer and B. Holmes (eds.) *Theories and Methods in Comparative Education* (Frankfurt am Main: Peter Lang, 1988). p.3.

23 E. H. Epstein, 'The Problematic Meaning of "Comparison" in *Comparative Education*', op. cit (note x), p.3.

In many ways, Jullien's positivist approach is a precursor to the international statistical surveys of education provided by UNESCO and the OECD that have been referred to above.

In more recent years the work of Harold Noah and Max Eckstein has not only continued within this positivist tradition but also developed it. In *Toward a Science of Comparative Education*, the authors champion the methods of empirical social science, their vision for research in the field made loud and clear.[24] 'Comparative education…emerges as the attempt to use cross-national data to test propositions about the relationship between education and society and between teaching practices and learning outcomes'.[25] For Philip Altbach and Gail Kelly,

> Noah and Eckstein… believed that a "science" could be developed only through use of methodologies borrowed from the social sciences that consisted of hypothesis formulation and testing and the use of quantification and statistics in the conduct of scholarship. The goal was to discover scientific laws governing school/society relations that could guide policy decisions.[26]

Almost thirty years after writing *Toward a Science of Comparative Education*, Noah and Eckstein point out that the impetus to write their seminal book arose in part from another 'concern'. In short, 'to instruct students about empirical research and to turn away from the strange lands and friendly people approach that characterized most comparative education courses at the time'.[27]

Comparative educational research from a positivist philosophical perspective invariably focuses on data in order to test hypotheses and draws attention to particular cause and effect relationships. How would it be possible to compare topics in history education from such a perspective? Using the scientific method would it be possible to measure and verify certain forms of historical data while, at the same time, identifying how and where the facts may be shrouded by ideological bias? To reiterate, positivist approaches are grounded in particular epistemological assumptions concerning the nature of knowledge and truth and the relationship

---

24   H. J. Noah, and M. A. Eckstein, *Toward a Science of Comparative Education* (New York, Macmillan, 1969).

25   H. J. Noah, and M. A. Eckstein, *Toward a Science of Comparative Education*, op. cit. (note 24), p.114.

26   P. G. Altbach and G. P. Kelly (eds.) *New Approaches to Comparative Education* (Chicago: University of Chicago Press, 1986), pp.4–5).

27   H. J. Noah, and M. A. Eckstein, *Doing Comparative Education: Three Decades of Collaboration* (Hong Kong: University of Hong Kong Comparative Education Research Center, 1998), p.9.

between researching subjects and educational objects. Comparisons of historical topics in history education across contexts will depend, therefore, on definitions of what history actually is – as an object.

What is History from a Positivist Perspective?

In his seminally important book *What is History?* E. H. Carr identifies the 'cult of facts' that emerged in the 19th century with the great German historian Ludwig von Ranke:

> When Ranke in the 1830s, in legitimate protest against moralizing history, remarked that the task of the historian was 'simply to show how it really was (*wie es eigentlich gewesen*)', this not very profound aphorism had an astonishing success. Three generations of German, British and even French historians marched into battle intoning the magic words *'Wie es eigentlich gewesen'* like an incantation... The Positivists, anxious to stake out their claim for history as a science, contributed the weight of their influence to this cult of facts. First ascertain the facts, said the Positivists, then draw your conclusions from them.[28]

For positivists history is conceived as an essentially factual account of past events. Moreover, since what counts as knowledge will always be considered necessarily 'objective' and therefore true, faithful accounts of the past must also be neutral accounts. The politics of historical knowledge is never acknowledged by the positivist. Indeed, this 'politics' is considered to be the very thing that obscures the linear and factual understanding of true history. Through the collection of facts about the past the positivist assumes to discover rather than construct history. Moreover, once discovered this history of facts and events, names, places, and dates, will be considered not as an interpretation, or as a culturally specific perspective, but as 'universal'. Indeed, 'the ultimate wisdom of the empirical... school of history', wrote Carr, is to '[f]irst get your facts straight, then plunge at your peril into the shifting sands of interpretation'.[29]

Positivists contrast true history with false, the single true and indeed universal account of events discovered through rational means against the many histories of the mystics and metaphysicians. It is upon the grounds of this understanding that alternative histories, pointing to struggles between ideological forces (critical theory) or to the role of tradition in understanding (hermeneutics) or to

---

28   E. H. Carr, *What is History?* (London: Penguin Books, 1990), pp.8–9.
29   E. H. Carr, *What is History?*, op. cit. (note 28), p.10.

the paradigmatic and political nature of truth through time (postmodernism), are rejected.

What are the Implications of Positivism for Comparing Syllabus Topics in History Education across Contexts?

The manner in which a topic such as World War II is approached in history education across contexts may be compared and evaluated from a positivist perspective as follows. First, the 'facts' concerning the conflict would need to be established through the empirical assessment of sources of evidence. Second, the place of these facts in the curricula, examinations, teaching approaches, textbooks and alternative learning packages across a pre-selected cluster of educational contexts would need to be measured. Since positivists argue that the facts exist 'out there' in the 'real world' independent of subjective interpretations, it will be assumed that an essentially true account of the Second World War exists – free from ideological bias. The extent to which World War II is treated in an unprejudiced way across settings will thus become the basis from which to assess its place in history education across systems.

It is important to understand that positivists will look for the causes of bias or of transparency. For example, certain versions of the conflict may be found closer to the 'positivist' definition of truth in some national contexts and further from the truth in others. Positivists would want to ask why history is treated more transparently in some systems compared to others. They would probably then go on to argue that some contexts are more politically transparent and democratic where others are more controlled. Let us not forget that positivism developed from empiricism and liberalism, the seeds of Enlightenment thinking, and represented a fundamental reaction against the autocracy of church and monarchy in the 18th century. It is for this reason that positivists are likely to champion not only science and the scientific method but also democracy as a means to maximise transparency in scientific endeavours and in education.

The following table may be used to identify the fundamentals of a positivist comparative education. Positivism is based in a particular theory of knowledge that, in turn, defines the parameters of the relationship between politics and knowledge. The theory of knowledge relies upon an essential conception of the relationship between subjects and objects, researcher and researched with fundamental implications for the making of comparisons.

	Theory of Knowledge / Reality	Relationship between politics and knowledge	Relationship between subject and object	Implications for making comparisons
Positivism	Facts exist 'out there' in the world. Truth can be known only through the use of scientific procedures.	True knowledge is neutral. Politics is a contaminating variable.	Passive and neutral. The 'centred' subject is free to discover 'autonomous' objects.	Using the scientific method the 'centred', 'autonomous' subject identifies and compares objects across contexts.

Critical theory

Critical theory is a vague term. In the 1930s, members of the Institute of Social Research in Frankfurt in Germany – the Frankfurt School – renamed their 'interpretation of Marxist theory' Critical Theory in order to divert attention from research activities in the wake of the rising tide of fascism.[30] However, the term is used today to describe not a particular school but rather the various forms of Marxism in all their variety. Indeed, since the fall of the Soviet Union, Marxism has become so unfashionable as to be renamed 'critical theory' across the fields of social and educational research. It is in this general way that I use the term 'critical theory'; Critical theory = Marxism in general.

Critical theory develops from the initial thesis proposed by Marx and Engels in the first section of *The Communist Manifesto*:

> The history of all hitherto existing societies is the history of class struggles… [in which] oppressor and oppressed, stood in constant opposition to one another, carried on an uninterrupted, now hidden, now open fight, a fight that each time ended, either in a revolutionary reconstitution of society at large, or in the common ruin of the contending classes.[31]

Like positivism, critical theory is a child of the Enlightenment. Thus, critical theorists will argue that the world contains a finite and ultimately knowable quantity

---

30   D. Held, *Introduction to Critical Theory: Horkheimer to Habermas* (Berkeley, University of California Press, 1980), p.13.

31   K. Marx, and F. Engels, *The Communist Manifesto* (London: Penguin, 1987), p.79.

of objects governed by laws, underpinned and driven by an essential rationality. However, it is not through adherence to bourgeois definitions of scientific rationality – the positivist championing of empiricism and the scientific method – that subjects are empowered to understand reality.

For critical theorists truth is defined according to the dynamic relationships that exist between subjects, the working class, the ruling class, and objects, the material world. In sharp contrast to positivists, therefore, the relationship between subjects and objects is not conceived to be neutral and passive but is instead characterised by alienation, oppression and tension. In this way subject and object are involved in a dramatic and ongoing struggle, an expression of the unequal social relations that underpin reality. Since subjects co-exist in a world of unbalanced and oppressive relations – with other classes and with nature – perpetuated and legitimated by the ideologies of ruling groups, they are conceived as alienated from the underlying truth and potentiality of their relationship to the world. Conservative ideologies giving the impression that inequalities are natural, or that capitalism and empirical science are given, are thus strongly criticised by critical theorists. In fact, the acceptance of such ideologies, particularly by those classes in society that experience the harsh realities of inequality most acutely, is perceived as an expression of 'false consciousness'.

Consciousness plays a central role in the philosophy of critical theorists. Indeed, the realisation of truth in the world and in history is accessible only through the raising of consciousness. It is consciousness that allows the subject to evaluate the world. Like positivism, critical theory is underscored by an essentially autonomous and 'centred' conception of the knowing subject. However, in sharp contrast to the positivist assumptions outlined above, objective reality cannot exist independently of the subject. In *Reason and Revolution*, discussing Hegel's *Phenomenology of Spirit*, Herbert Marcuse emphasises comprehension of 'the changing relationship between consciousness and its objects' as a means to understanding what is real. Thus:

> When experience begins, the object seems a stable entity, independent of consciousness; subject and object appear to be alien to one another. The progress of knowledge, however, reveals that the two do not subsist in isolation... 'The real,' which consciousness actually holds in the endless flux of sensations and perceptions, is a universal that cannot be reduced to objective elements free of the subject... [T]he world becomes real only by force of the comprehending power of consciousness.[32]

---

32 H. Marcuse, *Reason and Revolution* (London, Routledge & Kegan Paul, 1986), p.94.

In *History and Class Consciousness*, on a more overtly social and political level, Georg Lukacs writes with emphasis concerning the relationship between class, consciousness, knowledge and emancipation:

> Only the consciousness of the proletariat can point to the way that leads out of the impasse of capitalism. As long as this consciousness is lacking, the crisis remains permanent, it goes back to its starting-point, repeats the cycle until after infinite sufferings and terrible detours the school of history completes the education of the proletariat and confers upon it the leadership of mankind.[33]

The raising of consciousness facilitates awareness of the unfair state of social relations. It is synonymous with the completion of 'the education of the proletariat', enabling alienation and oppression to be overcome, and forming the essential basis for collective agency and praxis.[34] Knowing what you are is to know the world which, at the same time, is to know what to do about it. Consciousness reveals truth; it is the motor of emancipation, a revolutionary and progressive force.

Conscious of their place in the world, knowing subjects have the potential to exist in a state of harmony with objects. Indeed, liberated from oppressive social relations, subjects cease to be alienated from the world around them. With the raising of consciousness comes the opportunity for unfettered self-realisation, if not now then at some point in the future. Critical theory is thus underpinned by a Utopian vision of absolute freedom, the absolute standard against which the present is assessed. To return to Lukacs:

> The proletariat only perfects itself by annihilating and transcending itself, by creating the classless society through the successful conclusion of its own class struggle. The struggle for this society... is not just a battle waged against an external enemy, the bourgeoisie. It is equally the struggle of the proletariat against itself: against the devastating and degrading effects of the capitalist system upon its class consciousness. The proletariat will only have won the real victory when it has overcome these effects...[35]

The socio-economic and historical context in which subjects and objects are located is therefore essential to understandings of reality for critical theorists. Subjects and objects do not exist independently of each other or outside of any form of relation. On the contrary, the context in which subjects are located will directly affect relations

---

33   G. Lukacs, *History and Class-Consciousness* (London: Merlin Press, 1983), p.76.
34   M. Poster, *Critical Theory and Post-structuralism: In Search of a Context* (Ithaca: Cornell University Press, 1989), p.61. G. Lukacs, *History and Class-Consciousness, op. cit.* (note 33), pp.80–81.
35   G. Lukacs, *History and Class-Consciousness, op. cit.* (note 35), p.80.

to objects – indeed the reality of objects – just as much as the context of objects will affect the reality of subjects. To reiterate, the relationship between subject and object is characterised by ongoing struggle and tension for critical theorists. The subject remains subjected and oppressed as long as it remains alienated from this reality and from itself. Only through the raising of consciousness is it possible for subjects to rise above this reified world – and to identify what is true from false. In the words of Marx and Engels, oppressed social classes, 'have nothing to lose but their chains' and 'a world to win'.[36] It is Scott and Usher who remind us of the powerful appeal of critical theory for educational researchers in general:

> Critical theory and the approach it offers has resonated with educational practitioners and researchers. Its discourse of basic social needs, of distortions and of false consciousness, and its foregrounding of critical dialogue and praxis provide an appealing basis for theory and practice, particularly for educators committed to social action and change. Its refusal to separate research and knowledge (theory) from action (practice) demolishes the debilitating tension between theory and practice. An approach informed by critical theory provides one possible answer to both the epistemological question of what constitutes valid knowledge, and the ethical question of how it can best be used.[37]

During the 1970s several Marxist thinkers theorised education in capitalist societies. On the whole the conservative and reproductive role of schooling was emphasised, as well as the presence of deceptive 'hidden curricula' that gave the impression that inequalities between people were natural and could not be challenged. According to Louis Althusser, the late French Marxist, education performs a conservative function through the legitimisation of bourgeois ideology.[38] Along with the mass media, religion, culture and the family, education is conceived as an Ideological State Apparatus. Since the use of coercive control is limited to the police, the judiciary and to the armed forces – the Repressive State Apparatuses – it is the role of ideology to maintain the status quo and reproduce a malleable workforce; that is, 'to reproduce the conditions of production (productive forces and relations of production) in forms which secure submission to the dominant ideology'.[39]

---

36 K. Marx, and F. Engels, *The Communist Manifesto*, op. cit. (note 31), p.121.

37 D. Scott, and R. Usher, *Researching Education: Data, Methods and Theory in Educational Enquiry* (New York: Cassell, 1999), p.33.

38 L. Althusser, 'Ideology and Ideological State Apparatuses', in *Lenin and Philosophy and Other Essays* (New York: Monthly Review Press, 1971).

39 L. Thanh Khoi, 'Conceptual Problems in Inter-cultural Comparisons', in J. Schriewer, and B. Holmes (eds.) *Theories and Methods in Comparative Education* (Frankfurt am Main: Peter Lang, 1988), pp.91–92.

In *Schooling in Capitalist America* Bowles and Gintis argue that the organisation of education is closely connected with the hierarchical, atomising and deskilled needs of the capitalist economy.[40] Using 'statistical analysis' the authors 'attempt to demonstrate that social class structure is reproduced by schools which prepare various classes of children for their roles in the workplace by reinforcing class-based personality traits'.[41] In other words, where schools in middle class neighbourhoods will stress the need for students to excel, to be competitive and creative, schools in working class neighbourhoods will value compliance with the rules, in preparation for a life of low-skilled work in the capitalist economy.[42]

Learning to Labour: How Working Class Kids Get Working Class Jobs by Paul Willis is another important study that, with its emphasis on the reproduction of social class relations, was based in a critical theory perspective.[43] In this study Willis identifies the relationship between class identity, education and work. Indeed, according to Masemann, Willis 'postulates that working-class resistance to middle-class control, which legitimates the [working class] lads' identity in their own eyes, seals their identity as manual workers in the capitalist system'.[44] Other writers such as Basil Bernstein in *Class, Codes and Control* and Michael Apple in *Ideology and Curriculum* have made significant contributions to debates of this kind.[45]

Making Comparisons from a Critical Theory Perspective

Comparisons from a critical theory perspective will be grounded, as with all comparisons, in epistemological and ontological assumptions concerning knowledge, truth and existence. Essentially comparisons will be based in a particular understanding of the relationship between subjects and objects in class-based societies, consciousness

---

40 S. Bowles, and H. Gintis, *Schooling in Capitalist America: Educational Reform and the Contradictions of Economic Life* (New York: Basic Books, 1976).

41 V. Masemann, 'Critical Ethnography in the Study of Comparative Education', in P. G. Altbach and G. P. Kelly (eds.) *New Approaches to Comparative Education* (Chicago: University of Chicago Press, 1986), p.19.

42 T. Bilton et al (1981) *Introductory Sociology*, (London: Macmillan, 1981), pp. 386–387.

43 P. Willis, *Learning to Labour: How Working Class Kids Get Working Class Jobs* (Aldershot: Gower, 1977).

44 V. Masemann, 'Critical Ethnography in the Study of Comparative Education', in P. G. Altbach and G. P. Kelly (eds.) *New Approaches to Comparative Education* (Chicago: University of Chicago Press, 1986), p.21.

45 B. Bernstein, *Class, Codes and Control* (London: Routledge & Kegan Paul, 1977). M. Apple, *Ideology and Curriculum* (London: Routledge & Kegan Paul, 1979).

of unbalanced social relations being an essential prerequisite. Context-specific variables outside of the relationship between classes may be given some attention, since different capitalist societies will be assumed to be in different stages of development. However, the underlying 'truth' of dialectical class struggle will be assumed to be universal, as will the idea that all cultural, political and social configurations are determined by economic variables in the last instance. Consciousness of this reality will allow the critical theorist to see the 'wood for the trees' across international contexts. Indeed, cultural differences and particularities are likely to be understood in 'ideological' terms – deceptively shrouding the reality of inequity that lies beneath.

Researching subjects will not simply be driven to reveal truths across contexts, however. To repeat the words of Scott and Usher, quoted above, '[a]n approach informed by critical theory provides... answer[s] to both the epistemological question of what constitutes valid knowledge, and the ethical question of how it can best be used'.[46] In other words, the researcher is also conceived as an agent of change, an emancipator involved in the struggle for freedom. To conduct research, to write and to teach, these represent forms of praxis for the critical theorist: to expose inequities, to educate, and to raise consciousness.

Educational objects across contexts are thus conceived as expressions of bourgeois ideology, of social relations, economically determined, the latest stage in a broader historical process. Critical theorists are thus likely to use international statistical data provided by UNESCO, to expose inequities in capitalist societies. Yet the statistics themselves will be used only warily and with caution, since this form of data separates information from the contextual realities of economy, ideology and class conflict. Critical theorists are thus deeply sceptical of the positivist insistence on empiricism and the scientific method, since science is not perceived to be the great equaliser but another example of bourgeois ideology – neither neutral nor objective nor a guarantor of validity.

Finally, and in contrast to positivists, critical theorists will compare curricula across contexts by drawing attention to the misrepresentation of facts due to ideological bias. A handful of writers associated with comparative educational research have made contributions from a critical theory perspective. Michael Apple writes about 'the role of the school as a reproductive force in... unequal societies' and about 'the relationship between ideology and school knowledge'.[47] Importantly

---

46   D. Scott and R. Usher, *Researching Education: Data, Methods and Theory in Educational Enquiry* (New York, Cassell, 1999), p.33.
47   M. Apple, *Ideology and Curriculum* (London, Routledge & Kegan Paul, 1979), p.52 and p.54.

Apple points to the different ways that these relationships have been theorised by writers in different capitalist societies. Indeed, for Apple,

> It should not surprise us that that there is a rather extensive history of dealing with issues concerning the connections between culture and control on the continent and in England. For one thing, they have had a less hidden set of class antagonisms than in the United States.[48]

However, in Altbach and Kelly's important *New Approaches to Comparative Education*, Apple's paper, 'Ideology, Reproduction, and Educational Reform' provides readers with few comparisons and little in the way of examples, a tendency apparent in much of his work.[49] Apple develops a sophisticated approach – using the ideas of Antonio Gramsci, Raymond Williams and Pierre Bourdieu – to investigate 'the relationship between what curricular knowledge is accorded high status… and its economic and cultural effects'.[50] However, readers are left wondering if, by making speculative references to education in capitalist America he is, at the same time, generalising about education across the capitalist world in general. But Apple is not alone. On the whole, comparative education from a critical theory perspective tends to be high on theory while at the same time being low on examples.

Martin Carnoy's 'Education for Alternative Development' provides another good case in point. Writing in the mid-1980s the author's vision for education in the 'Third World' is underpinned by a strong Marxist sense of the inequities inherent across capitalist societies, both developed and developing, and of the role of education as one means in the greater struggle for non-capitalist forms of development. Essentially,

> observed inefficiencies and inequalities in education are the product of the capitalist organisation of production and the social class structure inherent in it… According to this analysis, it is difficult or even impossible to discuss serious changes in an inherently class-reproducing educational system… without discussing an overall strategy for changing the class structure of society and the dominant capitalist relations of production.[51]

---

48 M. Apple, *Ideology and Curriculum*, op. cit. (note 47), p.54.
49 P. G. Altbach and G. P. Kelly (eds.) *New Approaches to Comparative Education* (Chicago, University of Chicago Press, 1986).
50 M. Apple, *Ideology and Curriculum,* op. cit. (note 47), p.55.
51 M. Carnoy, 'Education for Alternative Development', in P. G. Altbach and G. P. Kelly (eds.), *New Approaches to Comparative Education* (Chicago: University of Chicago Press, 1986), p.76.

Carnoy makes several generalisations concerning social and educational problems faced by all countries in the capitalist Third World from Bangladesh to Senegal to Argentina. Thus, readers are informed how nearly 'every study of education in the Third World shows that the children of rural parents... [have, on] average [,] low levels of schooling, much lower than urban schooling', that '[t]he class-based nature of educational systems is particularly evident in those countries where state investment per year of schooling is from 20 to 60 times greater at the university level than at the primary level', and that 'in most Third World countries... differences are tremendously accentuated by the fact that a small, dominant group not only owns the means of production but also dominates the higher echelons of the state apparatus, including the technocratic elite'.[52] Carnoy argues that these generalisations are based upon evidence and 'on the basis of the empirical research available'.[53]

Carnoy argues that schools represent an important arena of class struggle. However, changing education alone will not lead to developments towards significantly greater equity in society. On the contrary, 'the development process, the educational process and the schooling process are part and parcel of the same whole... [and] inseparable from the same surrounding forces which influence them and bind them together'.[54] To change education significantly, society needs to be changed first. However, as an essential feature of society, struggles in education represent important battlegrounds for wider social change. Where education is seen to perform the conservative function of maintaining existing social relations, schools provide a platform from which conscious agents may 'push for educational alternatives which would create attitudes and skills more useful in an endogenous, worker-controlled development than in capitalist wage production'.[55] Ultimately, Carnoy evaluates current inequalities in education across capitalist developing countries against an equitable future – a socialist future – where meaningful work and participation are considered far more important than 'capital and property'.[56] In addition, it is against this ideal of equality that education in socialist countries, namely China, Cuba and Nicaragua, are judged far more favourably than in equivalent capitalist developing societies. Published five years prior to the collapse of the Soviet Union, four years prior to the reunification of Germany, and three years prior to the 'democratic

---

52   Carnoy, 'Education for Alternative Development', op. cit. (note 51), p.76–77.
53   Carnoy, 'Education for Alternative Development', op. cit. (note 51), p.81.
54   Carnoy, 'Education for Alternative Development', op. cit. (note 51), p.84.
55   Carnoy, 'Education for Alternative Development', op. cit. (note 51), p.86.
56   Carnoy, 'Education for Alternative Development', op. cit. (note 51), p.88.

revolutions' that swept through Central and Eastern Europe in 1989, Carnoy ends his paper on a no less radical note:

> The obstacles both to alternative development and alternative education are many ...
> even when the will to make radical changes is there. The drawbacks of socialist bu-
> reaucracies... are well known. But without the pursuit of a radical transformation in
> the relations of production and their underlying power relations, an alternative educa-
> tion – mass education and social inclusion – is essentially impossible to achieve...
> A fundamental implication of an analysis which sees capitalist development as
> inherently inequitable is that, to achieve a more equitable and inclusive development,
> radical transformations are necessary...[57]

Comparative educational research from a critical theory perspective emphasises the inequalities inherent in capitalist societies, class conflict and the need for radical transformations. Capitalism is so all-permeating that education and schooling – the legitimisation of certain forms of knowledge at the expense of other or alternative forms – is conceived as an effect of bourgeois ideology reproducing existing social relations. Like positivism, comparative education from a critical theory perspective is likely to draw attention to cause and effect relationships. Unlike positivism, it is consciousness of existing all-pervasive inequalities that leads the researcher to 'truth' across systems and not the scientific method. The 'class-conscious' critical theorist stands ultimately outside of reality in order to make assessments. How would it be possible to compare topics in history education from a critical theory perspective? Through raised consciousness is it possible to identify how and where truth may be shrouded in ideological bias? Essentially, comparative approaches will be based in particular epistemological assumptions concerning the nature of knowledge and truth and the relationship between researching subjects and educational objects. Comparisons of 'topics' in history education across contexts will depend on definitions of what history actually is.

What is History from a Critical Theory Perspective?

History from a critical theory perspective develops from a particular reading of Hegel, a teleological reading, conceived and appropriated by Marx. Indeed, Marx's reading of Hegel had an enormous influence on the way that subsequent generations of thinkers, conservatives, Marxists, and liberals, conceive Hegel. Accordingly, history is perceived as an unfolding story of the dialectical struggle between alienation,

---

57 Carnoy, 'Education for Alternative Development', op. cit. (note 51), p.90.

88

consciousness, freedom and oppression. It is marked by stages; each stage is characterised by specific social relations, material conditions and economic means; and it is through history that revolutionary ideas for action and radical change are propelled. That history, for Marx, develops dialectically through stages, that history is an ongoing process, comes initially from Hegel. According to E. H. Carr:

> Hegel was...the first philosopher to see the essence of reality in historical change and in the development of man's consciousness of himself. Development in history meant development towards the concept of freedom. But ... Hegel was politically too timid and, in his later years, too firmly entrenched in the Establishment of his day to introduce any concrete meaning into his metaphysical propositions... It was left for Marx to write the arithmetic into Hegel's algebraical equations.[58]

More recently Bottomore and Rubel point to how it can even be surmised that Marx remained, throughout his life, a disciple of Hegel, merely filling out with a more or less factual content the grandiose philosophy of history of his master.

> Marx, of course, grew up in the atmosphere of Hegel's philosophy, and used its technical vocabulary, especially in his early writings. He never abandoned his respect for certain aspects of the 'system'. But his own social theory had other intellectual sources besides Hegel and, as we should remember, it was also based on the empirical study of working-class life and movements.[59]

In the 'Afterword to the Second German Edition' of *Capital*, Marx's self-proclaimed debt to (his version of) Hegel, and particularly Hegel's dialectical method, is made loud and clear:

> The mystification which dialectic suffers in Hegel's hands, by no means prevents him from being the first to present its general form of working in a comprehensive and conscious manner. With him it is standing on its head. It must be turned right side up again, if you would discover the rational kernel within the mystical shell.[60]

Importantly, Marx combines a materialist conception of reality with a Hegelian conception of historical progress, development and agency. Thus, to return again to E. H. Carr:

> A disciple both of Adam Smith and of Hegel, Marx started from the conception of a world ordered by rational laws of nature. Like Hegel, but this time in a practical and concrete form, he made the transition to the conception of a world ordered

---

58   E. H. Carr, *What is History?* (London: Penguin Books, 1990), p.136.
59   T. Bottomore and M. Rubel (eds.) *Marx: Selected Writings in Sociology and Social Philosophy* (London: Pelican Books, 1983), p.17.
60   K. Marx, *Capital*, Vol. 1 (London, Lawrence & Wisehart, 1983), p.29.

by laws evolving through a rational process in response to man's revolutionary initiative.[61]

Although, like positivists, critical theorists argue that the world is filled with a finite and ultimately knowable quantity of objects, an objective material reality, governed by a universal rationality, social consciousness of reality is always determined by the location of social groups and agents in history. For critical theorists, therefore, the discipline of history is conceived as an analysis of past social struggles and processes that have brought society to its present condition; a history of ideologies and hegemonic relations and processes that have legitimised oppressive social relations in the interests of ruling groups. Reality is by no means self-evident. Indeed, for critical theorists, positivism, while appearing rigorous and scientific, is simply another element of the capitalist web of ideological deception. What is more, assumptions concerning objectivity, neutrality and science are seen to provide the grounds for little more than bourgeois history – a history of isolated names, dates and 'great men', with no conception of the dialectical forces that drive history forward.

The politics of historical knowledge is essential to critical theorists. Power is always conceived in repressive terms and in the hands of the powerful over the oppressed; it legitimates inequalities through persuasive forms of deception in the interests of ruling groups. This 'polities' obscures understandings of true history. But with raised consciousness, the critical theorist is able to look beneath the politics. History from a critical theory perspective is based, therefore, in conceptions of objective truth to be realised through the raising of consciousness through time. Critical theory thus provides a history of the 'becoming of freedom'; all historical stages, past and present, are judged against the pure and unfettered freedom of a utopian future.

What are the Implications of Critical Theory for Comparing Syllabus Topics in History Education across Contexts?

The manner in which a topic such as World War II is approached in history education across contexts may be compared and evaluated from a critical theory perspective as follows. First, historical, economic and social contexts in which national education systems are located would need to be identified. Are all the contexts being compared capitalist contexts, for example? Second, the place of World War II as a topic in the school history curricula, examinations, teaching approaches, textbooks, and alternative learning packages across contexts would need to be examined for ideological bias. In particular, critical theorists are likely to look for evidence of

---

61   E. H. Carr, *What is History?*, op. cit. (note 58), p.163.

nationalist interpretation, since few ideologies perpetuate the illusion that class differences do not exist more than nationalism does. Thus the reason why perspectives and approaches to the teaching of World War II appear different in, say, Japanese, US, and English contexts, would be put down to the role of nationalism in capitalist societies; a form of ideological deception diverting attention away from inter-class conflicts. As with the positivist approach, critical theorists will judge representations of history across contexts against a particular conception of what is considered to be true history. Unlike positivists, critical theorists will pay great attention to the socio-economic context in which educational ideas and practices are formulated and delivered. The more capitalist the society, the higher the likelihood that history education will be filled with ideological distortions or used in ways that, ultimately, will serve to legitimise the bourgeois order.

In the table below the essentials of a comparative education from the perspective of critical theory are contrasted with the earlier outlined positivist position. Critical theory and positivism are both forms of modernity thinking. However, as we have seen, the two perspectives are different in many respects.

	Theory of Knowledge / Reality	Relationship between politics and knowledge	Relationship between subject and object	Implications for making comparisons
Positivism	Facts exist 'out there' in the world. Truth can be known only through the use of scientific procedures.	True knowledge is neutral. Politics is a contaminating variable.	Passive and neutral. The 'centred' subject is free to discover 'autonomous' objects.	Using the scientific method the 'centred', 'autonomous' subject identifies and compares objects across contexts.
Critical theory	Truth exists in the world. Truth can be understood only through the raising of class-consciousness.	True knowledge is neutral. However, in class societies, pervasive social and political ideologies mask the truth.	Depends on the type of society. In class based societies the relationship will be dynamic, conflicting, and characterised by struggle.	With raised class consciousness the 'centred', 'autonomous' subject identifies and compares objects across contexts. The researcher will be motivated to discover truth and, in turn, raise the consciousness of others.

Postmodernism

If positivism and critical theory represent the theses of Enlightenment thinking, post-modernity thinking is the antithesis. On their own, postmodern perspectives, emphasising heterogeneity, plurality, and the fractured nature of knowledge are hard to define.[62] But to say that there are no features common to the ideas of those thinkers identified with the post-modernity project – intellectuals such as Lyotard, Baudrillard, Derrida, Deleuze and Foucault (in his archaeology and genealogy periods) – is equally contentious. In *The Postmodern Condition: A Report on Knowledge*, Jean-Francois Lyotard begins his description of the postmodern by describing the modern. Thus,

> I will use the term modern to designate any science that legitimates itself with reference to a metadiscourse ... [in the form of] ... an explicit appeal to a grand narrative, such as the dialectics of Spirit, the hermeneutics of meaning, the emancipation of the rational or working subject, or the creation of wealth... the Enlightenment narrative, in which the hero of knowledge works toward a good ethico-political end – universal peace...I define postmodern as incredulity towards metanarratives.[63]

Postmodern perspectives are often defined in terms of what they are not, the antonym or antithesis of modernism, the other of Enlightenment thinking. Writing in the early 1990s, Dunn argued that this practice had become 'a familiar operation. From universal to particular, from unity to disunity, from depth to surface, from origins to copies, from works to texts – in such paired abstract terms postmodernism...[is]...posited as a departure from modernist epistemology and aesthetics'.[64] A far more critical stance is taken by Stanley Aronowitz and Henry Giroux in their examination of Baudrillard's work which, they argue, 'represents more than a massive transgression of the boundaries that are essential to the logic of modernism'. Thus:

> In this perspective, there is no relevance to an epistemology that searches out the higher elevations of truth, exercises a depth reading, or tries to penetrate reality in order to uncover the essence of meaning. Reality is on the surface. Ideology, alienation, and values are all jettisoned in this version of postmodern discourse, and are subsumed within the orbit of a society saturated with media messages that have no

---

62 R. Usher and R. Edwards, *Postmodernism and Education* (London: Routledge, 1994).

63 J. F. Lyotard, *The Postmodern Condition: A Report on Knowledge* (Manchester, Manchester University Press, 1984), pp.xxiii–xxiv.

64 R. Dunn, 'Postmodernism: Populism, Mass Culture, and Avant-Garde', *Theory Culture & Society* (1991) 8 1, pp.111–135.

meaning or content in the rationalist sense. In this view, information as noise is passively consumed by the masses, whose brutish indifference obliterates the ground of mediation, politics and resistance.[65]

Aronowitz and Giroux's interpretation of Jean Baudrillard's ideas should not of course be accepted at face value; nor should we over-generalise about postmodernism based on the ideas of a small circle of critics. Indeed, with greater sympathy towards post-modernity thinking Usher and Edwards write as follows:

the postmodern, the term "postmodernism" notwithstanding, is not really a "system" of ideas and concepts in any conventional sense. Rather, it is complex and multiform and resists reductive and simplistic explanation and explication. The "message" (if such a term can be used for something so inchoate) is the need to problematise systems of thought and organisation and to question the very notion of systematic explanation.[66]

This being said, in a later work, Usher admits that post-modernity thinking appears to exhibit certain generic characteristics; 'that the "real" is unstable, in flux and contingent'.[67] From a postmodern perspective both positivism and critical theory are conceived as types of modernity thinking children of the Enlightenment different only superficially. Essentially, postmodernists reject modernist claims concerning the finite nature of knowledge and reality. Accordingly, underlying truths can never be known through the employment of the scientific method or via the raising of consciousness. Where positivism in the social sciences can be traced back to Comte, and critical theory to Hegel, post-modernity thinking exhibits the influence of Nietzsche: 'there are no eternal facts, just as there are no absolute truths'. Richard Rorty, however, discussing the influence of Nietzsche on Michel Foucault's work of the 1970s, points to the potential problems:

In presenting Foucault's Nietzschean attitude I am not commending it. I have no wish to do so, especially since much of Foucault's so-called 'anarchism' seems to me self-indulgent radical chic. Rather, I am contrasting his Nietzschean attitude with... Hegelian attitudes towards 'theory of knowledge' in order to emphasize the difficulty Foucault must face in attempting to offer... a theory of anything. Whereas the

65   S. Aronowitz, and H. A. Giroux, *Postmodern Education: Politics, Culture and Social Criticism* (Minneapolis: University of Minnesota Press, 1991), pp.65–66.
66   R. Usher, and R. Edwards, *Postmodernism and Education* (London: Routledge, 1994), p.1.
67   R. Usher, 'A critique of the Neglected Epistemological Assumptions of Educational Research', in D. Scott and R. Usher (eds.) *Understanding Educational Research* (London: Routledge, 1996), p.28.

Hegelian wants history to substitute for theory of knowledge and for philosophical theories generally, a Nietzschean must not want any substitute for theories. He views the very idea of 'theory' as tainted with the notion that there is something there to be contemplated, to be accurately represented in thought.[68]

Seeking to expose inconsistencies inherent in modernism and modernity thinking, post-modernists point to the ways in which the modern championing of universality and truth marginalises that which is other. Modernism is oppressive: it overly rationalises, destroying nuances, pluralities and differences. For this reason post-modernists reject truth, as well as the modernist championing of science, reason, progress and vertical knowledge hierarchies. Reality is considered not as something 'out there' to be discovered or realised, but as essentially constructed, paradigmatic and relative to context. No subject can escape its context and every object will be defined according to context. Where modernists champion the free 'centred' subject, autonomous according to the dictates of science or consciousness, the postmodern subject is always 'de-centred' bound to the nuances of context and locality. Postmodernism offers a relative perspective, therefore, subject and object existing in an essentially horizontal relationship based on relative difference – one to the other.

Postmodernist thinkers have changed the way we think about the politics of knowledge and the role of power in the legitimisation and production of knowledge.[69] Turning the Enlightenment argument – that knowledge gives rise to power – upside down, postmodernists use Nietzsche to argue that power is the essential factor defining what it is possible to know. In this way, different power configurations, across different spatial and temporal contexts, are assumed to validate different forms of knowledge and modernist claims to neutrality – through the appropriation of certain methods or the raising of consciousness – are assumed to be wholly false. For postmodernists, modernist truth claims to universality are considered highly pretentious – gaining legitimacy only according to the spatial and temporal contexts in which they are empowered to do so.

Making Comparisons from a Postmodern Perspective

The postmodern approach to making comparisons can be defined, once again, in relation to what it is not, contra positivism and critical theory. Thus the idea

---

68   R. Rorty, 'Foucault and Epistemology', in D. Couzens Hoy (ed.) *Foucault: A Critical Reader* (Oxford, Basil Blackwell, 1989), p.47.

69   M. Foucault, *Power/Knowledge: Selected Interviews and Other Writings 1972–1977* (Brighton: The Harvester Press, 1980).

that subjects can compare contexts using 'neutral' scientific procedures or raised consciousness is abhorrent to postmodernists. Indeed, these approaches will be considered not only to be overly rationalising but also highly destructive – insensitive to the particularities and differences that are very much the reality of local contexts. Arguing against the reduction of all knowledge to 'the empirical' or to 'the class struggle', comparisons from a postmodern perspective are likely to focus on those marginalised areas of knowledge that are silenced by oppressive modernist approaches. Writing during his middle period – characterised by his appropriation of Nietzsche's genealogical method – Foucault states clearly what he considers to be the central approach and object of his research:

> Genealogy must record the singularity of events outside of any monotonous finality; it must seek them in the most unpromising places, in what we tend to feel is without history – in sentiments, love, conscience, instincts; it must be sensitive to their recurrence, not in order to isolate the gradual curve of their evolution, but to isolate the different scenes where they engaged in different roles.[70]

Comparisons from a postmodern perspective involve, therefore, an investigation of exceptions, of those occurrences that do not form a pattern, of those marginalised items of evidence or sources or contingencies that challenge the existing orthodoxy and cast new light on what may be assumed to be given. Comparisons from a postmodern perspective will be driven by what might even be called an anti-epistemology. Objects for comparison will be considered to be necessarily fractured and heterogeneous. One instinctively wishes to think of objects as units, but from a postmodern perspective it might be better to think in terms of anti-units. Moreover, comparisons of educational objects across national contexts – examinations, teaching approaches, curriculum issues – will be understood not in terms of similarities but differences, the particularities essential to each context understood to be of central importance to understanding the identity of objects.

Postmodernists will thus replace the enlightened or 'centred' subject implicit in positivism and critical theory with a de-centred conception of the subject. This will have important consequences for the making of comparisons. Where the knowing modernist subject assumes to survey the world from on high, the postmodern subject can never escape the particularities of the context in which it is located. While subjects and objects are conceived in a dynamic and mutually re-constructive relationship – one to the other -the relationship is essentially a dynamic of particularities; that is, of contents without a sense of universally binding forms. Great emphasis

---

70   R. Rorty, 'Foucault and Epistemology', in D. Couzens Hoy (ed.) *Foucault: A Critical Reader* (Oxford: Basil Blackwell, 1989), p.46.

will be placed on analysing the contextual power relations that give rise to particular types of knowledge. The subject will likewise be enmeshed, saturated even, in contextual power relations. As an effect of power, the limits and parameters of the de-centred subject will thus be defined relatively from one context to the next.

Yet this is highly problematic. If all contexts are defined relatively, how can we differentiate meaningfully between them? Would they not all appear 'equally different'? Likewise, if all contexts are simply defined by relative differences, why should the subject feel motivated to compare? Indeed, if truth is merely an expression of power- relations in given settings, how is it even possible to evaluate or assess differences? Where the postmodernists are 'right to insist that power was chronically and inevitably involved in all social processes' the 'Nietzschean radicalization of power, which elevates it to the prime position in action and in discourse' is questionable resulting in a kind of nihilism – a denial of meaning and purpose.[71] In spite of this, some commentators, the philosopher of education Paul Standish, for example, argue that the tendency towards nihilism is too often over-stated or even misunderstood.[72] For Standish, the importance of postmodern and especially post-structuralist thought is expressed in the realisation that aspects of 'the other' are simply unknowable. In other words, beyond thought and experience, some aspects of the history of objects simply cannot be acted upon. Writing in the first person Standish writes as follows: 'The Other comes to me as having depths that I cannot know and, in order not to do violence, I must acknowledge this unknowability. This negativity is at the heart of things'.[73]

There has long been an anti-positivist 'relativist impulse' in comparative educational research.[74] This strand of the field has long been rooted in anthropological approaches. For Epstein, relativism in comparative education is distinctive because it 'avoids casting judgement on what is observed, including the practices and conduct of people who do not share the observer's values'.[75] Epstein makes

---

71 A. Giddens, *Politics, Sociology and Social Theory* (Cambridge: Polity Press, 1995), p.268.
72 P. Standish, 'Europe, Continental Philosophy and the Philosophy of Education', *Comparative Education* (2004) 40 4, pp.485–501.
73 P. Standish, 'Europe, Continental Philosophy and the Philosophy of Education', op. cit. (note 72), p.494.
74 E. H. Epstein 'The Problematic Meaning of "Comparison" in Comparative Education', in J. Schriewer and B. Holmes (eds.) *Theories and Methods in Comparative Education* (Frankfurt am Main, Peter Lang, 1988).
75 Epstein 'The Problematic Meaning of "Comparison" in Comparative Education', op. cit. (note 74), p.11.

the distinction between two types of relativism. First the 'cultural relativism' that formed the basis of the work of Vernon Mallinson in which 'the comparative study of education is a process of gaining knowledge about foreign schools in order to gain a better understanding of one's own system'.[76] Here education systems are seen to be unique and distinctive along national lines. They cannot be judged against some universal criteria – neither can policies be transferred. Rather we must study and identify differences across contexts in order to understand what is particular to education at home.

In his now famous paper, 'How Far Can We Learn Anything of Practical Value from the Study of Foreign Systems of Education?', Michael Sadler pursues a similar line of argument.[77] 'The practical value of studying in a right spirit and with scholarly accuracy the working of foreign systems of education' writes Sadler 'is that it will result in our being better fitted to study and understand our own'.[78] Again, this perspective is taken up later in the century by Kandel: 'the study of other systems helps to bring out into relief the meaning and significance, the strength and weakness of our own'.[79] Importantly, for Epstein, although cultural relativists speak of the distinctive nature of national education systems they are not 'ethnocentric' as such since they refrain from making judgements about systems. No system is better or worse than the next, merely different. We learn from other systems in order to improve our own system and no more.[80]

Epstein identifies 'phenomenology' as a second kind of relativism. Phenomenological approaches, we are told, provide strong critiques of positivism. Here education systems are perceived as 'living things'. Essentially, the particularities of a given system or educational phenomenon are conceived as real only in as much as we observe them as such. Where positivists assume that reality is 'out there' waiting to be discovered, phenomenologists argue that it is the observer who constructs reality. According to Epstein,

> Phenomenologists object to the positivist view of social facts as 'things'... Positivist inquiry ignores the 'internal logic' of conditions under study – the rules used by the participants themselves, including the observer, to generate 'facts' or 'variables'.

---

76 Epstein 'The Problematic Meaning of "Comparison" in Comparative Education', op. cit. (note 74), p.9.

77 M. Sadler, 'Study of Foreign Systems of Education', in: *Comparative Education Review* (1964) 1 3, pp.307–314.

78 N. Hans, *Comparative Education* (London: Routledge & Kegan Paul, 1951), p.3.

79 I. L. Kandel, *Studies in Comparative Education* (London: Harrap, 1933), p.xxiv.

80 Epstein 'The Problematic Meaning of "Comparison" in Comparative Education', op. cit. (note 74), p.11.

Unlike physical objects social phenomena are 'real' only insofar as we organize our activities in such a way as to routinely confirm their real existence; they have no innate 'real' properties.[81]

For Epstein, the phenomenological approach in comparative education is necessarily 'microanalytical', 'interactionist' and 'interpretive'.[82] This being said, Epstein's final assessment of phenomenology is highly critical, mirroring the critique of 'postmodernity' thinking that would sweep through the English-speaking academy in years to come. Indeed, where

cultural relativism... requires multicultural analysis, and therefore can be said to employ some reasonable concept of 'comparison'. This is not so for phenomenological approaches, which carry relativism to a nihilistic extreme that allows interpretation of highly idiosyncratic interactions within severely limited contextual boundaries.[83]

More explicitly 'postmodern thinking' has had an enormous influence on the social sciences in English-speaking countries since the 1990s. Where Marxism once dominated critical perspectives in the academy, the situation changed, in close connection with the fall of the Soviet Union and the former communist bloc. Today much research is grounded in the ideas of postmodern thinkers.

Of the major contemporary thinkers in comparative education Robert Cowen has engaged directly with the issue of postmodernism. Writing over a decade ago, Cowen remarks not only on how 'comparative education, as a university field of study, has been late in addressing issues of post-modernity' but also on the implications of postmodernism for the university itself.[84] Comparative education, like the university, 'is... part of the modernity project'.[85] Yet if different forms of knowledge are to be valued, one as much as the next, what is the role of comparative education and the university? In a later and no less perceptive paper, Cowen argues that while comparative educationists need to grapple with the new reality, '[i]t seems improbable... [that] our categories of educational description, which

---

81 Epstein 'The Problematic Meaning of "Comparison" in Comparative Education', op. cit. (note 74), p.11.

82 E. H. Epstein 'The Problematic Meaning of "Comparison" in Comparative Education', op. cit. (note 74), p14.

83 Epstein 'The Problematic Meaning of "Comparison" in Comparative Education', op. cit. (note 78), pp.15–16.

84 R. Cowen, 'Last Past the Post: Comparative Education, Modernity and Perhaps Post-Modernity', *Comparative Education* (1996) 32 2, pp.151–170.

85 R. Cowen, 'Last Past the Post ', op. cit. (note 84), p.151.

are about 150 years old and which have become our categories of analysis, will be useful much longer'.[86]

Rolland Paulston engages with the issue of postmodernism, coming out very much in favour of post-modernity thinking. In his article 'Mapping Comparative Education after Postmodernity' Paulston 'examines the postmodern challenge to how we have come to see, represent, and practice comparative and international education'.[87] For Paulston the 'ontological shift from an essentialist view of one fixed reality... to an antiessentialist view where reality constructs are seen to resist closure', should be embraced by practitioners of comparative education.[88]

What is History from a Postmodern Perspective?

Is there such thing as a postmodern history? Yet again, it is possible to define postmodern history in the same way that it is possible to define postmodernism in general – i.e. in relation to what it is not. Thus, against the modernist stress on discovery, linearity, rationality, and progress, postmodern histories emphasise construction, multiplicity, irregularity and relativity. Importantly, and owing to paradigmatic conceptions of knowledge, history is perceived to be anything but a developmental process towards absolute truth. The work of Thomas Kuhn in *The Structure of Scientific Revolutions* comes to mind here, as does that of the early Michel Foucault in *The Order of Things*.[89] In the former Kuhn points to the paradigmatic and essentially political nature of scientific research over time. Science is not about the discovery of truth towards absolute knowledge in any linear or progressive sense, but about the conformity of researchers to particular paradigmatic communities. Thus, what counts as true at one point in time may be considered false at another point in time, and from one scientific paradigm to the next.

---

86   R. Cowen, 'Comparing Futures or Comparing Pasts?', *Comparative Education* (2000) 36 3, Special Number (23), Comparative Education for the Twenty-First Century, p.341.

87   R. G. Paulston, 'Mapping Comparative Education after Postmodernity', *Comparative Education Review* (1999) 43 4, p.438.

88   Paulston, 'Mapping Comparative Education after Postmodernity', op. cit. (note 87), p.440.

89   T. Kuhn, *The Structure of Scientific Revolutions* (Chicago: University of Chicago Press, 1974). M. Foucault, *The Order of Things: An Archaeology of the Human Sciences* (London: Routledge, 1991).

In *The Order of Things* Foucault speaks of pseudo-paradigmatic epistemes, '"fundamental codes", generative grammars of cognitive language…more than world views…built in a still deeper layer of (un)consciousness'. For Foucault, at this early stage in his career, all claims to truth and knowledge are situated within epistemes. Thus, in the Western World, as epistemes have changed, from Renaissance to classical and from modern to contemporary, so the meaning of truth has changed. At this early 'archaeological' stage in his writing, Foucault attempts to demonstrate how the history of ideas has not developed in any rational or linear sense, but according to the all-pervasive epistemic structures that define an age. Accordingly it is from within the context of the contemporary episteme that we now understand knowledge and from which we construct our histories.

There are problems with the idea of a postmodern history, however. By rejecting universal truth/knowledge claims, how is it possible to define history in any generic sense? Does not the emphasis on plurality and difference, the valorisation of various contents, negate the idea of the *form* history? Where modernists contrast true history with false, the single true account of events discovered through rational means against the many histories of mystics and metaphysicians, postmodernists value plurality. Commonly this involves the discussion of multiple histories, of the history of the marginal and of the particular. On one level this is to be welcomed. However, through the rejection of universal truth claims, postmodernists negate the concept of history itself; that is to say, the epistemological means through which it is possible to say that different histories, on the level of content, are all, on the level of form, history. While postmodernists are right to question the modernist concept of a single universal history, the attempt to champion multiple histories while negating the idea of the generic concept – history – is equally problematic. But there is nothing new in this. To return to E. H. Carr, writing in 1961, 'we are offered here the theory of an infinity of meanings, none any more right than any other- which comes to the same thing' as 'the theory that history has no meaning'.[90]

What are the Implications of Postmodernist Perspectives for Comparing Syllabus Topics in History Education across Contexts?

In the comparison of the topic of World War II in history education across contexts the postmodernist will focus upon differences. In contrast to positivists and critical

---

90   E. H. Carr, *What is History?* (London: Penguin Books, 1900), p.26.

theorists, there will be no universal criteria against which to make judgements. Indeed, owing to the recognised otherness of each context postmodernists will show a distinct aversion to making assessments. The researching subject will point, as such, to the necessarily constructed and subjective nature of history education across contexts, differences understood as the effects of particular configurations of power. In this way, contrasting approaches to the topic of World War II will be understood as inevitable – as natural even – with no sense that a single correct interpretation of the conflict underlies differences.

On one level, this position ends up in practice as something oddly close to the positivist approach outlined above. Comparative research thus becomes an exercise in the empirical description of differences and particularities across contexts. This being said, critical evaluations will be denied by postmodernists since they are perceived to be unfairly insensitive to differences. Again the problems of relativism and agency alluded to above come into play here. Is the approach to teaching World War II as a topic in classrooms in Japan only different from that which occurs in, say, Sweden or England? Is every approach involving every interpretation to be understood as equally valid? With a completely relativised concept of the subject is it possible meaningfully to assess anything?

Concluding comments

In this chapter I have provided a general overview of three important philosophical perspectives – positivism, critical theory, and postmodernism – in order to assess their implications for comparative research on history education.

	Theory of Knowledge / Reality	Relationship between politics and knowledge	Relationship between subject and object	Implications for making comparisons
Positivism	Facts exist 'out there' in the world. Truth can be known only through the use of scientific procedures.	True knowledge is neutral. Politics is a contaminating variable.	Passive and neutral. The 'centred' subject is free to discover 'autonomous' objects.	Using the scientific method the 'centred', 'autonomous' subject identifies and compares objects across contexts.

101

	Theory of Knowledge / Reality	Relationship between politics and knowledge	Relationship between subject and object	Implications for making comparisons
Critical theory	Truth exists in the world. Truth can be understood only through the raising of class-consciousness.	True knowledge is neutral. However, in class societies, pervasive social and political ideologies mask the truth.	Depends on the type of society. In class based societies the relationship will be dynamic, conflicting, and characterised by struggle.	With raised class consciousness the 'centred', 'autonomous' subject identifies and compares objects across contexts. The researcher will be motivated to discover truth and, in turn, raise the consciousness of others.
Post-modernism	Knowledge is essentially constructed. Different societies have different understandings of knowledge. Truth is denied.	All knowledge is political. Knowledge is an effect of power. Different power = different knowledge.	Subjects and objects exist in context specific relationships. different context = different subject / object relationships.	Emphasis on the uniqueness of different contexts. Concern with types of knowledge that have been denied or marginalised by repressive truth regimes.

Key differences between the three perspectives are presented in the above table. As we have seen, each perspective is underpinned by a particular view on the nature of knowledge, on the politics of knowledge and on the relationship between subjects and objects. In addition, each perspective contains different methodological implications with regard to the making of comparisons.

ANTINOMY BETWEEN MODERNITY THINKING AND POST-MODERNITY THINKING

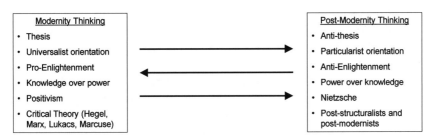

Fig. 3.1: *Antinomy between modernity thinking and post-modernity thinking*

In this chapter modernity thinking and post-modernity thinking have been posited as opposites, as portrayed in the diagram above. On the side of modernity thinking, the thesis of the Enlightenment project, we have positivism and critical theory. Positivism views the world from what is presumed to be the a-historical high ground facilitated by empiricism and science. Armed with the scientific method the positivist distinguishes between valid and invalid knowledge across contexts. Historical, political and cultural variables are seen to be impossible to measure and are therefore considered to be invalid. Critical theory offers a more radical approach. Here the high ground is provided through consciousness of the prevailing social and economic relations that exist in class societies, ultimately underpinning all forms of knowledge. Historical, political, and ideological variables are seen to be essential features of reality in class societies. Comparisons across contexts will therefore involve 'revealing' ideological deceit wherever it may occur. Both positivism and critical theory are based in a particular view of the 'centred' subject – a knowing subject empowered by knowledge that stands autonomous from social, historical and ideological forces in order to survey truth across contexts in the world.

Post-modernity thinking is the antithesis of modernity thinking – and is positioned against the Enlightenment project. According to postmodernists, the subject can never stand outside of history. Reality is always context-specific. There are no universal truths. The history of things in the world is far too complex ever to assume total knowledge. For postmodernists therefore the subject is 'de-centred', relativised and localised, an effect of contextual power relations. In sharp contrast to the positivists and the critical theorists, power is thus considered to be 'chronically and inevitably involved in all social processes... [with] logical primacy over truth'.[91] By arguing that the politics of knowledge is a deceptive mask shrouding underlying truths it is, according to postmodernists, the modernists that are deceived. Truth and knowledge are effects of power across contexts and no more. Different power = different knowledge.

Each of the perspectives outlined in this chapter has its supporters and its critics. It is my position, however, that each position has its merits if considered in moderation. Thus the positivist insistence on empirical reality is important. However, it is also crucial to recognise that there is a reality beyond the empirical. Likewise, critical theorists are right to focus on inequalities in society and their relationship to knowledge. Yet it would surely be overly reductionist to claim that all knowledge is determined, in the last instance, by class factors. Likewise, postmodernists are right to emphasise the importance of context and power. But to relativise knowledge to the point where 'anything goes' is surely to deny knowledge altogether, not to mention all motivations to act upon it.

Many of the problems outlined above are related to the conceptions of the subject that form an essential feature of each perspective. Modernist positions champion the 'centred' or autonomous subject. According to this position the enlightened subject is empowered. Postmodernist positions, on the other hand, stress the 'de-centred' nature of subjectivity. Here the subject is always enmeshed within relations of power, and unable to break out of an all-pervasive relativism. What I argue is that neither modernist nor postmodernist perspectives suffice. In other words, what is required is a concept of the subject that is neither purely 'centred' nor 'de-centred' in order to approach differences across contexts meaningfully. Based in a hermeneutic conception of reality – in an essential 'synthesis' of the thesis and antithesis outlined above – the subject may construct meaningful platforms from which to proceed, in order to make judgements and assessments of differences encountered across contexts – within specified limits. It is towards the possibility of constructing a hermeneutic approach to making comparisons that we turn in the following chapter.

---

91   A. Giddens, *Politics, Sociology and Social Theory* (Cambridge: Polity Press, 1995), p.264.

Chapter Four
The Philosophical Basis of Comparisons II – Towards a Hermeneutic 'Synthesis'

> All the great philosophical ideas of the last century – the philosophies of Marx, Nietzsche, phenomenology, German existentialism, and psychoanalysis – had their beginnings in Hegel.
>
> Maurice Merleau-Ponty, *Sense and Non-Sense*, 1964, p.63

> [W]ithin the circle of the philosophers of my generation who diagnose our times, Foucault has most lastingly influenced the Zeitgeist.
>
> Jurgen Habermas, *Taking Aim at the Heart of the Present*, 1989, p.107

In this chapter it will be argued that hermeneutic approaches provide a philosophical basis for making comparisons across contexts that incorporate important features of modernity and post-modernity thinking while avoiding the excesses of over- empiricism, class reductionism and relativism. Hermeneutic conceptions of reality will be posited as both an important synthesis and critique of the positions outlined in Chapter Three – hermeneutic perspectives providing a powerful alternative, suited to a truly dynamic comparative education for our times. With a dynamic conception of knowledge, the politics of knowledge, and of agency, it will be argued that hermeneutic philosophies provide the grounds upon which to construct methodologies that facilitate meaningful yet sensitive comparisons of syllabus topics in school history education across contexts. Hermeneutic approaches provide a perspective that is sensitive to cultural and linguistic differences while at the same time providing the subject with the space – the platform even – to make evaluations and assessments. Hermeneutic conceptions of truth and history enable the subject to take positions while acknowledging important limits.

4.1 Re-reading Hegel in the Spirit of Our Times

In Chapter Three Hegel was introduced as an Enlightenment thinker and as a kind of great grandfather of critical theory. However, it was also pointed out that this interpretation of Hegel was in part due to Marx's reading of Hegel and to the acceptance of this reading by subsequent generations. The significance of this 'orthodox' or 'classical' reading of Hegel cannot be underestimated and to this day remains as the 'standard' reading. Orthodox readings of Hegel place emphasis on the grand systematic design of his philosophy, the conscious subject playing an essential role on the road to freedom, to be realised through time. According to Peter Singer:

> Hegel's overriding aim... is straightforward: to demonstrate the necessity of absolute idealism. He seeks to do this by starting... from the bare concept of being, and showing that this concept leads by dialectical necessity to other concepts which more precisely and truly capture the nature of reality; and these other concepts in turn prove inadequate and require others, until finally we reach 'the absolute idea'.[1]

In *Hegel's Critique of Liberalism*, Steven Smith concedes, however, that Hegel is a philosopher open to interpretation. Yet ultimately Smith chooses to interpret Hegel in the orthodox way. Thus:

> A key task for anyone broadly sympathetic to Hegel's approach is to determine what kind of necessity or logic he claims to be operating with. After considering a number of possible candidates, I conclude that Hegel is operating with a ideological conception of necessity. This conception of teleological necessity leads, finally, to... Hegel's controversial views on the end of history.[2]

Alternative readings of Hegel – hermeneutic or at least pseudo-hermeneutic readings – interpret his ideas in a non-teleological way. Truth is granted but not as something to be realised absolutely through or at the end of history. Consciousness enables knowledge but never complete knowledge. Indeed, concepts such as truth, the subject, and consciousness are understood as having no identity outside of a relationship to another – untruth, the object and alienation. This is a dialectical relationship, a circular and ongoing relationship between

> the whole and the parts; the content is the whole and consists of its opposite, i.e., the parts (of the form). The parts are diverse from each other and they are what is independent. But they are parts only... insofar as, taken together, they constitute the whole. But the ensemble is the opposite and the negation of the part.[3]

According to orthodox readings of Hegel, dialectical struggles between opposites are necessarily resolvable in time. Pseudo-hermeneutic readings posit, however,

---

1   P. Singer, *Hegel* (Oxford: Oxford University Press, 1988), p.80.
2   S. B. Smith, *Hegel's Critique of Liberalism* (Chicago: University of Chicago Press, 1989), p.13.
3   S. B. Smith, *Hegel's Critique of Liberalism,* op. cit. (note 2), p.204.

that these relationships are necessarily un-resolvable. They are inescapable and ongoing. History moves forward dialectically, but not towards a *telos* – a Utopian end of history – but ad infinitum. Progress is not guaranteed. According to this reading, subjects can never stand outside of history, assuming complete autonomy. The parameters of space and time cannot be overcome. In *The Philosophy of Right*, Hegel makes it very clear that the subject has its limits:

> Whatever happens, every individual is a child of his time; so philosophy too is its own time apprehended in thoughts. It is just as absurd to fancy that a philosophy can transcend its contemporary world as it is to fancy that an individual can overleap his own age... If his theory really goes beyond the world as it is and builds an ideal one as it ought to be, that world exists indeed, but only in his opinions...[4]

It is from its necessary location in time and in space that the subject must appeal to truth. This appeal within limits provides the motivation for individual and collective agency and praxis.

Since the fall of the Soviet Union and the decline of Marxism as a critical force in the Western academy, teleological conceptions of the end of history – via Hegel and Marx – have become deeply unfashionable. Yet with the demise of the philosophy that appeared to prophesy the end of history we have arrived strangely at 'the end of history'.[5]

What is this era that we now live in? Francis Fukuyama argued that the inevitable collapse of communism signalled the triumph of liberalism as a universal ideology, a position that has received both strong criticism and acclaim. Looking at the world today capitalism if not liberalism is everywhere. Others have talked about the end of ideology. In those areas that were once highly ideological, government or the universities, for example, we see the end of the old ideological traditions that at one point defined debates. Politics without ideology, without left and right, is the politics of power alone – the realm of Machiavelli – politics without ethics. This frightening scenario would seem to suggest that the postmodernists were right. Yet in many ways the present *Zeitgeist* is so much more than a simple championing of the local and contextual effects of power. In the information age the interface between global and local, between the subject and knowledge, across space and time, has taken on a dynamic new meaning. Masses of information – a vast plurality – is available universally, signalling a new hermeneutic synthesis between whole and parts, and the continued need for a vigorous and dynamic conception of subjects as agents.

---

4   G. W. F. Hegel, *Philosophy of Right* (Oxford: Oxford University Press, 1967), p.11.
5   F. Fukuyama, 'The End of History?', *National Interest* (1989) 16, pp.3–18.

I consider the current age as a form of Hegelian synthesis, beyond the modernist thesis and its postmodern antithesis. However, this interpretation – using Hegel after post-modernity – is rooted in a pseudo-hermeneutic understanding of Hegel's thought. Accordingly, history is not conceived as ending at some absolute *telos* – the Prussian State or the dictatorship of the proletariat or Fukayama's liberal Utopia – but rather as an ongoing and dynamic process between whole and parts, agents and objects, power and knowledge. Synthesis here is thus understood not as an end, but as the expression of those relationships that define the Spirit of the contemporary age.

This chapter is not concerned solely with Hegel. Far from it, in what remains of the chapter I will focus in greater depth on the work of those thinkers identified directly with the hermeneutic tradition, particularly that of Gadamer, who, it is argued, looks back to Hegel and forward to a place beyond post-modernity. As in Chapter Three I will focus on the implications of hermeneutic philosophy for making comparisons and on definitions of history from a hermeneutic perspective. Following this I will turn to the later works of Foucault, the ultimate synthesis in the current synthesis, where he moves from his formerly relativist position – located inside the post-modern antithesis – to a new 'ontology of the present'.[6]

4.2 Gadamer and the Hermeneutic Tradition

Providing an interpretation of reality that is neither modernist nor postmodernist, hermeneutic perspectives are concerned with the relationship between language, meaning, interpretation and existence. With hermeneutics, ontological as opposed to epistemological dimensions are especially emphasised. Thus, what it means to be in the world is considered to be more directly important than definitions of the nature of knowledge. Indeed, the latter will depend on the former. In this way, knowledge is conceptualised neither along vertical axes of truth nor along horizontal axes of difference but, rather, as a circular and ongoing relationship, a process tied to the existence of subjects in the present, objectivity bound with subjectivity and vice versa. Josef Bleicher in his study *Contemporary Hermeneutics* begins by providing the following definition:

> Hermeneutics can loosely be defined as the theory or philosophy of the interpretation of meaning... The realization that human expressions contain a meaningful component, which has to be recognized as such by a subject and transposed into his own system of

---

6   M. Foucault, *The Politics of Truth* (New York, Semiotext(e), 1997), p.171.

values and meanings, has given rise to the 'problem of hermeneutics': how this process is possible and how to render accounts of subjectively intended meaning objective in the face of the fact that they are mediated by the interpreter's own subjectivity.[7]

Hermeneutic perspectives provide an important alternative to the philosophical positions outlined in Chapter Three. While, on one level, the hermeneutic endeavour may be viewed as the precursor to much postmodern thinking since it is characterised by an attempt 'to find a place for the "subjective"', hermeneutics should not be conceived in opposition to truth and objectivity.[8] Rather the subjective dimension in all interpretations of reality is considered to be an important aspect of objective reality. Finitude and particularity are valued and respected by hermeneutic thinkers not simply as the other of modernity or Enlightenment thinking but as the road to knowledge and innovation. 'The incapacity for completeness', Gadamer tells us, 'has a positive side: it reveals the true infinity of the mind, which constantly surpasses itself... and in doing so also finds the freedom for constantly new projects'.[9] In this way, hermeneutic theorists reject the modernist quest for the whole truth and for unity.

But the championing of local knowledge by postmodern thinkers is seen to be equally problematic. To argue that knowledge is only subjective and relative destroys the concept of meaning. Knowledge is not arbitrary. From a hermeneutic perspective reality is thus conceived very much as an ongoing process in which 'unity and multiplicity are fundamentally in dialectical relationship to each other', whole and parts existing in a constantly developing and indeed fluid symbiosis. Usher describes these features of the hermeneutic perspective as follows:

[I]nterpretations are always circular. The interpretation of part of something depends on interpreting the whole, but interpreting the whole depends on an interpretation of the parts. As an example, think of what happens when you read a book – the meaning of the book depends on the meaning of each of its chapters (the parts), yet each chapter's meaning depends on the meaning of the whole book. This determination of meaning in the interaction of part and whole is called the hermeneutic circle of interpretation. Knowledge-formation is therefore conceived as circular, iterative, spiral – not linear and cumulative as portrayed in positivist/empiricist epistemology.[10]

7   J. Bleicher, *Contemporary Hermeneutics: Hermeneutics as Method, Philosophy and Critique* (London: Routledge & Kegan Paul, 1980), p.1.

8   D. Scott and R. Usher, *Researching Education: Data, Methods and Theory in Educational Enquiry* (New York: Cassell, 1999), p.25.

9   H. G. Gadamer, *Truth and Method* (London: Sheed & Ward, 1989), p.426.

10   R. Usher, 'A critique of the neglected epistemological assumptions of educational research', in D. Scott and R. Usher (eds.) *Understanding Educational Research* (Lon-

Suddenly we are back with Hegel. Yet the hermeneutic tradition is commonly conceived outside of the Hegelian horizon or, at least, critical of Hegel. Indeed, Hegel is described by Gadamer in *Truth and Method* as 'an absolute thinker'.[11] Thus Gadamer conforms to an orthodox reading of Hegel. Upon these grounds, it becomes impossible to

> accept Hegel's explanation of the unity of world history through the concept of spirit. That spirit reaches its culmination in the perfect self- consciousness of the historical present, which constitutes the significance of history, [and] is an eschatological self-interpretation which basically supersedes history by turning it into a speculative concept.[12]

Yet the distance from Hegel is questionable. In *The Broken Middle*, the late Neo-Hegelian philosopher and social theorist Gillian Rose quotes the 'shrewd comment on Gadamer's relation to Hegel' made by Wolfhart Pannenberg. Here, *Truth and Method* is understood as 'a partly open, partly tacit debate with Hegel.' Thus:

> It is a peculiar spectacle to see how an incisive and penetrating author has his hands full trying to keep his thoughts from going in the direction they inherently want to go. Gadamer's book [Truth and *Method*] offers this kind of spectacle when he strives to avoid the Hegelian... mediation of the truth of the present by means of history.[13]

Gadamer's hermeneutics owes much to the philosophy of Dilthey.[14] Dilthey would identify a fundamental relationship between the human and the natural sciences, the spiritual and the physical. Contrasting spheres were conceived to be essentially different and yet inter-dependent. Dilthey would be strongly critical of the kind of pure idealism championed by orthodox Hegelians. The material exists in its own right. Thus,

> If one were to imagine pure spiritual beings in a realm of persons in a realm of persons which consisted only of such beings, then there coming- to-be, preservation, and development, as well as there extinction... would be dependent on purely spiritual conditions. Their well being would be based on their relation to a world of spirit, their contact with each other and their interactions would be effected through purely

don, Routledge, 1996), p.19.

11   Gadamer, *Truth and Method*, op. cit. (note 9), p.343.

12   Gadamer, *Truth and Method*, op. cit. (note 9), p.210.

13   G. Rose, *The Broken Middle* (Oxford: Blackwell, 1992), p.6.

14   W. Dilthey, *Introduction to the Human Sciences*, 1983. [Internet] Available from <http://www.marxists.org /reference/subject/philosophv/workd/ge/dilthey.htm> [Accessed 19 December 2006].

mental means, and the lasting effects of their actions would be of a purely spiritual sort… In reality, however, an individual comes into being, survives, and develops on the basis of the functions of an animal organism.[15]

Nevertheless, for Dilthey, the separation of the spiritual and the material, the mental and the physical, is purely an abstraction for reality is constituted always by both sides.[16] 'Whatever the metaphysical facts may be' writes Dilthey 'man as a life-unit may be regarded from the two points of view that we have developed: seen from within he is a system of mental facts, but to the senses he is a physical whole'.[17]

In Gadamer's hermeneutics, subjects are always mediators between the ideal and the material. Gadamer, like Hegel, points to the necessary place of history and background in the formulation of perspectives. This 'background' is an integral feature of all interpretations of reality and truth, to deny it is to deny what is real. Subjects are even seen to act according to pre-assumptions and prejudices in interactions with objects, important contextual factors. Where Enlightenment thinking, based in reason, identifies 'prejudice… as the source of all error', in the hermeneutics of Gadamer, prejudice has its place as an integral part of reality.[18] Thus:

> What appears to be a limiting prejudice… in fact belongs to historical reality itself. If we want to do justice to man's finite, historical mode of being, it is necessary to fundamentally rehabilitate the concept of prejudice and acknowledge the fact that there are legitimate prejudices. Thus we can formulate the fundamental epistemological question for a truly historical hermeneutics as follows: what is the ground for the legitimacy of prejudices?[19]

In the same way, subjects are always conceived as contextually located within traditions. Again this 'situatedness' constitutes an element of the subject's objective reality. Where Enlightenment thinking posited 'tradition as an antithesis to the freedom of reason', and romantics champion tradition over reason, Gadamer provides a third perspective. Thus:

> It seems to me… that there is no such unconditional antithesis between tradition and reason. However problematical the conscious restoration of old or the creation of new traditions may be, the romantic faith in the "growth of tradition," before which all reason must remain silent, is fundamentally like the Enlightenment, and just as prejudiced. The fact is that in tradition there is always an element of freedom and of

15 Dilthey, *Introduction to the Human Sciences*, op. cit. (note 14).
16 Dilthey, *Introduction to the Human Sciences*, op. cit. (note 14).
17 Dilthey, *Introduction to the Human Sciences*, op. cit. (note 14).
18 Gadamer, *Truth and Method*, op. cit. (note 9), p.279.
19 Gadamer, *Truth and Method*, op. cit. (note 9), p.277.

history itself. Even the most genuine and pure tradition does not persist because of the inertia of what once existed. It needs to be affirmed, embraced, cultivated. It is, essentially, preservation, and it is active in all historical change. But preservation is an act of reason though an inconspicuous one.[20]

Contextual variables, local, specific and particular, are thus understood as playing an essential role in Gadamer's hermeneutics. More generic variables are, however, similarly important, the concepts of time and language, for example. The hermeneutic conception of the subject contrasts with modernist pretentions to timelessness as much as the postmodern negation of time. Developing from the ideas of Heidegger, Gadamer's predecessor, the expression of the dialectic between subjective and objective reality exists in time, not outside of it or without it. And it is from this dynamic 'situation' in the present, that the subject's hermeneutic horizons are formulated.[21] Horizons define the parameters but also the conscious possibilities of the subject as an agent located in space and time and in context. To return again to Gadamer:

> Every finite present has its limitations. We define the concept of "situation" by saying that it represents a standpoint that limits the possibility of vision. Hence essential to the concept of situation is the concept of "horizon". The horizon is the range of vision that includes everything that can be seen from a particular vantage point. Applying this to the thinking mind, we speak of narrowness of horizon, of the possible expansion of horizon, of the opening up of new horizons, and so forth. Since Nietzsche... the word has been used in philosophy to characterize the way in which thought is tied to its finite determinacy... On the other hand, "to have a horizon" means not being limited to what is nearby but being able to see beyond it.[22]

Horizons may be broadened through the incorporation of alternative or additional horizons; that is, through the fusion of horizons: a form of 'intersubjective agreement where different and conflicting interpretations are played out and possibly harmonized...despite differences'.[23] Through the fusion of horizons, 'an enlargement or broadening of one's own horizon' occurs, providing a new and refined platform from which to proceed.[24]

---

20   Gadamer, *Truth and Method*, op. cit. (note 9), p.281.
21   J. Bleicher, *Contemporary Hermeneutics: Hermeneutics as Method, Philosophy and Critique* (London: Routledge & Kegan Paul, 1980), p.110.
22   Gadamer, *Truth and Method*, op. cit. (note 9), p.302.
23   D. Scott and R. Usher, *Researching Education: Data, Methods and Theory in Educational Enquiry* (New York: Cassell, 1999), p.29.
24   R. Usher, 'A critique of the neglected epistemological assumptions of educational research', in D. Scott, and R. Usher (eds.) *Understanding Educational Research* (Lon-

Any description of Gadamer's ideas would be incomplete without some discussion of the centrality of language and the ontological dimension in hermeneutic philosophy. Where modernists and postmodernists have tended to debate the championing or the negation of epistemology, hermeneutic thinkers are concerned first and foremost with the meaning of existence in the world. Indeed, the focus moves away from what it is possible to know to what it means to exist. This emphasis on ontology is grounded, in turn, in a particular conception of the relationship between language and understanding. Developing according to Heidegger's hypothesis that 'language is the house of Being', there can be 'no world outside language' for hermeneutic thinkers.[25] 'Everything', claims Schleiermacher, 'presupposed in hermeneutics is but language'.[26] Understood as 'the universal medium of humanity' language becomes that whole in relation to which individual parts acquire their meaning' and the necessary pre-condition for all understandings, existence and being in the world.[27] Interpretation cannot ensue without or before language. Language is the medium for all interpretations and meanings.[28]

Hermeneutic approaches provide frameworks for approaching problems in a circular fashion, an investigative ontology, subjects employed in an ongoing process of engagement and re-engagement, definition and re-definition, in a continued attempt to broaden horizons, in order to interpret the meaning of reality and existence.

Making Comparisons from a Hermeneutic Perspective

In some ways, hermeneutic perspectives offer something of a middle way in the making of comparisons, between the modernist and postmodernist perspectives outlined in Chapter Three. Yet it is important not to assume that this reference to 'middle' takes anything away from the power and potentiality of the hermeneutic synthesis. Making comparisons from a hermeneutic perspective is a truly dynamic enterprise. Thus, the comparison of objects across contexts will ensue according to the location of the subject here in the present. At the same time, the meaning

don, Routledge, 1996), p.22.

25 J. Bleicher, *Contemporary Hermeneutics*, o. cit. (note 21), pp.115–116.

26 F. Schleiermacher and A. Bowie, *Schleiermacher: Hermeneutics and Criticism: And Other Writings* (Cambridge: Cambridge University Press, 1998), p.381.

27 J. Bleicher, *Contemporary Hermeneutics*, op. cit. (note 21), p.2.

28 J. Bleicher, *Contemporary Hermeneutics*, op. cit. (note 21), p.116.

of the subject's contextual location will be defined in relation to the objects being compared.

Hermeneutic interpretations are, to reiterate, always circular and ongoing. The subject surveys objects from a contextual platform, the arrangement of the objects impacting on the platform of the subject and so on – like navigating a vessel across a channel of water. The subject controls the vessel in relation to the conditions – the objects. In some contexts the conditions will be variable, in others constant. The subject brings its own background to the context. The horizons developed by the subject during the crossing will express the dynamic interplay between subjective background and objective conditions. The subject-object relationship is therefore essentially regenerative – expressing the ontology of the subject as it exists in the ongoing present. Essentially there will be no single, timeless way to cross the channel. At the same time the subject cannot simply take the vessel across the channel in 'any old way'. As an engaged agent, the subject will need to choose a way forward. This will involve the making of comparisons as well as the assessment and evaluation of situations.

For hermeneutic thinkers comparisons across contexts are pursued in acknowledgement of the specific parameters and limits of subjectivity. There is no neutral platform outside of time from which to formulate an all-encompassing horizon. Comparisons from the perspectives of positivism or critical theory are therefore rejected. To reiterate, the idea that truth may exist outside of time and space is considered to be a fiction. On the other hand, hermeneutic thinkers never deny the existence of truth. Truth exists and is objectively expressed – in the contextual realities of the subject as it exists in time. Where modernist thinkers identify truth with 'the whole' and postmodernist thinkers reject truth through the championing of 'the parts', hermeneutic thinkers conceive truth as the expression of the relationship between the whole and the parts. To make comparisons from a hermeneutic perspective is, therefore, to compare relationships

Hermeneutic approaches to making comparisons are intrinsically complex and sophisticated. After all, to acknowledge the limits of the subject is at the same time to recognise its practical potentiality. Can any subject make comparisons? The answer to this question would be given in ontological terms by the hermeneutic thinker; that is to say, existentially. While the most skilled of navigators is unlikely to guide the vessel across the channel successfully in all situations, a subject lacking all skills of navigation is unlikely to reach the other side, save through chance. In other words, meaningful engagement with objects will depend on the background of the subject. But can all objects be compared? The meaningful comparison of a cluster of objects requires a certain level of selectivity – an evaluative criteria. Going back to our 'channel crossing' example, upon what grounds is it possible to choose a suitable harbour for the vessel? From a distance the shoreline is likely to appear as a two-dimensional horizon, the subject deciphering between potential harbours and non-harbours only with great difficulty. But moving closer, the horizon will change. The intricacies of the shoreline will come into focus and the relationship between subject and objects will change. Some areas of the shoreline that appeared, from a distance, as potential harbouring points may be completely unsuitable when viewed close up. These will need to be dropped. The subject will then be left with a cluster of suitable harbouring points. As soon as these have been identified, meaningful comparisons may ensue.

Very few comparative educationists work from an explicitly hermeneutic perspective. This being said, the work of scholars like Patricia Broadfoot may appear conducive to hermeneutic ways of thinking. The relationship between contexts, comparison, and the potential for subjective agency appears as an essential feature of her work.[29] The comparative education of George Bereday may appear strongly hermeneutic if interpreted in a particular way, re-theorised through the ideas of Gadamer. For Bereday cultural and linguistic immersion defines the horizon of the researcher, qualifying the subject to research objects, and enabling comparisons to ensue meaningfully. Cultural and linguistic immersion brings researchers into meaningful proximity with the contexts being researched. Likewise, this proximity will determine the extent to which contexts will fall inside or outside of the researcher's horizon. The relationship between Gadamer and Bereday will be expanded upon in greater depth in the following chapter.

Comparative educational research from a hermeneutic perspective will emphasise the relationship between subjects and objects in the context of language, interpretation, meaning and existence. Unlike those working from a positivist or critical theory position, hermeneutic thinkers are likely to draw attention not to the epistemological mechanisms through which it is possible to ascertain true knowledge across contexts, but to the ontological relationship between the researching subject – existing in the present, in the world – and objects – i.e. what does the comparison of a particular set of objects tell us about our own existence?

---

29   R. Alexander, P. Broadfood and D. Phillips, D. (eds.) 'Learning from Comparing: New Directions' in *Comparative Educational Research*, Vol. 1: Contexts, Classrooms and Outcomes (Oxford, Symposium Books, 1999). P. Broadfoot, 'Editorial: structure and agency in education: the role of comparative education', *Comparative Education*, 38 1, 2002, pp.5–6.

In contrast to postmodernism, hermeneutic research will not deny the concept of truth since to do so would be tantamount to reducing knowledge and, more importantly, existence, to an arbitrary relativism.

How would it be possible to compare topics in history and social science education from a hermeneutic perspective? Essentially, comparative approaches will be based in particular assumptions concerning the nature of existence and the relationship between researching subjects in the present and educational objects. Comparisons of syllabus 'topics' in history and social science education across contexts depend, once again, on definitions of history.

What is History from a Hermeneutic Perspective?

The hermeneutic perspective provides a wholly different concept of history compared with the modernist and postmodernist positions outlined in Chapter Three. First, the idea of a single factual history 'out there' in the modernist sense is rejected. Yet so too is the postmodern notion that there can only be multiple histories. For hermeneutic thinkers, it must be remembered, whole and parts are constituted in dialectical relationship to each other. Bound by language, the object – history – is thus conceptualised in a dynamic and circular relationship with subjective interpretations and vice versa. Essentially, this vital inter-relationship is subjective as well as objective. It is subjective in the sense that all interpretations are relatively located, affected necessarily by pre-understandings and prejudices, traditions and context; it is objective in the sense that situated parts are understood to have no meaning outside of a relationship to a defining whole – that is, the form history. Essentially, history is conceived as fluid, dynamic, characterised by movement, but not necessarily progressing. In Gadamer's interpretation of the hermeneutics of Dilthey, history is perceived as an ongoing relationship between universality and particularity. The presence of Hegel is unmistakable:

> [H]ermeneutics... involves the whole business of historical research itself. For what is true of the written sources, that every sentence in them can be understood only on the basis of its context, is also true of their content. Its meaning is not fixed. The context of world history – in which appears the true meaning of the individual objects, large or small, of historical research – is itself a whole, in terms of which the meaning of every particular is to be fully understood, and which in turn can be fully understood only in terms of these particulars. World history is, as it were, the great dark book, the collected work of the human spirit...[30]

---

30 Gadamer, *Truth and Method*, op. cit. (note 9), p.177.

In 1961, one year after Gadamer published *Truth and Method*, E. H. Carr's position appears strongly hermeneutic in his discussion of what it means to be an historian. Thus:

> We sometimes speak of the course of history as a 'moving procession'. The metaphor is fair enough, provided it does not tempt the historian to think of himself as an eagle surveying the scene from a lonely crag... Nothing of the kind! The historian is just another dim figure trudging long in another part of the procession. And as the procession winds along, swerving now to the right and now to the left, and sometimes doubling back on itself, the relative position of different parts of the procession are constantly changing... New vistas, new angles of vision, constantly appear as the procession – and the historian with it – moves along. The historian is a part of history. The point in the procession at which he finds himself determines his angle of vision over the past.[31]

For hermeneutic thinkers, history is active, and it is always being done, for the researcher, the student, the teacher can never stand outside of the hermeneutic circle universal to all interpretations and meanings. History is understood, therefore, not simply in epistemological terms, in which a theory of knowledge, historical knowledge, of truth, provides closure. On the contrary, following Gadamer's 'ontological turn', history must be understood on the level of ontology, since historical knowledge is shaped, necessarily, by our ongoing investigations in relation to our own existence in the perpetually changing present.

What are the Implications of Hermeneutics for Comparing Syllabus Topics in History Education across Contexts?

The researcher working from a hermeneutic perspective will endeavour to make comparisons across contexts in a meaningful way. Making comparisons according to the absolute standards of positivism and critical theory will be rejected, therefore, since modernist truth claims are seen to be fictional. But the postmodernist focus on differences will also be rejected since the championing of relativism is seen to turn the business of comparing into an arbitrary affair.

From a hermeneutic perspective, the comparison of a syllabus topic such as World War II will involve a heightened acknowledgement of the researcher's ongoing relationship to the objects being researched. Gadamer makes it clear that unless 'the knowing subjectivity has the freedom to have...[the various]...

---

31   E. H. Carr, *What is History?* (London: Penguin Books, 1990), pp.35–36.

members of the comparison at its disposal' the making of comparisons can 'often give false legitimacy to superficial and arbitrary reflection'[32]. This means that the approximate distance between the subject and each of the objects in the cluster being compared cannot be overly varied. How is it possible to equalise the gap? Like the subject navigating the vessel across the channel, the meaningful engagement with clusters of objects will depend on the background of the subject. To begin with, since language is considered to be the gateway to meaning, the researching subject will be seen to require a good knowledge of the languages of the countries being compared. An in-depth cultural understanding gained from extended periods of immersion in each of the countries would also be considered highly beneficial. This being said, knowing the languages of only some countries in the cluster, or having experienced periods of extended immersion in only some contexts and not others, would unbalance the entire process.

On approaching the objects of comparison the researching subject will also be expected to acknowledge, to as great an extent as may be possible, the pre- understandings, prejudices and traditions that are likely to affect the research process. To reiterate, denial of the presence of these subjective elements is tantamount to denying what are seen to be essential features of reality.

As with the example of the choice of harbour confronting the navigator, the researcher will need carefully to select the cluster of countries it is planning to research. Random comparisons lack meaning. In each context, the syllabus topic as a whole will be composed of several parts. These parts will be configured differently from one context to the next – each part like a star in a constellation. In England, for example, the syllabus topic of World War II as an object, as a whole, is composed of several context-specific parts – e.g., the National Curriculum for history, the external examination syllabi, approaches to teaching history, production and use of educational media, types of school, external factors, etc. In contrast, in Japan, or perhaps the United States, the syllabus topic of World War II will be composed of a different constellation of parts. In some cases there will be overlap. Nevertheless, the task of the researcher will be to understand the relationship between whole and parts from context to context.

---

32   Gadamer, *Truth and Method*, op. cit. (note 9), p.234.

From Hegel through Hermeneutics towards Foucault

In this chapter, hermeneutic thinking has been presented as part of a wider Hegelian synthesis, beyond the modernist thesis – proposed by positivism and critical theory – and its postmodern antithesis. To do this Hegel's ideas have been re-positioned. Where Marx was traditionally placed with Hegel, as the extension of Hegel, with Nietzsche as the other to Hegel, that is to say contra Hegel, I am proposing that Marx and Nietzsche are the extension of the two halves of Hegel's dialectic. Essentially, by engaging with Hegel in contrasting ways, Marx and Nietzsche are seen to express the antinomy between acceptance and hostility, the thrusting pulse of Hegel's dialectic developing in the world of ideas and actions after Hegel. In the 20th century, the ideas of Marx and Nietzsche found expression and extension through the critical theory tradition and postmodernism. In *The Broken Middle*, Gillian Rose describes 'this epoch of the Hegelian vortex-ring' by quoting the astute comments of Blanchot:

> One cannot 'read' Hegel, except by not reading him. To read, not to read him – to understand, to misunderstand him, to reject him – all this falls under the authority of Hegel or doesn't take place at all... Hegel the impostor: this is what makes him invincible... master of irony...[33]

The importance of Hegel's thought lies with his dialectical method, with the concept of history as process, and the idea of 'mind as activity'[34]. Indeed, dialectic is understood as keeping a check on the potential excesses of non- dialectical thinking. Even the concepts of reason and the absolute cannot break away from a dialectical relationship to that-which-they-are-not. Reason outside of a dialectical relationship to non-reason has no identity. Where the orthodox or pro-Enlightenment reading of Hegel proclaims the epistemological basis of an absolute truth that lies, ultimately, beyond the dialectic, the pseudo-hermeneutic reading of Hegel championed in this chapter posits a method, a way of being in the world – a dialectical ontology – that is neither pro-Enlightenment nor anti-Enlightenment, but both and neither.

It would be a mistake to assume that Gadamer's hermeneutics represent an explicit extension of the reading of Hegel being proposed here. Yet it is Gadamer's ongoing debate with Hegel, his attempt to break away from Hegel that leads him, implicitly, ultimately, back to Hegel. Of course, Gadamer's

---

33 Rose, G., *The Broken Middle* (Oxford, Blackwell, 1992), pp.3–4.
34 D. Held, *Introduction to Critical Theory: Horkheimer to Habermas* (Berkeley: University of California Press, 1980, p.203.

thought is composed of a multiplicity of elements, many of which do not have their origins in Hegel. The emphasis on language is an important and essential addition, emerging directly from the influence of Heidegger. Indeed, this gives Gadamer's approach its distinctive flavour in the concern to interpret and discern the meaning of interactions between subjects and objects. Yet it is important to acknowledge that Gadamer's ideas did not develop as a reaction to the debates that raged in the English speaking academy during the late 1980s and early 1990s even if hermeneutic philosophy got caught in the crossfire. The fact is that Gadamer's ideas precede the antinomies raised by the modernity/post-modernity debate by a quarter of a century, his philosophy representing a much earlier attempt to overcome the oppositions. In many respects, his work appears, therefore, to look back past Heidegger to Hegel and forward to a location beyond post-modernity.

Is it possible to look ahead to a location beyond one's time? As 'a child of his time' Gadamer's horizon is necessarily limited. Indeed, reading his work today, there is something that immediately strikes the reader as non-contemporary. Something is missing, something is not addressed; something is lacking but must be recognised as an essential factor in any contemporary understanding of society. In Truth and Method Gadamer lacks a sophisticated conception of the workings of power. For this we must turn to Foucault.

4.3 Foucault's 'Ontology of the Present' and the Spirit of Critique

The work of Foucault represents the most advanced contribution to the hermeneutic approach. It is the synthesis within the synthesis, the latest layer fused to the hermeneutic horizon. As with Hegel, Foucault here in Chapter Four is a different Foucault from the one that we met in Chapter Three. Unlike Hegel, this is not due to an alternative reading of Foucault but rather to Foucault's re-reading of the tradition to which he belonged. In particular, towards the end of his life, Foucault re-discovered the work of Kant and, like Hegel, his work ensued thereafter via an interpretation of Kant. In particular by engaging with Kant on the seminal question 'Was ist Aufklarung?' [What is Enlightenment?] Foucault is drawn closer to the work of the neo-Marxist Frankfurt School which, at the same time, involves a repositioning in relation to Nietzsche. While Nietzsche remains an important influence on Foucault's work, I would argue that the engagement with Kant and the Frankfurt School actually pulls Foucault into line with Hegel.

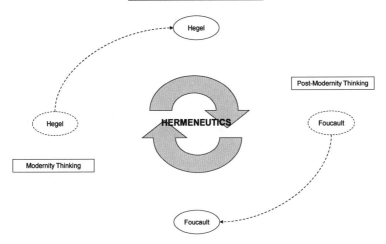

Fig. 4.1:   Hermeneutic re-configuration

For obvious reasons, Foucault's work is commonly associated with other French post-modernity thinkers. In the attempt methodically to unearth truth assumptions deemed universal in the area of mental health and across the human sciences, for example, his early 'archaeology period' of the 1960s represented a clear challenge to modernity thinking. During the 1970s Foucault's work continued as a dismantling exercise. In particular, in what came to be known as his 'genealogy period', knowledge is re-conceptualised in terms of relations of power, or 'Power/ Knowledge'. In this period, truth is understood neither 'outside power, or lacking in power...'. It is not 'the reward of free spirits, the child of protracted solitude, nor the privilege of those who have succeeded in liberating themselves'.[35] Rather,

> Truth is a thing of this world: it is produced only by multiple forms of constraint. And it induces regular effects of power. Each society has its regime of truth, its "general politics" of truth: that is, the types of discourse which it accepts and makes function as true and false statements, the means by which each is sanctioned; the techniques and procedures accorded value in the acquisition of truth; the status of those who are charged with saying what counts as true.[36]

35   M. Foucault, 'The art of telling the truth', in M. Foucault (1988) *Politics Philosophy Culture: Interviews and Other Writings 1977–1984* (New York: Routledge, 1984), p.72.
36   M. Foucault, 'The art of telling the truth', in M. Foucault (1988) *Politics Philosophy Culture: Interviews and Other Writings 1977–1984* (New York: Routledge, 1984), p.73.

Where Foucault's ideas are clearly influenced by Nietzsche throughout his career, this appears to be especially the case during the 1960s and the 1970s.[37] Indeed it might even be possible to consider the 'genealogy period' as simply Nietzsche in modern clothes. As Merquior points out, knowledge and truth are located relatively during these early and middle periods, the expression of contextual power-relations, 'the very opposite of the Enlightenment's ideal: culture-bound instead of universal, epoch-relative instead of cumulative'.[38] During this period, Foucault's intellectual enterprise appears in the vanguard of post-modernity thinking: relativist, emphasising context, concerned with the marginalisation of specific forms of knowledge by oppressive truth regimes.

It is difficult to say the precise point at which Foucault moves away from relativism. Commonly the transition is considered to take place somewhere in the long interval between the first volume of *The History of Sexuality* in 1976 and the subsequent follow-up volumes that appeared in the 1980s. Foucault is famous for trying to avoid categorisation. Yet in this interim period, in certain debates, he is forced to take a position. In the interviews that make up the small volume *Remarks on Marx*, conducted in 1978, Italian journalist Duccio Trombadori consistently puts Foucault on the spot with difficult questions on power, the subject and political agency. Interestingly, Foucault's responses hint at new intellectual influences. In particular, he openly recognises the close proximity of his own work to that of the Frankfurt School.

What is the significance of this? Comprising some of the very best German thinkers of the early to mid 20th century, the Frankfurt School provided an eclectic and multidisciplinary approach to philosophy and social theory. In their *Dialectic of Enlightenment*, first published in 1947, Adorno and Horkheimer deliver a profound analysis of 'the indefatigable self-destructiveness of enlightenment' and the reasons 'why mankind, instead of entering into a truly human condition, is sinking into a new kind of barbarism'.[39] For Adorno and Horkheimer the ultimate legacy of the Enlightenment could be found in the inequities of capitalism, in the barbarism of fascism, and in the illusion of Soviet communism. Where Enlightenment

---

37   D. Couzens Hoy (ed.) *Foucault: A Critical Reader* (Oxford: Basil Blackwell, 1989). B. Smart, 'The Politics of Truth and the Problem of Hegemony', in D. Couzens Hoy (ed.) *Foucault: A Critical Reader* (Oxford: Basil Blackwell, 1989).

38   J. G. Merquior, *Foucault* (London: Fontana Press, 1991), p.55.

39   T. W. Adorno, and M. Horkheimer, *Dialectic of Enlightenment* (London: Verso, 1992), p.xi.

philosophies championed progress, the outcome was 'disaster triumphant'.[40] Yet, importantly, Adorno and Horkheimer's 'critique of philosophy… refuses to abandon philosophy'.[41] Where they reject the orthodox Enlightenment thesis, they do not champion its anti- thesis either. Enlightenment and anti-Enlightenment thinking are conceived as painfully connected in an ongoing dialectic leading downwards. But hope remains as long as philosophy and critical thinking are in some way preserved. For Martin Jay, writing specifically on the work of Adorno:

> Rather… than seek to remove philosophy… Adorno stubbornly insisted that its fatal entanglement with the world was an irreversible development that must be squarely, if painfully, faced. His task then was to find a way to preserve the critical power of philosophy that was immanent in a fallen world.[42]

In *Remarks on Marx*, Foucault concedes that 'the Frankfurt people had tried ahead of time to assert things that I too had been working on for years to sustain' and that 'correctness and theoretical fecundity would have asked for a much more thorough acquaintance with and study of the Frankfurt School'.[43] Later, in the same section, Foucault continues as follows:

> When I recognize all… [the] …merits of the Frankfurt School, I do so with the bad conscience of one who should have known them and studied them much earlier than was the case. Perhaps if I had read those works earlier on I would have saved useful time, surely: I wouldn't have needed to write some things and I would have avoided certain errors. At any rate, if I had encountered the Frankfurt School while young, I would have been seduced to the point of doing nothing else in life but the job of commenting on them. Instead, their influence on me remains retrospective, a contribution reached when I was no longer at the age of intellectual "discoveries".[44]

This is Foucault in 1978 at the age of 52. The passage is written very much 'in hindsight' but in several important respects it lacks foresight. The comment on saving time is sadly ironic since, as we now know, Foucault would only live for a further six years. In addition, Foucault concedes that he had reached a time in his life that no longer involved intellectual discoveries. That there were intellectual parallels between his ideas and the concerns of the Frankfurt School is not conceived, therefore, at this stage, as providing any kind of basis for new projects, let

---

40   T. W. Adorno, and M. Horkheimer, *Dialectic of Enlightenment* (London: Verso, 1992), p.3.
41   T. W. Adorno, and M. Horkheimer, *Dialectic of Enlightenment* (London: Verso, 1992).
42   M. Jay, *Adorno* (London: Fontana, 1984), p.57.
43   M. Foucault, *Remarks on Marx* (New York, Semiotext(e), 1991), p.117.
44   M. Foucault, *Remarks on Marx* (New York, Semiotext(e), 1991), pp.119–120.

alone a new direction. But in the years to come, in the twilight of his life, Foucault develops a new position, a new standpoint, imbibed with a new intelligence. Indeed, in the works of the 1980s, the later volumes of *The History of Sexuality*, and in his essays and interviews on Kant, Foucault's development of ideas in light of work by members of the Frankfurt School becomes increasingly explicit.

The constitution of the self, or of how 'we constitute ourselves as moral agents' provides the intellectual thrust for the final volumes of *The History of Sexuality*.[45] Likewise, through engagement with Kant, Foucault considers the limits and the possibilities of the subject. What is Enlightenment? What is the subject's relationship to the present? Upon what grounds is it possible to perform critique? Central to this enterprise is what Mark Poster refers to as Foucault's 're-examination of the Enlightenment'; an attempt 'to redefine the limits of reason in relation to the question of self-constitution'.[46] Where Foucault continues to insist on the need for empirical precision, as identified during the archaeology period, and on the need to conceive knowledge in relation to power, as conceived during the genealogy period, his position on the legacy of the Enlightenment changes. Where he had constructed strong 'critiques of the Enlightenment, Foucault now reversed himself.' Indeed, '[t]here was for him something in the Enlightenment which the methods of archaeology and genealogy did not confront, some "attitude" of the Enlightenment which had to be preserved'.[47] In 1984, Foucault provides the following explanation of the philosophical current underpinning his new enterprise:

> I have been seeking, on the one hand, to emphasize the extent to which a type of philosophical interrogation – one that simultaneously problematizes man's relation to the present, man's historical mode of being, and the constitution of the self as an autonomous subject- is rooted in the Enlightenment. On the other hand, I have been seeking to stress that the thread that may connect us with the Enlightenment is not faithfulness to doctrinal elements, but rather the permanent reactivation of an attitude – that is, of a philosophical ethos that could be described as a permanent critique of our historical era.[48]

During his last works Foucault confronts us with a perspective that is neither modern nor post-modern. Indeed,

---

45   M. Foucault, *The History of Sexuality,* Vol.1, (London: Penguin, 1976), p.341.
46   M. Poster, Critical Theory and Post-structuralism: In Search of a Context (Ithaca: Cornell University Press), pp.56–58.
47   M. Poster, Critical Theory and Post-structuralism: In Search of a Context (Ithaca: Cornell University Press), p.58.
48   M. Foucault, 'The art of telling the truth', in M. Foucault, *Politics Philosophy Culture: Interviews and Other Writings 1977–1984* (New York: Routledge, 1988), p.42.

rather than seeking to distinguish the "modern era" from the "premodern" or the "postmodern," I think it would be more useful to try to find out how the attitude of modernity, ever since its formation, has found itself struggling with attitudes of "countermodernity".[49]

Is this Foucault's dialectic of Enlightenment? Essentially, his approach 'does not mean that one has to be "for" or "against" the Enlightenment.' On the contrary, he states clearly

> It even means precisely that one has to refuse everything that might present itself in the form of a simplistic and authoritarian alternative: you either accept the Enlightenment and remain within the tradition of its rationalism (this is considered a positive term by some and considered by others as a reproach); or else you criticize the Enlightenment and then try to escape from its principles of rationality (which may once again be seen as good or bad).[50]

Foucault's interpretation of the Enlightenment and of subjectivity changes during this final stage of his career. While he acknowledges the positive legacy of the Enlightenment, Foucault remains sceptical of orthodox modernity thinking; that is, of 'faithfulness to doctrinal elements'.[51] Yet at the same time, while remaining sympathetic to what might be called postmodern concerns for 'the theoretical and practical experience that we have of our limits' he argues without question that this 'does not mean that no work can be done except in disorder and contingency.' On the contrary, '[t]he work in question has its generality, its systematicity, its homogeneity, and its stakes'.[52] Likewise, where Foucault continues to reject the notion of the autonomous 'centred' subject, he moves away from the idea of the 'de-centred' subject, lacking in autonomy, a subjugated effect of contextual power relations. Instead, Foucault re-defines the subject in a pseudo-hermeneutic way that is neither solely centred nor de-centred but somehow both. Here, Enlightenment thinking is understood as facilitating a particular philosophical sensibility, an ethos or critical Spirit, 'seeking to give new impetus, as far and wide as possible, to the undefined work of freedom'.[53] Again, according to Poster,

---

49   M. Foucault, 'The art of telling the truth', in M. Foucault, *Politics Philosophy Culture: Interviews and Other Writings 1977–1984* (New York: Routledge, 1988), p.39.

50   M. Foucault, 'The art of telling the truth', in M. Foucault, *Politics Philosophy Culture: Interviews and Other Writings 1977–1984* (New York: Routledge, 1988), p.43.

51   M. Foucault, 'The art of telling the truth', in M. Foucault, *Politics Philosophy Culture: Interviews and Other Writings 1977–1984* (New York: Routledge, 1988), p.42.

52   M. Foucault, 'The art of telling the truth', in M. Foucault, *Politics Philosophy Culture: Interviews and Other Writings 1977–1984* (New York: Routledge, 1988), p.47.

53   M. Foucault, 'The art of telling the truth', in M. Foucault, *Politics Philosophy Culture: Interviews and Other Writings 1977–1984* (New York: Routledge, 1988), p.46.

Accepting his own finitude, his own historicity, his own debt to the Enlightenment, Foucault proposes that the philosopher commit him – or herself and take responsibility for that commitment. The subject becomes an active agent, a point of intelligibility, a self that constitutes itself in relation to history.[54]

The one aspect of Enlightenment thinking that must be preserved is, therefore, the space to perform critique. This requires an understanding of our limits; that is, of the precise space in which freedom to perform critique is possible. This zone of de- subjugation, similar to Hegel's 'sphere of liberty', must be theorised.[55] Where in the genealogy period Foucault appears like Nietzsche in contemporary clothes, he is now closer to Adorno. But there are important differences. Adorno's work is marked by an overwhelming sense of disappointment and of melancholia. In his work, the hopes and aspirations of his radical generation are tragically doomed. Foucault's later works, on the other hand, are marked by an incredible sense of optimism. After what appeared like a collapse into the abyss of nihilism he finds a toe hold from which to proceed meaningfully. Yet Foucault contributes an extra dimension, something profound and especially contemporaneous that pushes him forward to a new space ahead of Adorno and the Frankfurt School, and Gadamer, even beyond his former self.

Power

Foucault's theory of power is commonly identified with his middle genealogy period of the 1970s. Essentially, power is not conceived as synonymous with repression or violence, but as a relation of forces configured to influence, persuade, 'incite,…induce,…seduce,…make easy or difficult,…enlarge or limit, … make more or less probable, and so on'.[56] Writing on 'Foucault's great theses on power' his friend Gilles Deleuze tells us of how '[a]n exercise of power shows up as an affect'.[57] Here the actions of the subject are conceived as affects of power relations, persuaded, influenced and, ultimately, subjugated. Knowledge too is theorised as an affect of power, a subjugated object relative to the politics, persuasions and influences of the day. According to Foucault, writes Mark Olssen '[t]ruth… is ultimately political in nature' expressing 'power strategies operative in a given

54 M. Poster, Critical Theory and Poststructuralism: In Search of a Context (Ithaca: Cornell University Press), p.61.

55 G. W. F. Hegel, *Philosophy of Mind* (Oxford: Clarendon Press, 1990), p.251.

56 G. Deleuze, *Foucault* (Minneapolis, University of Minnesota Press, 1990), p.70.

57 G. Deleuze, *Foucault* (Minneapolis, University of Minnesota Press, 1990), p.71.

society at a given time.' Likewise, 'the subject' is understood to be 'constituted discursively and institutionally by power-knowledge organised in disciplinary blocks'.[58] But during the 1980s, even Foucault appears conscious of the problems posed by this position. In particular, he seems to realise that the subject, in order to perform critique, could not be totally subjugated. In his later works, by de-subjugating the subject, at least enough to have an awareness of its limits, his conception of truth and knowledge, and of the relationship between knowledge and power is re-adapted and brought profoundly up to date.

The implications of this transformation are best understood in relation to the other positions that we have engaged with. In positivism and critical theory, the two strands of pro-Enlightenment or modernity thinking identified in Chapter Three, where 'unknowing subjects' may be trapped in the contextual politics of the day, deceptively persuaded, the 'knowing subject' is free to discover truths about objects. Here knowledge of truth will lead to power and control, true knowledge allowing the subject to rise above contextual politics. This position I will call knowledge/power. In contrast, for post-modernity thinkers, Foucault in his genealogy period, for example, truth is an affect of power, the persuasion of a particular time and place. As such there is no such thing as true knowledge outside of contextual politics. This position may be called power/knowledge.

Yet in Foucault's later works, truth is understood as neither totally subjugated to relations of power nor as totally de-subjugated from relations of power. We are thus left with a pseudo-hermeneutic position that is neither solely power/knowledge, nor knowledge/power. Essentially, while knowledge and subjectivity are understood as affects of power, they are not considered solely as affects. Truth is no longer denied but neither are the politics of persuasion. Here Foucault moves to a position between power/knowledge and knowledge/power that is at once beyond both positions. And it is from this location that the limits of reason are defined, and from which the subject may perform critique aware of its limits. Thus,

> above all, one sees that the core of critique is basically made of the bundle of relationships that are tied to one another, or one to the two others, power, truth and the subject. And if... individuals are subjugated in the reality of a social practice through mechanisms of power that adhere to a truth... I will say that critique is the movement by which the subject gives himself the right to question truth on its effects of power and question power on its discourses of truth... Critique would essentially ensure

---

58 M. Olssen, 'The School as the Microscope of Conduction: Doing Foucauldian Research in Education', in J. D. Marshall (ed.) *Post-structuralism, Philosophy, Pedagogy* (London: Kluwer Academic Publishers, 2004), p.65.

the desubjugation of the subject in the context of what we would call, in a word, the politics of truth.[59]

'What is philosophy' writes Foucault in 1980, 'if not a way of reflecting, not so much on what is true or false, as on our relationship to truth?'[60] During the 1980s, Foucault provides a circular, pseudo-hermeneutic concept of the subject. Liberated through an awareness of its limits the subject engages ad infinitum with objects, aware that knowledge is the expression of a relation between truth and the politics of truth. Similar to the hermeneutics of Gadamer, the subject proceeds meaningfully owing to its own relative de-subjugation. In this way, the subject is cast as an agent with intent and purpose, expressing the critical Spirit that, according to Foucault is the Enlightenment's essential legacy. In this final enterprise, Foucault places overriding emphasis on what it means to exist as a subject, in the present, in the world. In other words, like Gadamer his focus is ontological, concerned with the limits and possibilities of being 'in the detail of the given moment, which is pregnant with decision and bursting under the pressure of anticipated possibilities'.[61]

In his last works, Foucault concedes overwhelmingly, that he is 'a child of his time', as others had done before him, and with whom he now identified. In the Spirit of the contemporary age, Foucault now claims to offer a philosophical perspective that 'will concern what might be called an ontology of ourselves' or 'an ontology of the present'. Indeed, 'it is this form of philosophy', Foucault now writes, 'that, from Hegel, through Nietzsche and Max Weber, to the Frankfurt School, has founded a form of reflection in which I have tried to work'.[62]

With the sun setting on his own life, and in profound acknowledgement of his own limits, it is not Gadamer nor even Adorno but Foucault who is propelled spiralling to the extended limit of the 'Hegelian vortex-ring'. Soaring from the Nietzschean flank, he surveys an altered horizon, a new frontier, in the twilight, when objects appear most complex, casting long shadows, grey upon grey. Suspicious to the very end of simplistic modernist claims to truth 'in the broad light of day', Foucault nevertheless rejects the unseeing relativism of post-modernity

59   M. Foucault, *The Politics of Truth* (New York, Semiotext(e), 1997), p.32
60   M. Foucault, *Politics Philosophy Culture: Interviews and Other Writings 1977–1984*, L. D. Kritzman (ed.) (New York, Routledge, 1988), p.330.
61   J. Habermas, 'Taking Aim at the Heart of the Present', in D. Couzens Hoy (ed.) *Foucault: A Critical Reader* (Oxford, Basil Blackwell, 1989), p.105
62   M. Foucault, *Politics Philosophy Culture: Interviews and Other Writings 1977–1984,* L. D. Kritzman (ed.) (New York, Routledge, 1988), p.95

thinking's 'eternal night'. In the end, his new- found foresight is fed by hindsight, in an ongoing hermeneutic; as he looks ahead, he looks back, to Hegel: The owl of Minerva spreads its wings only with the falling of the dusk'.[63]

NEW CONFIGURATION

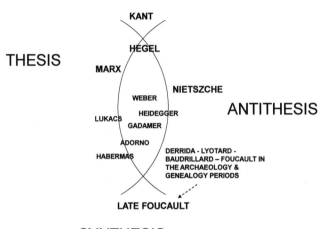

Fig. 4.2:   New configuration

In Figure 4.2 I depict the trajectory of continental thought from Kant to Foucault. After engaging with Kant, Hegel and his philosophy are understood driving the antinomies of modern and contemporary thought. The ideas of Karl Marx represent an explicit if radical extension of the classical Hegelian thesis. No less radical, Nietzsche's philosophy casts itself against the classical Hegelian thesis, 'will to power' contra reason, forming the basis of an antithesis. These responses to Hegel, the two sides of the dialectic, are understood affecting developments through to the contemporary era. In the early 20th century, on the side of the thesis, Lukacs would develop his own Hegelian- Marxism that, in turn, would influence the Frankfurt School and Habermas. On the side of the antithesis Nietzsche would be revered and championed by French post-modernity thinkers, contra Hegel and Marxism.

But some thinkers can be positioned between the oppositions. Weber's sociology fuses Marxist and Nietzschean elements. Heidegger's existentialism would be

---

63   G. W. F. Hegel, *Philosophy of Right* (Oxford, Oxford University Press, 1967), p. 13.

strongly influenced by the anti-Hegelian and existentialist Kierkegaard, and his understanding of 'infinite time' would appear close to Nietzsche's 'eternal return', his focus on 'being' and 'time' representing an implicit dialogue with Hegel. As we have seen, Gadamer's hermeneutics appear as an extension of Hegelian thinking while, at the same time, he is strongly influenced by his teacher, Heidegger. And Adorno, although a member of the Marxist-Hegelian Frankfurt School, would be highly sympathetic to the ideas of Weber and Nietzsche. Yet it is Foucault, in the last stage of his career, having read Kant and the Frankfurt School, who is understood moving into a position not simply 'between' the oppositions but 'beyond' them, into the location of synthesis. As such, Foucault in his last works is understood to be the philosopher of our times, his thought and ideas, his concepts and use of language, providing a powerful means for critique in the contemporary age. As Habermas concedes, among 'the circle of the philosophers… who diagnose our times, Foucault has most lastingly influenced the *Zeitgeist*'. [64]

Making Comparisons from the Perspective of Foucault's 'Ontology of the Present'

Making comparisons from the perspective of Foucault's later works offers a dynamic extension of the hermeneutic position outlined above. As in hermeneutics, the comparison of objects across contexts ensues according to the location of the subject in the present. Likewise, the meaning of the subject's contextual location will be defined in relation to the objects being compared. The subject will survey objects from a contextual platform – a zone of de-subjugation – informed by its own background. This zone will define the limits of the subject's horizon.

The essential dynamic between subjects and objects will be circular, on-going and regenerative, the subject conceived as an active agent existing in dynamic relationships with truth and power. Importantly, comparisons across contexts will be pursued in acknowledgement of the specific parameters and limits of the subject. At the same time, the contexts being compared will be understood as clusters of relationships. Comparisons from a totally de-subjugated (knowledge/power) position or from a totally subjugated (power/knowledge) position will be denied. It is, therefore, from its position of relative desubjugation, that the subject is in a position not only to describe clusters of relationships but also to perform critique.

---

64   J. Habermas, 'Taking Aim at the Heart of the Present', in D. Couzens Hoy (ed.) *Foucault: A Critical Reader* (Oxford: Basil Blackwell, 1989), p.107

As 'an ontology of the present' emphasis will be placed on what it means to exist as a subject in the present in relation to the objects being compared. What are the implications of the differences observed? What do they tell us about ourselves, about our limits and the extent of our freedom? This will inform the parameters of what can and cannot be compared. In a sense, the zone of de-subjugation – of autonomy – is tantamount to a qualification. If the subject has experiences of the contexts being compared, through cultural and linguistic immersion in each of the contexts, the basis upon which to make comparisons, for knowing what can and cannot be said, becomes greater. The freedom to compare is therefore dependent on a precise understanding of our limitations, not simply in academic terms but linguistically and experientially. When we compare a cluster of objects we therefore perform a simultaneous examination of ourselves. Who am I to say this or that about x, y and z? In addition, it is only through examining ourselves that the objects we choose to compare may be identified. The choice to compare x, y and z will depend on who we are as subjects; that is, on our understanding of our own limits. For some subjects z may be inside the limits of what it is possible to compare, for others outside.

Foucault's ideas are frequently utilised by researchers of education. 'The appeal of Foucault,' comments Olssen, 'was that he problematised the meta-narratives of the enlightenment and advocated the possibility of treating all knowledge and forms of pedagogy as contingent, specific, local and historical'. In addition, his ideas 'permitted... the realisation of historically constituted forms of knowledge and pedagogy as "regimes of truth"'.[65] As these comments suggest, it is Foucault's ideas of the 1960s and 1970s that have proved most popular in educational research. The work of James Marshall provides an additional case in point. Marshall uses Foucault to critique liberal understandings of education that are based in Enlightenment conceptions of personal autonomy. For Marshall the subject is necessarily an effect of power, 'our conception of ourselves as "free agents"... an illusion'.[66]

Few, if any, educational researchers utilise the Hegelian imbibed/ pseudo-hermeneutic reading of Foucault that I have advocated. This being said, Olssen's work on the origins of educational psychology is based in what he refers to as a close 'materialist' reading of Foucault's work of the 1980s[67]. Olssen is,

65 M. Olssen, *Michel Foucault: Materialism and Education* (London, Bergin & Garvey, 1999), p.75.
66 J. D. Marshall (ed.) (2004) *Post-structuralism, Philosophy, Pedagogy* (Dortrecht, Kluwer Academic Publishers, 2004), p.77.
67 M. Olssen, *Michel Foucault: Materialism and Education* (London, Bergin & Garvey, 1999), p.76.

furthermore, keen to point to the limits of relativism. Thus, '[unless Foucault is to suffer death through incoherence his approach must entail a minimal universalism' and '[t]he principle of difference itself must entail a commitment to certain non-negotiable universal values if it is to function as a principle at all'. Unlike the position of Poster or of myself, however, Olssen's reading of Foucault's later works suggests that this minimal universalism needs to be 'added' when, I would argue, it is implicit. 'Although Foucault himself never articulated such a notion,' writes Olssen, 'I believe that such a push is warranted'[68]. In my view, Olssen is both overly cautious and mistaken.

I know of no researchers of comparative education working explicitly from the late Foucauldian hermeneutic perspective described above. However, it could be argued that the combined work of the great methodologists of comparative education, Edmund King and Brian Holmes may, if interpreted in a particular way, appear not only strongly hermeneutic but conducive to a Hegelian/late Foucauldian reading. King's emphasis on the processes of hypothesis generation in the context of relative cultural and linguistic variables is implicitly hermeneutic. Difficult to read, easily misunderstood, 'the problem solving approach' of Brian Holmes appears equally hermeneutic as well as being conducive to certain Foucauldian conceptual attachments. Both approaches encourage the researcher to engage with educational contexts in a regenerative and dynamic way.

Contexts are likewise understood to be made up of constituting parts or factors that I would interpret as practices of power, that shape educational objects. Likewise, the subject is conceptualised, and this is especially clear in the work of Holmes, with a degree of space from which to perform critique, and make judgements and recommendations within specified limits. This interpretation of the work of King and Holmes will be discussed in far greater depth in Chapter Six.

How would it be possible to compare topics in history education from the perspective of Foucault's 'ontology of the present'? Again, comparative approaches will be based in particular assumptions concerning the nature of existence and the relationship between researching subjects in the present and educational objects defined in terms of relationships of truth and power. The comparison of syllabus 'topics' in history education across contexts will depend, once again, on definitions of history.

---

68   M. Olssen, *Michel Foucault: Materialism and Education* (London, Bergin & Garvey, 1999), p.176.

What is History from the Perspective of Foucault's 'Ontology of the Present'?

In his early archaeology and genealogy periods Foucault seeks to dismantle 'the history of the historians', purposefully exposing the limits and vulgarities of reason in history and of the history of reason.[69] Here the rational, objective, linear, progressive, and teleological 'pretensions' of modernist histories, the legacy of the Enlightenment, are dismissed as myth. Reason brings insanity as much as the psychiatric cure. Knowledge is a construction, the effect of configurations of power through time.

The subject is located only relatively in relation to other subjects and objects. Totally subjugated to power, the subject is ironically disempowered. The change of position in Foucault's later works, his re-assessment of the Enlightenment contribution, gives rise to a different understanding of history. While remaining critical of modernist histories he now makes it clear that history cannot be denied. Thus,

> I think that the blackmail which has very often been at work in every critique of reason or every critical inquiry into the history of rationality (either you accept rationality or you fall prey to the irrational) operates as though a rational critique of rationality were impossible, or as though a rational history... a contingent history of reason, were impossible[70].

With power and knowledge conceived in a dynamic relationship, truth neither totally subjugated to power nor totally de-subjugated from power, we are no longer presented with an anti-epistemology. Knowledge cannot be considered only as a relative or arbitrary construct, power is the effect of knowledge as much as knowledge is the effect of power. Similarly, within this framework the subject is no longer horizontally located, but instead enters what I will call the Foucauldian circle of inquiry with truth and power: a hermeneutics of power. Suddenly, it is possible not simply to passively describe relative differences across space and time but to actively engage in the assessment of differences as a critical subject – empowered – within specified limits and parameters.

Within the Foucauldian circle of inquiry ontological considerations gain new resonance, history becoming an ongoing activity without end, and it is always being done, inextricably linked to being in the world. As a result, while single modernist 'objective' histories are rejected, so too is the idea that history is

---

69 J. G. Merquior, *Foucault* (London, Fontana Press, 1991), p.26.
70 M. Foucault, *Politics Philosophy Culture: Interviews and Other Writings 1977–1984*, L. D. Kritzman (ed.) (New York, Routledge, 1988), p.27.

arbitrary and completely 'subjective'. With this comes the idea that there really is such a thing as history, an object, which, at the same time, is engaged with in a continual process of circular re-definition with the historical perspectives of subjects in the present. Essentially, historical knowledge must be understood in a circular relationship with configurations of power but not simply as an effect of power. Similarly, subjects are no longer conceived as 'all powerful', modernism's all conscious subject, or 'powerless', relativised out of existence, but 'empowered', in a circular relation to historical knowledge and power, of which they are well placed to make evaluations and assessments.

What are the implications of Foucault's 'ontology of the present' for comparing syllabus topics in history education across contexts? As with hermeneutics, the researcher working from the perspective of Foucault's 'ontology of the present' will refrain from making comparisons according to the absolute standards of positivism and critical theory while, at the same time, rejecting the postmodernist denial of standards. In turn, the comparison of syllabus topics across contexts will involve a heightened acknowledgement of the limits of subjectivity, of what can and cannot be said and/or known about syllabus topics as complex and sensitive cultural objects. The approximate distance between the subject and each of the objects in the cluster of contexts being compared will depend, therefore, on the extent to which the subject is de-subjugated, engagement with clusters of contexts depending on the background of the subject.

A respect for cultural difference will be seen as essential. Linguistic and cultural immersion in contexts will thus be considered as an important aspect of the subject's platform. Yet contexts will not be defined merely in terms of differences. To reiterate, where the totally de-subjugated modernist subject will downplay the importance of differences, the totally subjugated postmodernist subject will see nothing but differences. Yet from a late Foucauldian perspective the subject may perform critique from a limited platform of de-subjugation. In part, the limits of subjectivity, of what can and cannot be said, will be defined, therefore, in terms of the subject's knowledge and experience of the cultural and linguistic differences that exist across the contexts being compared. The researcher will need carefully to select the cluster of countries that it is planning to research. Selection will depend not only on the outward rationality or justification for comparing the cluster of contexts but on the background of the researcher in relation to the contexts being compared – i.e., has the researcher spent extended periods of time in each of the contexts? Can he or she speak the necessary languages?

Syllabus topics such as World War II will be located across contexts according to practices of power and knowledge. As with traditional hermeneutics, these practices will make up the parts, a complex web of points and intersections, around the syllabus topic as an object. The shape of the syllabus topic will differ from one context to the next, an expression of the topic as a concept in relation to the push and pull of the influencing parts. To compare the topic will require, therefore, a detailed knowledge of the configuration of the various practices of power and knowledge in each of the contexts.

As with the hermeneutic approach outlined above, it is useful to consider the syllabus topic as a constellation – each push and pull factor like a constituent star. Again to use the example of England, the syllabus topic of World War II is composed, necessarily, of several context-specific parts – e.g., the National Curriculum for history, the external examination syllabi, teaching approaches, the production and use of educational media, types of school, external factors, etc. Some of these factors will exist in contexts other than England while others will be specific to the particular context. As with conventional hermeneutics, the task of the researcher will be to understand the relationship between whole and parts from context to context. However, since each of the parts will be understood as a practice of power and knowledge, some will be considered to be more influencing than others.

To return to the constellation metaphor, some stars are brighter than others. In the constellation for England, for example, the National Curriculum is a bright star along with the external examination syllabi. The Internet as a resource is a brightening star, the school history textbook a fading star. In Japan, on the other hand, the textbook remains as an exceptionally bright star alongside government censorship of texts and the university entrance examinations. But the Internet remains relatively remote. There are other variables, practices of power and knowledge, push and pull factors, stars, of course.

However, if we wanted to compare and fully understand the meaning of the Second World War as a syllabus topic in Japan and England, we would need to do much more than simply compare how, say, the war is portrayed in school textbooks from each country. The textbook is not a centred object. It is not at all equal as an influencing factor across the two contexts. Instead it would be much better if we isolated those practices of power and knowledge that have the greatest influence; sub-clusters made up of the brightest stars. We would then need to consider why this is the case, and then proceed to assess the effects.

4.4 Summarising Hermeneutic Approaches

Making Comparisons when Subject and Object are neither Absolutely 'Centred' nor Absolutely 'De-centred'

In Chapter Three, the implications of both centred and de-centred conceptions of the subject for making comparisons were discussed. Essentially, a centred 'autonomous' notion of subjectivity is synonymous with a centred 'autonomous' understanding of objects. Thus the positivist using the scientific method or the critical theorist with raised consciousness will consider themselves fully empowered to perceive absolute truths in objects. The relationship between de-centred conceptions of subject and object works in the same way. In other words, the de-centred or 'relativised' subject contemplates objects as de-centred and relative. Postmodern researchers consider themselves to be relatively located as subjects. For this reason, they argue that it is impossible to conceive absolute truths in objects. Let us not forget that essentially the subject is an object, whether 'centred' or 'de-centred', modern or postmodern, and whatever is held to be true for the subject will be held to be true for the object.

The hermeneutic conception of the subject put forward in this chapter – expressing the synthesis that begins and ends with Hegel via Gadamer and late Foucault – is different because it offers an understanding of the subject and, therefore, of the object, that is neither centred nor de-centred. This position can be defined 'in terms of what it is not'. In other words, the researching subject is conceived unable to take a position that is absolutely autonomous and 'centred' OR absolutely relative and 'de-centred'. Defining this position 'in terms of what it is', this means that the subject is conceived relatively centred which is, at the same time, to be relatively de-centred. Again, what is considered to be true for the subject will, moreover, carry over to the object.

Syllabus topics in history education are contextual objects. In addition, from a hermeneutic perspective, the relationship between the researching subject and the syllabus topic is necessarily dynamic, as is the relationship between the syllabus topic and other objects. As suggested above, where some aspects of the syllabus topic will be universal to several contexts – e.g., the fact that a given topic on a given theme will be taught and examined across contexts a, b, c, d, and e – the particularities of each context will dynamically re-figure or shape the topic. Syllabus topics across contexts will express generality, therefore, in the sense that they can be defined as objects across contexts and specificity in the sense that they are defined by the context in which they are located. It cannot be assumed that the topic is ever, therefore, wholly centred and stable, defined by universal parameters, regardless of local context. But neither can it be assumed that the parameters of the topic are wholly de-centred and destabilised either; that is to say, absolutely relative to location. If this were the case, general concepts that enable us to make sense of specificity, concepts such as 'syllabus', 'curriculum', and 'history', for example, would be rendered meaningless. The question is, therefore, how is it possible to conceptualise the syllabus topic as an object that is neither centred nor de-centred?

From the perspective of hermeneutics, relationships between subjects and objects are always circular. I like to use the metaphor of constellations to conceptualise the relationship between variables in different cultural contexts since it enables the researcher to visualise particular power/knowledge configurations. However, to understand that variables are dynamic and fluid – neither centred nor de-centred – it is also useful to think in terms of orbits, placing the various parts of the constellation into inter-dynamic motion.

It is often assumed that the Moon orbits a centred Earth, or that the planets orbit a centred Sun. In the section of my family atlas entitled 'Where Earth Belongs: the Solar System' the relationship between the Sun, the planets and their satellites is presented in exactly this way. However, the reality of the situation is that while the Moon does in fact orbit the Earth, the Earth also orbits the Moon. The same is true of the Sun and its planets. The system of Earth and Moon is not, therefore, centred about the Earth's core, but around somewhere between the Earth and the Moon, the point around which the two bodies orbit. In the same way, just as 'the Sun keeps its planets under strict control' the planets influence the relative position of the Sun. In spite of its larger size and gravitational influence, the Earth is never more than 'relatively' centred in relation to the Moon. The same would be true of the Sun in relation to the planets. There are no absolutely centred objects in our solar system. On the other hand an absolutely de-centred conception of the solar system, would deny the system altogether. This can best be understood by imagining that gravity no longer existed. Suddenly the underpinning relationship between the Sun, the planets and their satellites would be extinguished, each body drifting arbitrarily into space.

To say that the syllabus topic is only relatively centred is also to say that it is relatively de-centred. It is to say that while the topic is understood affected by contextual variables and factors it is, at the same time, conceived exerting its influence on the variables and factors. An absolutely centred conception of the syllabus topic would not acknowledge the influence of contextual variables. Likewise, an absolutely de-centred conception would deny the 'gravity' or universality of the syllabus topic as a relatively centred object across contexts. It is essential, however, that the syllabus topic is considered as nothing more than 'relatively centred'. A relatively centred topic is defined by the fact that it is relatively de-centred by the influencing variables that pull the topic away from the absolute centre but never to an absolutely de-centred position. This conception of the syllabus topic as an object, neither absolutely centred nor absolutely de-centred, but relatively centred and relatively de-centred, is essential, providing the conceptual basis for what I will call Constellation Dynamics.

Constellation Dynamics

Constellation Dynamics enables us to picture the syllabus topic as neither totally centred nor totally de-centred. Essentially, it helps us to envision the hermeneutic and/or circular relationship that exists between syllabus topic and influencing variables. The following diagrams are used to illustrate relationships in a purely hypothetical context.

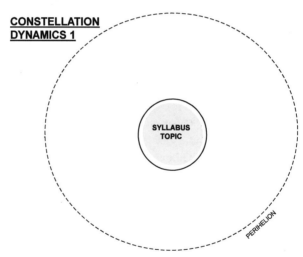

Fig. 4.3:   Constellation Dynamics 1

In this first diagram, 'Constellation Dynamics I', we see an absolutely centred syllabus topic. It appears like the sun in the centre of the solar system but there are no planets. Here we see the syllabus topic positioned 'as if free' from the influence of push and pull variables. In the next diagram, however, the influencing factor of Examinations is recognised and introduced. With the acknowledgement of this factor the topic is relatively de-centred; that is to say, pulled away from the absolute centre.

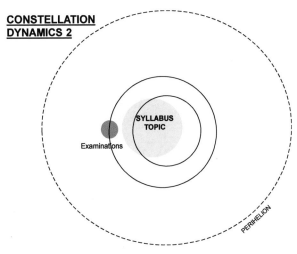

Fig. 4.4:   *Constellation Dynamics 2*

In 'Constellation Dynamics 3' the additional influencing factor – Official Curriculum – is acknowledged. Due to its size in the diagram it is obviously an important variable – in some ways more important than Examinations. However, it orbits at a greater distance from the centre. In some ways, therefore, it may be less important. Nevertheless, as soon as this variable is positioned we see that the shape and location of the syllabus topic changes while remaining relatively centred.

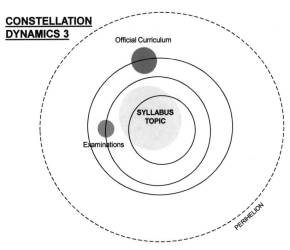

Fig. 4.5:   *Constellation Dynamics 3*

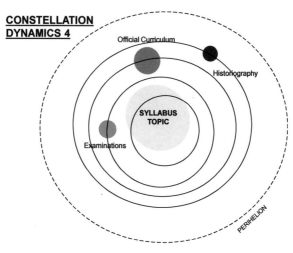

Fig. 4.6:   Constellation Dynamics 4

In 'Constellation Dynamics 4' another variable is acknowledged – Historiography – smaller than the previous two and more remote it nevertheless exerts some influence. Indeed, the shape and relative position of the syllabus topic is transformed again through the recognition of this newly added contextual factor. Importantly we see that while the influencing variables are understood as pulling the topic away

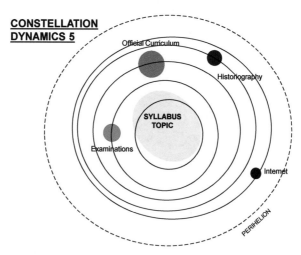

Fig. 4.7:   Constellation Dynamics 5

140

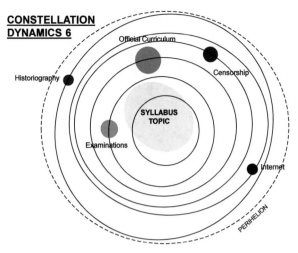

Fig. 4.8: *Constellation Dynamics 6*

from the absolute centre – through the process of relative de-centring – the topic is never absolutely de-centred. In other words it remains relatively centred; the relative conceptual centre around which the orbiting parts gravitate.

In the diagrams for 'Constellation Dynamics 5' and 'Constellation Dynamics 6' two additional influencing factors are recognised Internet and Censorship. These

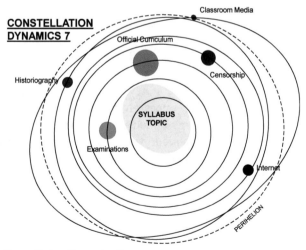

Fig. 4.9: *Constellation Dynamics 7*

are smaller and more remote than any of the previously acknowledged variables. Censorship even comes close to the edge of the syllabus topic's perihelion, the outer circle marking the most remote point at which a variable may influence a given topic and vice versa. Yet again the syllabus topic is reshaped, however, in dynamic interplay with the influencing factors while remaining relatively centred.

Finally, we recognise the small and highly remote influencing variable of Classroom Media. Here the orbit is elliptical at times extending well beyond the edge of the 'perihelion' of the syllabus topic. What does this signify? When a variable is conceived as such it means that influence is exerted only in some cases within the given context but by no means as universally as, for example, Official Curriculum or Examinations. In other words, some types of classroom media may be used only sporadically or by some teachers but not by others. Syllabus topics in different contexts will be influenced by similar variables in different ways. The emphasis here is not therefore on the same variables having the same influence regardless of context (as suggested, for example, in Marxist theory) or on the necessary definition of different contexts using different variables (as championed by the postmodernists). On the contrary, I am arguing that we need to identify the same variables across contexts in order to assess their different effects in different contexts. Engaging with syllabus topics in this way we can 'challenge... taken for granted assumptions embedded in conventional discourse' by our 'use of rigorous and systematic explanations of similar phenomena in different cultural, geographic ... or chronological settings'.[71]

Constellation dynamics draws on the hermeneutic tradition from Hegel through to Foucault via Gadamer, allowing the researcher to visualise the relationship between a syllabus topic and influencing variables in a way that is neither absolutely centred nor absolutely de-centred. Of course the concept of variables 'orbiting' the topic is a purely metaphorical device used to suggest the dynamic, circular and hermeneutic relationship that exists between concepts and objects in motion. Essentially, to analyse a given topic and the variables that influence it, the motion of the constellation would need to be momentarily frozen in time. This momentary freezing resembles the acknowledgement of a 'zone of de-subjugation' for the subject. As a 'frozen' constellation the last diagram featured above would look, therefore, something like the following:

---

71   P. Broadfoot, 'Editorial: Structure and Agency in Education: the Role of Comparative Education', *Comparative Education*, 38 1 (2002), p.5.

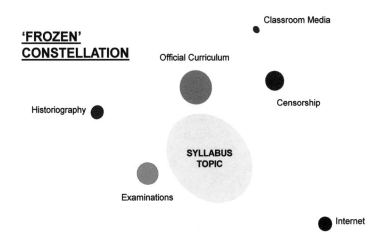

Fig. 4.10: *'Frozen' Constellation*

4.5 Concluding Comments

In this chapter I have considered the philosophical basis for making comparisons from the position of a hermeneutic synthesis beyond the modernist thesis and its postmodern anti-thesis. I have argued, moreover, that this synthesis is rooted in a particular pseudo-hermeneutic reading of Hegel; that is to say, it is above all, a Hegelian synthesis. I have argued that this approach provides a dynamic philosophical basis for comparative education in the contemporary age. The work of Gadamer and Foucault, during the 1960s and the 1980s, respectively, is considered as a dynamic extension of the synthesis. Gadamer's emphasis on language and meaning is considered to be of pivotal importance. In addition, as the most advanced expression of the current synthesis, Foucault's last works on the hermeneutic relationship between truth, power and the subject are championed. These positions, it is argued, form the basis for the construction of robust yet sensitive methodologies in comparative education. Perhaps most importantly, I would maintain, with the special emphases on the limits of critique, on the importance of language, and on the relationship between knowledge and power, the hermeneutic approach provides an abstract conceptual basis especially suited to the comparison of sensitive syllabus topics in history education.

	Theory of Knowledge / Reality	Relationship between politics and knowledge	Relationship between subject and object	Implications for making comparisons
Positivism	Facts exist 'out there' in the world. Truth can be known only through the use of scientific procedures.	True knowledge is neutral. Politics is a contaminating variable.	Passive and neutral. The 'centred' subject is free to discover 'autonomous' objects.	Using the scientific method the 'centred', 'autonomous' subject identifies and compares objects across contexts.
Critical theory	Truth exists in the world. Truth can be understood only through the raising of class-consciousness.	True knowledge is neutral. However, in class societies, pervasive social and political ideologies mask the truth.	Depends on the type of society. In class based societies the relationship will be dynamic, conflicting, and characterised by struggle.	With raised class consciousness the 'centred', 'autonomous' subject identifies and compares objects across contexts. The researcher will be motivated to discover truth and, in turn, raise the consciousness of others.
Post-modernism	Knowledge is essentially constructed. Different societies have different understandings of knowledge. Truth is denied.	All knowledge is political. Knowledge is an effect of power. Different power = different knowledge.	Subjects and objects exist in context specific relationships. different context = different subject / object relationships.	Emphasis on the uniqueness of different contexts. Concern with types of knowledge that have been denied or marginalised by repressive truth regimes.

	Theory of Knowledge / Reality	Relationship between politics and knowledge	Relationship between subject and object	Implications for making comparisons
Hermeneutics	Epistemological concerns with knowledge replaced by ontological concerns with reality. Objective reality has a necessarily subjective component.	Truth is neither purely neutral nor simply and effect of power. While reality is understood including a political element, it can never be simply reduced to the political.	Subjects and objects exist in circular ongoing relationships. The relationship is essentially dynamic and regenerative.	Emphasis placed on the limits of the subject in relation to the contexts being compared. Objective comparisons can only ensue across contexts that fall within the subject's research horizon.

In the above table, hermeneutic perspectives are contrasted with the modern and post-modern perspectives outlined in Chapter Three. Essentially, each perspective is underpinned by a specific view on the nature of knowledge and reality, on the politics of knowledge, and on the relationship between subjects and objects. Furthermore, each perspective contains different methodological implications with regard to the making of comparisons.

In the next two chapters, philosophy will be fused with methodological considerations. This will bring us closer to defining the parameters of a robust model approach for comparing a syllabus topic such as the Second World War across contexts. In Chapter Five Gadamer will be used to re-interpret Bereday. In Chapter Six, the Hegelian way of thinking championed in this chapter will be used to reassess the Edmund King/Brian Holmes dialectic. It is to these considerations that we will now turn.

Chapter Five
Hermeneutic Readings of Past Masters I – Re-interpreting Bereday's Emphasis on the Importance of Language and Contextual Immersion Using Gadamer

> It is... Hegel who testifies to the dialectical element in experience... He conceives experience as skepticism in action... one's experience changes one's whole knowledge... The experiencer ... has acquired a new horizon...
>
> Hans-Georg Gadamer, *Truth and Method*, 1989, pp.353–354

Making comparisons across cultures is a practical undertaking. Moving on from the abstract concerns of Chapter Three and Chapter Four it is now time, therefore, to focus on the more overtly methodical dimensions that will underpin the comparative research of syllabus topics in history education. Essentially, philosophy and method are intimately connected, fundamental questions over the relationship between subject and object and the limits of the subject having overwhelmingly practical ramifications.

In this chapter, and in the following chapter, I will re-interpret the ideas of three of the great Past-Masters of comparative education in light of the hermeneutic perspectives, the 'syntheses', discussed in Chapter Four. First I will turn to the work of George Bereday. Based at Teachers College, Columbia University, Bereday's contribution to the development of comparative education as a field was considerable. Much of his work involved the practice of comparative education in and across the countries in which he was a specialist, e.g. the United States, the Soviet Union, and various countries of Europe and Latin America.[1] However, Bereday's most lasting contribution was in the area of methodology. In this chapter,

---

1   G. Z. F. Bereday and L. Volpicelli (eds.) *Public Education in America* (New York: Harper, 1959). G. Z. F. Bereday and R. V. Rapacz, 'Kruschev's Proposals for Soviet Education', *Teachers College Record*, 60 3 (1958), pp.138–149. G. Z. F. Bereday and J. Pennar (eds.) *The Politics of Soviet Education* (New York: Praeger, 1960). G. Z. F. Bereday 'School Systems and Mass Demand: A Comparative Overview', in G. Z. F. Bereday, (ed.) *Essays on World Education* (New York: Oxford University Press, 1969).

I will focus specifically on Bereday's insistence that 'residence abroad... [and] a knowledge of foreign languages' are 'prime requisites for sound comparative analysis'.[2] Using Gadamer, I argue that the emphasis on 'preparation for study' defines the limits of the comparative educationist's research horizons. In the next chapter, Chapter Six, I re-interpret the work of Edmund King and Brian Holmes from a dialectical perspective. Rather than perceiving the two thinkers in irreconcilable opposition I argue that they can be seen representing the two halves of a single pseudo-hermeneutic approach to comparative education. In both chapters I point to the way in which these interpretations facilitate the proposed methodological approach that forms the basis of this thesis.

5.1 Bereday's Comparative Method in Education: An Introduction

Published in 1964, *Comparative Method in Education* is George Bereday's most important contribution.[3] Along with a handful of books by other authors, the work is a key text for all involved in comparative education. In this study, Bereday argues the case for comparative education as a distinct field and practice, its justification and purpose being both practical and esoteric.

On the practical level, comparative educational research allows us 'to deduce from the achievements and mistakes of school systems other than... [our] ...own,' and 'to be aware always of other nations' points of view'.[4] Likewise, for Bereday 'reformers in one country cannot ignore relevant precedents in other countries'.[5] By likening 'education' to 'a mirror held against the face of a people', however, Bereday argues that the lessons learned extend far beyond the field. We study foreign education because we 'want to know', on an esoteric level, both about other peoples in the world and by inference about ourselves.[6] How are students taught and examined? What knowledge is valued? What is the role of government in the education system? How much autonomy is permitted to local actors? The answers to these questions will tell us many things not only about education but societies in general.

---

2   G. Z. F. Bereday, *Comparative Method in Education* (New York: Holt, Rinehart and Winston, 1964).
3   Bereday, Comparative Method in Education, op. cit. (note 2).
4   Bereday, *Comparative Method in Education*, op. cit. (note 2), p.4.
5   Bereday, *Comparative Method in Education*, op. cit. (note 2), p.7.
6   Bereday, *Comparative Method in Education*, op. cit. (note 2), p.5.

Bereday proposes a practical approach to undertaking comparative educational research, beginning with detailed single-context area studies, followed by broader comparative analyses. His method is inductive and pseudo-positivist, moving through stages of description, interpretation, juxtaposition and finally comparison. That hypotheses are formulated after the initial collection of data is an important feature of the method.

The first stage, description, involves 'the systematic collection of pedagogical information in one country'.[7] Here, the researcher is required to become familiar with 'primary, secondary and auxiliary sources.' Bereday recommends 'a solid program of school visitations' to complement '[s]ource reading'. In all circumstances, visits should be carried out according to 'definite systematic rules', neither randomly nor 'according to what the hosts are willing to show'.[8]

This is followed by a stage of interpretation, involving the subjection of 'pedagogical data to scrutiny'.[9] Interpreting data will involve social, political, historical and economic analysis, to discern the meaning of the information collected. According to Bereday:

> Interpretation consists of using one after another the approaches and methods of different social sciences to see what light they may shed upon the collected pedagogical evidence. By exposing the data to a rosette of different disciplines one emerges with an evaluation of not only educational happenings but also of their causes and connections. It is the why rather than the how that permits one to embark upon direct comparison.[10]

Only after interpreting the data can the researcher move on to the stage of juxtaposition, the 'simultaneous review of several systems to determine the framework in which to compare them'.[11] Here the researcher attempts to identify 'a unifying concept and hypothesis' by juxtaposing what has been described and interpreted across contexts. Bereday refers to 'the principle of compulsory education' or 'the presence of nationalism' across curricula as examples of 'a guiding idea' that may arise from 'the juxtaposition.' The final stage involving comparison, 'entails a simultaneous treatment of several and all countries studied to prove the hypothesis derived from the juxtaposition'.[12] For Bereday, 'these four steps point the way to the future of

---

7   Bereday, *Comparative Method in Education*, op. cit. (note 2), p.27.
8   Bereday, *Comparative Method in Education*, op. cit. (note 2), pp.12–13.
9   Bereday, *Comparative Method in Education*, op. cit. (note 2), p.19.
10 Bereday, *Comparative Method in Education*, op. cit. (note 2), p.21.
11 Bereday, *Comparative Method in Education*, op. cit. (note 2), p.27.
12 Bereday, *Comparative Method in Education*, op. cit. (note 2), p.22.

comparative education'.[13] Essentially, the horizon of the comparative researcher will change with experience, the scale of projects increasing over time. Indeed, Bereday argues that researchers must first begin with the analysis of particular problems, as 'an apprenticeship' before they can move on to 'total analysis'.[14]

Bereday's approach is underpinned by a distinct empiricism. As mentioned above, Bereday undoubtedly postulates that hypotheses may be formed after the collection of data. Brian Holmes even argues that this represents 'Bereday's... systematic acceptance of Mill's inductive method':[15]

> Bereday proposed in Comparative Method in Education that data should first be collected and classified. In order to do this research workers must acquire language skills and be trained to observe aspects of school systems at first hand. Thus equipped they could collect and classify empirical data objectively.[16]

Holmes suggests that Bereday's 'commitment to the colligation of information was perfectly in line with the proposals of Jullien'.[17] This logic underpins Bereday's approach to making comparisons too. As Holmes reminds us:

> For Bereday the comparative approach begins when information... is juxtaposed in order to highlight differences and similarities. This procedure clearly depends upon the classification of material and from it comparative hypotheses are derived. Such hypotheses state the purpose for which comparison is to be made.[18]

Bereday's methodology appears linear in its approach. The trained researcher collects raw data from which hypotheses are formed from which 'the formulation of "laws" or "typologies" that permit an international understanding' may be established.[19] Holmes recognises this as Bereday's acceptance of 'Mill's goal, the discovery of general laws'.[20]

---

13   Bereday, *Comparative Method in Education*, op. cit. (note 2), p.28.

14   Bereday, *Comparative Method in Education*, op. cit. (note 2), p.23.

15   B. Holmes, *Comparative Education: Some Considerations of Method* (London, George Alien & Unwin, 1981), p.63.

16   Holmes, Comparative Education: Some Considerations of Method, op. cit. (note 15), p.59.

17   Holmes, Comparative Education: Some Considerations of Method, op. cit. (note 15), p.59.

18   Holmes, Comparative Education: Some Considerations of Method, op. cit. (note 15), p.62.

19   Bereday, *Comparative Method in Education*, op. cit. (note 2), p.25.

20   Holmes, Comparative Education: Some Considerations of Method, op. cit. (note 15), p.62.

5.2 Bereday and the Empirical Dimension

From the discussion so far, it would appear that Bereday's ideas are anything but hermeneutic in orientation. Linear and hierarchical as opposed to circular, his approach can easily appear in the vanguard of modernity thinking, in line with 'the positivism of postwar social scientists'.[21] Does this mean that we should throw Bereday on to the scrap heap? I would suggest not. On the contrary, there is much of value in his work that draws our attention to the fundamental importance of the empirical dimension in comparative educational investigations.

Which is right: induction or deduction? Brian Holmes argues against Bereday's position of induction. As a champion of deduction he claims that even though '[d]ata collection is important' it is 'not… at the first stage of inquiry'.[22] Intuitively I want to agree with Holmes. Does not the collection of data begin with guiding hypotheses, concepts or theories that tell us what to look for when we go out to collect data? Will not the research community or orientation to which we belong affect the kind of data we select? However, it is equally important to question the meaning of a hypothesis without data. Like the polemic between materialism and idealism – Orthodox Marxists versus Left Hegelians – the contest between induction and deduction is in fact a chicken and egg debate and, quite frankly, a waste of intellectual energy. I would suggest instead, therefore, that data need to be conceived not over and above or 'prior to' the hypothetical, but in combination with it, the empirical and the theoretical understood as integral components of an ongoing dynamic.

This circular understanding of the relationship between data and hypotheses, the empirical and the rational, the material and the ideal, induction and deduction, takes us back to the key protagonists of the hermeneutic synthesis that we encountered in Chapter Four. In Hegel this is none other than the dialectic between the 'actual' and the 'rational'; in Gadamer, between '[r]eal experience' and 'planning reason'; in Foucault, between the 'empirical field' and 'theoretical questions'.[23]

The empirical is important but has no meaning unless theorised. Theory is, likewise, meaningless without an empirical object to theorise. Bereday's emphasis on

---

21   Holmes, Comparative Education: Some Considerations of Method, op. cit. (note 15), p.59

22   Holmes, Comparative Education: Some Considerations of Method, op. cit. (note 15), p.60

23   G. W. F. Hegel, *Philosophy of Right* (Oxford: Oxford University Press, 1967), p.10. H. G. Gadamer, *Truth and Method* (London: Sheed & Ward, 1989), p.357. M. Foucault, *Politics Philosophy Culture: Interviews and Other Writings 1977–1984*, in L. D. Kritzman (ed.) (New York: Routledge, 1988), p.257.

the empirical dimension in comparative education is useful, therefore, as long as it is not championed at the expense of the theoretical. Our experience of a foreign education system will be both empirical and conceptual – a dynamic.

While Holmes identifies Bereday's approach with positivism, there is nevertheless something exceptionally warm, experiential and qualitative about Comparative Method in Education that strongly suggests something else. Even when his method is clearly inductive, Bereday does not champion the scientific method as some kind of great equaliser. If anything, Bereday's emphasis on the importance of language and overseas experience suggests that there are limits to what we can research, no matter how scientific our approach. For Bereday, theoretical and methodological training as a comparative researcher must be combined with knowledge of languages, and extended periods of time spent in the foreign contexts under investigation, in the attempt to ensure high quality research. In some cases, involving the quantitative comparison of macro-educational units, focusing on, for example, the school leaving age across OECD countries, knowledge of languages may not appear crucial. But in the case of projects comparing micro-educational units, for example, the delivery and reception of curriculum subjects in history or geography or literature, it will be considered essential.

In the English-speaking countries, under libertarian pressures to 'perform' and to produce, comparative 'academic' research sometimes ensues without meeting these necessary linguistic and experiential prerequisites. All too frequently, projects are carried out by researchers who have no knowledge at all of the necessary languages, and who have no direct experience of the countries they are investigating. Research is undertaken via the use of unofficial translations and ad hoc solutions. In turn, the superficial results yielded by these studies, often tantamount to a kind of journalism, are written up and published masquerading as academic research.

5.3 Language and the Development of Research Horizons

In his early paper 'Some Discussion of Methods in Comparative Education' Bereday refers to 'inadequate language' alongside 'infrequent travel and scant training in academic disciplines' as a 'binding shackle' in comparative educational research.[24] Ten years later, Bereday remains highly concerned with the question

---

24 G. Z. F. Bereday, 'Some Discussion of Methods in Comparative Education', *Comparative Education Review*, 1 1, pp.13–15, in particular p.14.

of language prowess and international research. 'What are the language skills that researchers need?' he asks. 'Can one study an area... without the knowledge of the respective languages? Does one need to be a general polyglot to do global studies in comparative education?'[25]

In the section of *Comparative Method in Education* entitled 'Preparation for Study' Bereday engages readers in a fascinating discussion on the place of language prowess and travel in comparative educational research. Bereday begins by providing his perspective on the approach to comparative education practised by a significant number of his fellow Americans:

> [W]hen Americans interest themselves in foreign educational systems... [a]ll too often they not only do not learn how to understand their neighbor's point of view; they seem to refuse to permit him to have one. By neglecting, first of all, to learn his language, most Americans forget that he speaks not in halting English but fluently with thoughts and idioms all his own. Secondly, by unwise travel, even when undertaken for educational purposes, whatever is gleaned from his neighbor's life is limited to the gilded and the quaint. And lastly, by not making an effort to understand the foreigner's point of view, specialists in international studies seldom succeed in driving a wedge into the nationalistic and racial parochialisms.[26]

In the early 1960s Bereday writes optimistically that 'the United States is emerging from the age of linguistic isolation'.[27] Yet as we now know, English has become more dominant as the language of business and diplomacy than in any previous era. Where the study of English as a second language is rising globally, the study of foreign languages in the English speaking countries appears in decline. This is highly problematic for the purposes of comparative educational research, especially when investigations involve the close study and comparison of micro-educational units. According to Bereday, it is often the case that 'wrong judgements are caused by inadequate knowledge of the language of the country under analysis.' Likewise, he claims with emphasis that a 'lack of knowledge of... language[s] bedevils understanding between peoples everywhere'.[28]

Language prowess is the key to gaining a 'deeper knowledge' of a foreign country's education system, drawing our attention 'not only to its faults but also its

---

25 G. Z. F. Bereday, 'Reflections on Comparative Methodology in Education, 1964–1966', *Comparative Education*, 3 3 (1967), pp.169–187, in particular p.170.

26 Bereday, *Comparative Method in Education,* op. cit. (note 2), p.131.

27 G. Z. F. Bereday, 'Comparative Education at Columbia University', *Comparative Education Review*, 4 1 (1960), pp.15–17, in particular p.133.

28 Bereday, 'Comparative Education at Columbia University', op. cit. (note 27), p.132.

richness, not only to its gross outlines but also to its delicate nuances'.[29] With no knowledge of foreign languages how can we consult primary documents, conduct interviews, or observe situations without resorting to guesswork? In such cases, the context will fall outside of the researcher's horizon of possibilities, unable to proceed since 'serious comparative research... requires an unhampered access to primary sources and firsthand informants'.[30]

Essentially language prowess enables the researcher to access an object of study at a sophisticated level of consciousness. It enables a fusion of horizons between the researching subject and the object. 'For the purposes of true communication and research,' writes Bereday, a knowledge of language lets one in on the intimate secrets of the nation under study.[31] Language is one of the keys to a spiritual union with a country, as travel is another. It is good education, too. To be privileged to read each and the same day about current events, not in one but in two or more languages, not from one but from several national points of view, is a lesson in humility and understanding not easily matched anywhere.[32]

Acknowledging the importance of language as a prerequisite for comparative educational research, Bereday is highly sceptical of the tendency, 'to dismiss the necessity for knowledge of languages on the grounds that it can be circumvented by the use of interpreters'. According to Bereday, '[e]ven when excellent interpreters... are available... [t]he delicate nuances and undertones of languages are never caught'.[33] Bereday continues in this highly suspicious tone as follows:

> The job of translation is... an extremely exacting intellectual activity... Even the best interpreters tire quickly; their efficiency rapidly diminishes after the first half an hour. What is true of good interpreters is truer still of mediocre ones. The misinterpretations, understatements and poorly rendered sentiments in such cases are incessant. An interpreter not... at home in... [the] languages with which he is working... will inevitably "edit" the translations, will substitute easier words for the more difficult, or shorter for longer sentences.[34]

Knowledge of foreign languages is therefore a fundamental dimension of Bereday's approach to comparative education. While recognising that it is possible to 'cite examples of good works written by people who did not have a background

---

29 Bereday, 'Comparative Education at Columbia University', op. cit. (note 27), p.133.
30 Bereday, 'Comparative Education at Columbia University', op. cit. (note 27), p.133.
31 Bereday, 'Comparative Education at Columbia University', op. cit. (note 27).
32 Bereday, 'Comparative Education at Columbia University', op. cit. (note 27), p.139.
33 Bereday, 'Comparative Education at Columbia University', op. cit. (note 27), p.135.
34 Bereday, 'Comparative Education at Columbia University', op. cit. (note 27), p.136.

in the language of the country analyzed,' Bereday states unequivocally that 'full command of several foreign languages should be the ideal'.[35] In turn, developing language skills must form an essential element in the training of every comparative educationist. Bereday concludes his discussion of 'The Importance of Language' with considerable foresight, uncannily in touch with the rigours and demands of the current *Zeitgeist*:

> In the forever-expanding horizon of educational interchanges, there needs to be... a hard core of tough, seasoned, trained specialists. To maintain such a core, a body of recognized requirements must be evolved in comparative education. A seal of approval among those aspiring to be numbered among specialists should include language skills... Given their history, Americans should be a nation of polyglots. They will certainly not rise to the challenges calling out to them from every corner of the globe if they permit students of foreign cultures to be less.[36]

In the work of Gadamer, language is understood as the expression of a hermeneutic relationship between parts and whole. On the side of the parts, different languages express a variety of contexts. On the side of the whole, languages are not simply identified through their differences but according to the rationality that makes them all languages. In *Truth and Method*, Gadamer writes as follows:

> Certainly the variety of languages in which linguistics is interested presents us with a question. But this question is simply how every language, despite its difference from other languages, can say everything it wants. Linguistics teaches us that every language does this in its own way. But we then ask how, amid the variety of these forms of utterance, there is still the same unity of thought and speech.[37]

For Gadamer, language is understood as a vehicle of reason, experience and meaning. Knowledge of languages gives the subject a particular level of access to contexts as objects. A world without language is literally unthinkable. Nevertheless, to argue the case for the universality of language as a concept is not to say that there is one language for every particularity. On the contrary, 'every language is a view of the world... because of what is said or handed down in this language.' Likewise, '[i]t is not learning a foreign language as such but its use, whether in conversation with its speakers or in the study of its literature, that gives one a new standpoint'.[38] Essentially, language for Gadamer enables

35   Bereday, 'Comparative Education at Columbia University', op. cit. (note 27), p.141.
36   Bereday, 'Comparative Education at Columbia University', op. cit. (note 27), p.142.
37   Gadamer, *Truth and Method*, op. cit. (note 23), p.402.
38   H Gadamer, *Truth and Method*, op. cit. (note 23), pp.441–442.

the subject to engage in new relationships with objects, to develop backgrounds while defining new horizons.

In the discussions on hermeneutics in Chapter Four, Gadamer's remarks on 'comparative method' were quoted and embellished upon. He is without doubt exceptionally wary of the comparative approach. This is due in large part to his sense of the unequal distances existing between the researching subject and the various contexts being compared. For meaningful comparisons to ensue the subject must have a relatively similar level of familiarity with each context. This makes a lot of sense. We cannot compare x with y and z if we know next to nothing about x. In other words, all three contexts must be located inside the subject's research horizon for comparisons to ensue.

Bereday's ideas can be re-interpreted using Gadamer. According to Bereday a practitioner's limits will be defined, in part, according to his/her knowledge and experience of contexts. Regardless of whether the researcher begins with data collection or with the formulation of hypotheses it is, nevertheless, knowledge of foreign languages and cultural immersion in given contexts that will enable meaningful comparative investigations to proceed. In other words, contexts x, y and z can only be compared if the researching subject has spent extended periods in contexts x, y and z and possesses a knowledge of the languages used in each of the contexts.

5.4 The Hermeneutics of Contextual Immersion: Travel and Residence Overseas

In addition to language acquisition, Bereday emphasises the crucial importance of travel and contextual immersion as bases for the practice of comparative educational research. The researcher must have first-hand experiences of the cultures that he or she plans to compare. Ideally, this means periods of 'prolonged residence abroad'.[39] Thus,

> The path of training along which a student of comparative education must be coaxed needs to include travel and residence abroad… the familiarity born of travel is one of the prime requisites for sound comparative analysis. From travel flows understanding. To meet a culture in daily contact and in a thousand unforeseen situations is to acquire the feel for the tenor of life that is hard to match otherwise.[40]

---

39 Bereday, 'Comparative Education at Columbia University', op. cit. (note 27), p.143.
40 Bereday, 'Comparative Education at Columbia University', op. cit. (note 27), p.143.

Again this brings us back to Gadamer's understanding of the importance of experience. Like language, experience brings the subject into meaningful proximity with objects. Experience is constituted historically, dynamically, dialectically, in time and in space. Crucially, and brilliantly, Gadamer argues that it is through experiences that we may define our limits and, by inference, our possibilities.

[E]xperience is experience of human finitude. The truly experienced person is one who has taken this to heart, who knows that he is master neither of time nor the future. The experienced man knows that all foresight is limited and all plans uncertain.[41]

Like Foucault, Gadamer recalls Hegel's 'owl of Minerva' that 'sets out only with the falling of the dusk'; experience brings wisdom, a profound understanding of the limits of reason, of what cannot be done. Interpreting Bereday in this way, the highly travelled person is likely to be intensely aware of places not visited, of the locations that he or she is unable to comment upon, and of the many languages and dialects neither spoken nor understood. Yet this self-understanding of limits is not synonymous with modesty. In the name of rigour, the researcher of comparative education, aware of what cannot be done, is simultaneously sensitised to what can be done and 'done well'. As a trained educational researcher, I can compare countries x and y to high standards because I have lived in both countries and speak the necessary languages. Perhaps this cannot be said of country z. An awareness of limits becomes, therefore, a way of defining standards. As well as being able to conceptualise a context, we ideally need to have experienced it too, as an 'expatriate' or through 'several visits'. According to Bereday '[n]o one should venture to speak or write on foreign education on less than such authority'.[42]

Bereday's message is a simple one: robust comparative research cannot ensue without overseas experiences. We cannot select a group of countries for analysis simply because they fall neatly into some external rationale. 'Quick reading about a country' simply will not do.[43] The parameters and possibilities of any comparative research project will be defined by linguistic and experiential limits:

Workers in the field are expected to have resided or visited for extended periods of time in the country or countries of specialisation. This... permits them to follow closely and continuously not only the changes of educational organization, or even of educational philosophy, but also all other relevant facts of politics, economics,

---

41   Gadamer, *Truth and Method*, op. cit. (note 23), p.357.
42   Bereday, 'Comparative Education at Columbia University', op. cit. (note 27), p.145.
43   Bereday, 'Comparative Education at Columbia University', op. cit. (note 27), p.146.

culture and society. In areas of specialization, comparative educators are expected to acquire a deft touch, to sense the spirit of the culture.[44]

In many ways Bereday's vision for the comparative educational researcher expresses the concept of agency that we encountered in our discussions of Hegel, hermeneutics and Foucault in Chapter Four. Such a researcher is a linguist and a traveller, an agent constantly engaged, treading the path between the limits and the possibilities as they arise. Experiences of foreign countries form part of the researcher's essential background from which it becomes possible to formulate horizons:

> To travel abroad discerningly is to acquire a vision that will make one sensitive to the difficulties of assuming the role of an educational expert. A few days is enough to make one wonder and perhaps to worry. The easy generalizations that one is prone to formulate under the impact of other impressions begin to look less certain upon visual contact. One begins to be less sure that one knows much … [E]ven a short trip is enough to implant bewilderment; but it is from doubts that enlightenment will come[45].

PREPARATION FOR STUDY

Fig. 5.1:   *Preparation for study*

44   Bereday, 'Comparative Education at Columbia University', op. cit. (note 27), p.143.
45   Bereday, 'Comparative Education at Columbia University', op. cit. (note 27), p.145.

The relationship between training in educational research methodologies, international experience and knowledge of foreign languages can be observed in the above diagram. In order to conduct comparative studies involving several countries the researching subject will need to be either a single polymath or a team involving more than one researcher. It is important to understand here that, following Hegel, the subject need not be defined in purely individual terms, but as a collective, a community. If a researcher has linguistic knowledge and experience of two settings, but wishes to incorporate a third setting, he or she will need to work with an additional researcher, who possesses linguistic knowledge and experience of the third setting. In respect to this minimum requirement, rich and meaningful research projects of a high standard may ensue.

In his important review of *Comparative Method in Education*, Edmund King welcomes Bereday's insistence on the need for language training and overseas residence.[46] 'Being an accomplished linguist and restless traveller' writes King, 'Professor Bereday rightly emphasises the importance of language and residence in person'. However, King also draws attention to the problem of exclusivity that could easily ensue as a result of Bereday's approach.

> Scholarship, integrity, ability to see the total context…, and awareness of complementary disciplines – all these are prerequisite, as Professor Bereday insists; but so is the receptiveness which resists the temptation to be exclusive. Our discipline is holistic, a skill of synthesis. There is a real risk that insistence on specialist standards in this or that may be an unsuspected hankering for… hierarchical eminence with deferential acolytes. We in Comparative Education must be on guard against adopted prescriptions for exclusion.[47]

However, as King then goes on to clarify, standards can be maintained through teamwork, in other words, while language and contextual immersion are important pre- requisites, if researchers lack ability in a specific language they will not be excluded from undertaking research on the condition that they work with someone who DOES speak and understand the language. The researcher can be 'complemented by others'.[48]

---

46   E. King, 'Book review, Comparative Method in Education by G. W. Z. Bereday', *Comparative Education*, 1 1, (1964), pp.37–38, in particular p.38.
47   E. King, 'Book review, Comparative Method in Education by G. W. Z. Bereday', op. cit. (note 46), p.38.
48   E. King, 'Book review, Comparative Method in Education by G. W. Z. Bereday', op. cit. (note 46), p.38.

Language, Cultural Immersion and the Horizons of this Researcher

The horizons of this researcher have been defined by experiences. In addition, these experiences have made him acutely aware of his limits. As a trained educationist, involved in research and teaching in comparative and international education, I strongly acknowledge that the vast majority of contexts exist, at the present time, beyond my research horizons. In what follows, and for the sake of explication, I will use my own case as an example.

Following Gadamer and Bereday what contexts am I qualified to research? On the basis of my experience and knowledge of languages which overseas contexts lie within my horizon as a researching subject and which do not? Likewise, which contexts lie teetering on the edge of my horizon and how can I rectify this situation?

I have lived in six countries: England, Sweden, the United States, Japan, China and Argentina. I have also spent an extended period of time in Italy. In all of these countries, I have been directly involved in education either as a student or as an educator. A native Briton, I attended compulsory education in England, Sweden and the United States and higher education in England.

Do all of these countries fall within the comparative research horizon of this author? Potentially, the answer to this question is yes. However, at this present time the answer would have to be no. This relates to my current knowledge of the languages used in these countries. As a native English speaker I am, of course, able to conduct comparative research on education in England and the United States. Moreover, my current knowledge of Swedish is close to sufficient to pursue research there. A concentrated period of full immersion would pull the standard up, a requirement that also applies, to some extent, to the other Nordic countries (with the exception of Finland). During my time living in Hiroshima, I studied Japanese for a total of two-and-a-half years. On leaving the country in 1999 I had a fair grasp of the language. However, in the years that have passed this ability has diminished. In addition to this, I have not revisited the country since 1999. In this sense Japan as a research context has gradually slipped back from my investigative horizon. I imagine that four to six months of full immersion would bring Japan back to the foreground. I lack the ability to speak Chinese and/or Spanish. However, I do possess knowledge of Italian. This improved during my visit to Rome where I attended an intensive language immersion course.

These countries can be contrasted with those in which I have spent shorter periods of time, for educational purposes. I spent ten days in the former Soviet Republic of Moldova, where I was invited to lecture at the Ion Creanga State Pedagogical

University. This visit was important in terms of improving my first hand knowledge of the country and has led to further activities. Yet I do not speak Romanian, and so I am unlikely ever to carry out research on 'primary sources' there. I have also made four trips to Germany since 2002. Three of these were research-oriented. The other was for purposes of international exchange organised by the Goethe Institute. These were useful trips enabling me to develop an initial impression of German society beyond that of the holidaymaker. However, I do not speak German. Using Gadamer and Bereday, it could be argued that Moldova and Germany are currently positioned on the remote edge of my research horizon. English speaking countries where I have visited only for leisure purposes may also be located in this distant outer realm. I have visited Canada and Australia, for example, on several occasions. A single extended visit to either of these countries would bring them into closer proximity for the purposes of conducting quality research.

Finally there are those contexts that lie completely outside of my research horizon. This includes most countries of the world: for example, those countries that I have visited for leisure purposes but where I do not speak the native language e.g. France, Malaysia, Brazil, Morocco, etc., and those English-speaking countries that I have never visited, e.g. New Zealand. Remotest of all, are those countries that I have never visited where the native tongue is not English, e.g., Russia, Vietnam, Chad, Mexico etc.

RESEARCH HORIZONS AS THEY RECEDE WITH DISTANCE

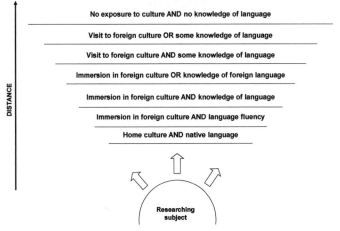

Fig. 5.2: Research horizons as they recede with distance

As the subject looks out from its location in time and space, international contexts will appear at varying distances. Some will appear in the foreground, some will appear in the middle distance while others will appear remote and far off – at the horizon's edge. Some contexts will not be visible at all. Crucially, the researcher's experience of contexts as well as his/her knowledge of languages will determine the distance between subject and contexts. In the above diagram I have attempted to rationalise this understanding of proximity.

At the bottom of the diagram we see the hypothetical location of the researching subject. The arrows indicate the direction faced. Looking out across the vista the relative proximity of contexts is depicted by the banded categories that recede progressively one after the next. The subject's home context appears in the direct foreground followed by those foreign contexts where the researcher has resided and possesses language fluency. Next we have those contexts resided in where language abilities exist if not at a level of fluency. Then there are the contexts where the researcher speaks the language but has never visited, or contexts where the researcher has spent extended periods but does not have a grasp of the language. More distant are those contexts that the researcher has visited, but not for extended periods, and where the researcher may have only some knowledge of the languages. On the remote edge of the horizon can be found those cultures to which the researcher has only made brief visits.

RESEARCH HORIZONS: LIMITS AND POSSIBILITIES

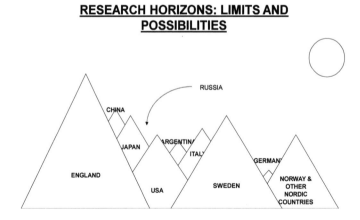

Fig. 5.3:   Research horizons: limits and possibilities

The diagram above depicts the horizon of this educational researcher as a range of mountains. Each mountain represents a particular educational system. The closer the mountain is to the foreground, the easier it will be to scale. England looms large and accessible in the foreground. As a native Briton and English speaker this researcher can approach it fairly easily. To the right lies the smaller mountain of Sweden. Not as accessible as England it nevertheless lies well within reach, on experiential and linguistic grounds. This can also be said of the mountains representing the United States and the other Nordic countries. More remote we see the mountains representing Japan and Italy.

These would become more accessible with renewed experience and continued language training. High and far off we see the relatively inaccessible peaks representing China and Argentina. Without language prowess these cannot currently be scaled. The mountain representing Germany, on the distant edge of the horizon, is barely discernible, accessible only with time, effort and great stamina. Finally we see that the mountain representing

Russia lies somewhere over the horizon, not visible from this researcher's current location in time and space. Having never visited Russia and being unable to speak the Russian language, the author is only aware that it exists from the stories and tales of others.

There are other factors that will affect the researcher's proximity to contexts. Edward Said's concept of 'Orientalism' draws attention to the stereotypes that may underpin Western perceptions of non-Western cultures.[49] Said points out with emphasis how Westerners have tended, unfairly and unjustly, to evaluate 'oriental' cultures and societies in Western terms. Through Said's work, we may understand that there is such a thing as cultural as well as linguistic and experiential proximity to contexts. In my own case, as a Westerner, I must be particularly sensitive, therefore, when making assessments of history education in, for example, Japan or China.

The horizon of the researching subject will change according to philosophical perspective. That is to say, the range of mountains will appear different depending on the lens through which they are observed. From the perspective of a positivist, for example, use of the scientific method will be seen to facilitate the investigation of a far wider range of contexts – a universal horizon even. Equipped with the scientific method the positivist researcher is perceived as empowered to discover truths wherever they lie. And all contexts will be understood as underpinned by the same fundamental truths. What cannot be measured, moreover, will be considered of little or no relevance since it does not possess the status of knowledge. Those working

---

49   E. Said, *Orientalism* (New York, Pantheon, 1978).

from a critical theory perspective will assume, likewise, that consciousness gives the researcher access to an unlimited range of contexts. Language and cultural immersion will be seen to be of secondary importance for understanding the universal truths that underpin reality in all capitalist societies. Postmodern perspectives, on the other hand, will be so context-specific that the concept of 'horizon' becomes difficult to justify. Indeed, using the metaphor of the mountain range, the postmodernist can be likened to a climber stuck to the side of a single peak, caught up in the fine details of the moment, concentrated on the surroundings of the immediate location.

Re-interpreting Bereday using Gadamer, the limits and possibilities of the comparative researcher are thus redefined. The subject looks out across a horizon, a rich and varied topography, aware of the limitations imposed by time and by space. There is no all-encompassing horizon from which to view objects. At the same time the concept of horizon is never denied. Rather, an intense awareness of proximity to contexts provides the grounds and the parameters to formulate horizons. Only then can comparisons proceed in a meaningful way.

5.5 Background and Prejudice

In the discussions of Chapter Four we touched on the importance given to the place of background, tradition and prejudice in the work of Gadamer. Every subject is the expression of its background; all knowledge is interpreted and located within a tradition. And the subject can never totally escape prejudices.

In many ways the concept of background is similar to the idea of experience encountered earlier in this chapter. Experiences form the background of the subject, in turn, it is this background that will define, to some extent, the perception of objects. Just as the meaning or understanding of the context will change according to philosophical perspective, the subject identifies different features in the object according to background. This was recognised by that other great methodologist of comparative education, Edmund King:

> [T]he subject who sees an object is directly or unconsciously aware of himself looking at it. That is to say, a man seeing a fish in a pond looks at it as an angler, as a zoologist, as an aquarist, as an aesthete, or as someone thinking of supper... [A] great deal more than the transmission of light from the object to the retina goes into anyone's perception of an object.[50]

---

50   E. King, *Comparative Studies and Educational Decision* (London, Methuen, 1968), pp.27–28

In the same way 'educational objects' across contexts will be viewed and understood differently depending on the background of the observer. The parent, the student, the politician, the university educated banker, the worker who left school with no qualifications, the person who has lived in many countries, the person who has lived in no other country than the one where they were born. All are likely to observe and understand educational phenomenon in different ways. The same would even be true of educationists working in different traditions, even comparative educationists. However, this is not to say that anything goes. The extent to which researchers may approach objects meaningfully will depend on their 'background' of training.

While language skills and international experience are considered to be essential, Bereday places considerable emphasis on the need for students and researchers of comparative education to pursue area studies. 'There is no doubt' writes Bereday 'that the mastery of descriptive details of an educational system... is an indispensable precondition of serious comparative study'.[51] Likewise, 'the area approach' allows 'for work' at an 'in depth' level.[52] In his early papers Bereday applauds those universities in the United States that offer courses that allow students to understand the broader 'area' context in which an educational system is located. To begin to understand education in Japan, for example, the student or researcher will need to acquire background knowledge on Japanese history, culture, politics and society in general.[53] According to Bereday, this background knowledge is considered to be indispensable.

In many ways, this focus on 'context' echoes the work of Sadler. As editor of the *Comparative Education Review*, Bereday reprinted 'Sir Michael Sadler's "Study of Foreign Systems of Education"' in 1964.[54] At that time, Bereday claimed that Sadler's essay of 1900 'remain[ed] remarkably relevant'.[55] In the following passage, now famous, Sadler's emphasis on the relationship between school and society reminds us of the hermeneutic relationship between whole and parts.

---

51   G. Z. F. Bereday, 'Some Methods of Teaching Comparative Education', *Comparative Education Review*, 1 3 (1958), pp.4–9, in particular p.4.
52   Bereday, 'Some Methods of Teaching Comparative Education', op. cit. (note 51), p.4.
53   Bereday, 'Some Methods of Teaching Comparative Education', op. cit. (note 51), p.5.
54   G. Z. F. Bereday, 'Sir Michael Sadler's "Study of Foreign Systems of Education"', *Comparative Education Review*, 1 3 (1964), pp.307–314.
55   G. Z. F. Bereday, 'Sir Michael Sadler's "Study of Foreign Systems of Education"', op. cit. (note 54), p.307.

In studying foreign systems of Education we should not forget that the things outside the schools matter even more than the things inside the schools, and govern and interpret the things inside... A national system of Education is a living thing, the outcome of forgotten struggles and difficulties, and "of battles long ago." It has in it some of the secret workings of national life.[56]

If we are to understand an education system as the expression of the 'workings of national life' then we must study aspects of national life. For Bereday this means full immersion in the life, language, and culture of a given society. It means cultivating one's background knowledge in order to understand the background and context of the educational phenomenon being observed. It also means understanding the traditions that underpin a given society that, in turn, gave rise to its system of education, expressing particular values with regard to knowledge, teaching and learning.

As we saw in Chapter Four, tradition plays an important role in the philosophy of Gadamer. Indeed, we can never wholly escape tradition, and, essentially for Gadamer, it would be undesirable to do so. To reiterate, Gadamer sees 'no unconditional antithesis between tradition and reason'. To recognise 'the truth of tradition' is crucial to an understanding of reality and existence.[57] Bereday's position on tradition, outlined above, can be interpreted from the perspective of Gadamer's hermeneutics. However, to conduct research on history education across contexts Gadamer's understanding of prejudice is particularly useful. Like traditions, a degree of prejudice is seen to be an unavoidable component of reality. The researcher cannot be cleansed of all prejudices. Indeed, the 'Enlightenment's discreditation of the concept of "prejudice"' is perceived in itself to be an expression of prejudice[58]. From the outset we need to be aware that prejudice will play a part in our research decisions, judgements and thinking:

> The overcoming of all prejudices, this global demand of the Enlightenment, will itself prove to be a prejudice, and removing it opens the way to an appropriate understanding of the finitude which dominates not only our humanity but also our historical consciousness.[59]

Does this mean that all prejudices are justified? Far from it, a totally prejudiced view is seen to be as unreasonable as a totally unprejudiced view. Nevertheless, all views will be seen to contain a degree of unconscious prejudice.

---

56 G. Z. F. Bereday, 'Sir Michael Sadler's "Study of Foreign Systems of Education"', op. cit. (note 54), p.310.

57 Gadamer, *Truth and Method*, op. cit. (note 23), p.281.

58 Gadamer, *Truth and Method*, op. cit. (note 23), p.277.

59 Gadamer, *Truth and Method*, op. cit. (note 23), p.276.

Bereday's position on 'cultural bias' as outlined in *Comparative Method in Education* may be interpreted in light of the ideas of Gadamer.[60] In the first instance, Bereday is strongly critical of the 'hidden pitfall' of prejudice in 'comparative education'. 'These prejudices,' writes Bereday, 'which everyone in some way derives from his own culture, are [a] major block to communication between peoples'.[61] Some pages later he refers to 'cultural bias' as 'the plague of comparative methodology, tragic in a discipline expressly dedicated to the breaking down of ethnocentrism'[62]. Writing in the post-war 1960s, and imbibed with a strong sense of optimism, Bereday appears to champion the Enlightenment ideal that cross-cultural research projects should and indeed could be pursued free from bias. Yet in response to his own question: 'Can... cultural bias be avoided?' Bereday replies with a strong tinge of realism that '[p]robably it cannot', conceding in the end, that 'it can' at best 'be minimized'.[63]

Echoing Gadamer, Bereday recognises the limits experienced by the researching subject. In particular, Bereday concedes that, in the absence of 'international... standards', the researching subject 'is justifiably left to evaluate foreign experiences in terms of its own criteria''. Since the subject is necessarily located in time and in space, it can never totally avoid contextual variables that may lead to bias. Essentially, to 'minimise' prejudice,

> The student must be sensitive to the fact that different "chemistry" is set in motion when he looks at his own country and when he studies practices abroad. He must increase his readiness to acknowledge some measure of accuracy in the appraisal of his own character by others.[64]

As argued earlier in this chapter, knowledge of languages and overseas experience may also provide the necessary means to develop our sensibilities. Thus for Gadamer:

> [B]y entering foreign-language worlds, we overcome the prejudices and limitations of our previous experience of the world, [but] this does not mean that we leave and negate our own world. Like travellers we return home with new experiences.[65]

---

60 Bereday, Comparative Method in Education, op. cit. (note 2)
61 Bereday, *Comparative Method in Education*, op. cit. (note 2), p.156.
62 Bereday, *Comparative Method in Education*, op. cit. (note 2), p.159.
63 Bereday, *Comparative Method in Education*, op. cit. (note 2), p.166.
64 Bereday, *Comparative Method in Education*, op. cit. (note 2), p.166.
65 Gadamer, *Truth and Method*, op. cit. (note 23), p.448.

This being said, it is Bereday who recognises 'another complication'. Through the acquisition of foreign languages and overseas travel the researcher develops a perspective and a point of view with a peculiarity that is all its own. In comparative education, the requirements of the field… bring into the discipline an unusually high proportion of uprooted people, who, through the accident of having been "blown across" the world, have acquired the desired competence. These people cannot help projecting into their comparative work their personal longings and fears.[66]

What do we bring to research contexts? The discussion in this last section has drawn attention to the importance of background and prejudice in the context of comparative educational research. Indeed, we have seen how, in the work of both Gadamer and Bereday, prejudice is considered to be an unavoidable feature of reality. While on the one hand, travel and language prowess are perceived as sensitising the researcher to cultural difference contra prejudice, these experiences may in fact lead to new biases and 'complications'. For Gadamer, to claim a neutral position above prejudice is a form of denial. Bereday appears far more wary of the idea of prejudice per se. It is omnipresent but needs to be 'minimised'. Essentially, however, important aspects of Bereday's ideas may be interpreted from a hermeneutic perspective. Background and bias are core elements affecting the subject's relationship to contextual objects. This dynamic is circular and conditional on the researcher's relationship to contexts in time and space.

5.6 Concluding Comments

In this chapter we have looked closely at Bereday's assertion that linguistic prowess and overseas travel are fundamental prerequisites in comparative educational research, especially where it involves close investigations of topics in history education. In turn, these ideas have received theoretical justification using Gadamer's hermeneutic conceptions of language, experience, and the formulation of horizons. Essentially, the researching subject proceeds to compare contexts in profound acknowledgement of its limits. These limits are defined theoretically, according to definitions of the subject, knowledge, and existence, as well as in linguistic and experiential terms. Building on 'the philosophical bases of comparisons' outlined in Chapter Four, the concerns of this chapter have brought us forward towards the construction of a comparative methodology.

---

66   Bereday, *Comparative Method in Education*, op. cit. (note 2), p.160.

Bereday envisions the 'ideal' researcher of comparative education in the form of a polymath – an individual along the lines of the Renaissance model. Such a researcher will have a strong grounding in several social sciences and knowledge of foreign languages and will have lived in several countries. Using Gadamer the researcher is conceived in an ongoing relationship with contexts. Owing to the subject's background and experience, contexts will appear at various distances across the field of vision, accessible with varying degrees of ease or difficulty. In addition, proximity between subject and objects will be necessarily fluid depending on the ongoing development and interaction of influencing factors.

Which contexts fall inside a given horizon and which do not? Which contexts can be meaningfully compared? These questions throw light on the central concerns of this chapter. But how are the features of a given educational context configured and how may a single context be approached? In Chapter Six, we will focus on these questions using the work of Edmund King and Brian Holmes.

Chapter Six
Hermeneutic Readings of Past Masters II – Isolating and Approaching Educational Contexts through a Re- interpretation of the Brian Holmes / Edmund King Dialectic

[T]hinking does not need to conduct itself polemically...

G. W. F. Hegel, *The Encyclopaedia Logic*, 1991, p.35

In Chapter Four I introduced the hermeneutic synthesis as a philosophical basis for making comparisons. Essentially this synthesis was defined in the sense outlined by Hegel, posited as a step beyond thesis and anti-thesis, the antinomies of modernity and post-modernity thinking. I argued that Gadamer and especially Foucault were the logical extension of this way of thinking in the contemporary historical era. From the hermeneutic perspective the subject is understood as acting within the limits of a particular zone of de-subjugation, 'the agent... in his existent sphere of liberty'.[1] It is, moreover, this zone or sphere that defines the limits and the possibilities of critique; that is to say – the extent and potential of critical Spirit.

In Chapter Five we moved towards a series of more methodical considerations by re-interpreting the work of Bereday using Gadamer, in order to define the research horizon of the subject. Within an overall hermeneutic framework the emphasis was again placed on the definition of limits. What contexts are researchers in a position to investigate and what contexts are 'out of bounds'? In practical terms the limits of the subject will be defined not only according to the research training received but also in relation to the researcher's overseas experience and knowledge of foreign languages. This was understood to be especially the case for comparative researchers focusing on curricular subjects such as history across contexts.

On the way to comparing complex educational objects, it is now important to consider the 'approach' to a given context. This is an extremely important consideration. Given that there may be two, three, or four objects looming on the research horizon, how do we begin to chart the array of variables and particularities that characterise the educational locations? Returning to the example of this

---

1   G. W. F. Hegel, *Philosophy of Mind* (Oxford: Clarendon Press, 1990), p.251.

author's research horizon as a range of mountains, as sketched in Chapter Five, we might imagine isolating one of the peaks and approaching it. As we move closer we will be able to describe the details that mark its surface. Guided by hypotheses we will assess what we find against an ideal- typical conception of the context.

In this chapter I will re-interpret the work of two past-masters of methodology in comparative education, Brian Holmes and Edmund King. Traditionally, the two thinkers have been conceived and used as opposites. Arriving at the field from vastly contrasting backgrounds, Holmes and King appear as an antinomy, one clashing against the other with great force and energy. Brian Holmes, the physicist who is remembered for emphasising the importance of the scientific method using Popper and Dewey, Edmund King, the classicist with a humanistic approach and a natural ear for languages. One appears as the anti-thesis of the other's thesis. This has been the view of the vast majority of researchers in comparative education and not without good reason. Yet this need not be the case. First, a close and highly particular reading of work by the two authors does not necessarily suggest antinomy. Indeed, it can even be said that there is much overlap between the work of the two thinkers if viewed in a particular way. Second, the lesson taught by Hegel, and expressed in the hermeneutic way of thinking that runs through this book, enables us to re-theorise the relationship between oppositions and contradictions, from being and nothing to becoming, from thesis and anti-thesis to synthesis. In *The Encyclopaedia Logic*, Hegel's position on the importance of antinomy between positions is made loud and clear:

> the setting-up of the antinomies remains a very important result... and one that is worthy of recognition; for what is brought out in this way... is the factual unity of the determinations which... understanding clings to in their separation from one another.[2]

What understandings may be 'brought out' from an assessment of the different positions offered by Holmes and King? Is there any sense that 'their contradiction, has disappeared in their relation' one to the other, that beyond their head to head battle we may arrive at 'a unity in which' the opposing perspectives 'are only moments'?[3] To move beyond perceived differences to a third position, a synthesis, would be a highly ambitious undertaking. Is it possible or even desirable to do so? Without any doubt, there is much of value in the work of both

2   G. W. F. Hegel, *The Encyclopaedia Logic* (Indianapolis: Hackett, 1991), p.94.

3   Hegel, *The Encyclopaedia Logic,* op. cit. (note 2), p.146.

men. To favour the ideas of one at the expense of the other could be understood as 'one-sided' and, more essentially, as favouring 'the merely negative result of the dialectic'.[4] In this chapter, I will argue, on the contrary, that elements of the work of both thinkers may be consolidated into a complementary approach, 'a positive result', if the antinomy between the two is understood in a dialectical or hermeneutic way.[5]

I will focus first on the work of Holmes then on the work of King. I will draw special attention to each man's procedure of isolating and approaching a given educational context. A final section in which the work of the two thinkers is synthesised will then follow these expositions. In many ways, the internal format of this chapter emulates the dynamic presented in Chapters Three and Four. First the two positions are presented, followed by a re-thinking and consolidation of the oppositions in the form of a synthesis.

6.1 Isolating and Approaching Educational Contexts in the Work of Brian Holmes

Brian Holmes is not easy to read and therefore easily misunderstood. A trained physicist, Holmes attempted to develop a methodology for use in comparative educational research based primarily in the philosophy of science. Using a particular interpretation of the ideas of Karl Popper and John Dewey, Holmes devised his 'Problem Solving Approach', a speculative methodology that enabled evaluations and recommendations to be made within specified limits. As Erwin Epstein points out, Holmes's methodology represents, in itself, an 'attempt at synthesis' between positivist and relativist currents.[6] Later in the piece in question, Epstein describes Holmes's position as

> the most genuinely eclectic in the Comparative Education literature... Indeed, that approach acknowledges the role of "sociological laws" as fundamental, but always as "hypothetical, contingent, and refutable under given circumstances"[7].

---

4   Hegel, *The Encyclopaedia Logic,* op. cit. (note 2), p.129 and p.131.
5   Hegel, *The Encyclopaedia Logic*, op. cit. (note 2), p.131.
6   E. H. Epstein, 'The Problematic Meaning of "Comparison" in Comparative Education', in J. Schriewer and B. Holmes (eds.) *Theories and Methods in Comparative Education* (Frankfurt am Main: Peter Lang, 1988), p.16.
7   Epstein, 'The Problematic Meaning of "Comparison" in Comparative Education', op. cit. (note 6), p.20.

This refreshingly hermeneutic 'third-way' is essential to the work of Holmes from the 1950s to the 1980s.[8] In his essay, *Causality, Determinism and Comparative Education as a Social Science*, Holmes writes as follows:

> I believe that our understanding of social affairs... requires that we accept an intermediate position between pure chance and perfect determinism. The distinction between normative and sociological theories and laws offers a framework within which an intermediate position can be developed. If men and women are freely to make rational decisions it is not possible to accept either of the antithetical extremes – namely perfect social determinism or perfect social indeterminism.[9]

By theorising a position in comparative education that operated beyond the antinomy between determinism and indeterminism, Holmes was ahead of his time. Yet his use of language is not only difficult but also highly misleading. Holmes insists on using 'scientific' terminology wherever possible. In his work, we read a lot about 'laws' and 'logical prediction', and about 'observable events', 'piecemeal social engineering', 'a science of education and planning' and about 'testing'.[10] This, it could be argued, did little more than to generate a major communication barrier between Holmes and his peers.

Some positivists, such as Noah and Eckstein, commented favourably on Holmes's acceptance of 'laws', perhaps identifying the term with the definition used in their own work. However, Holmes states unequivocally that 'in *Toward a Science of Comparative Education*", Noah and Eckstein, 'placed their discussion of functional propositions and correlationship statements... in a framework I do not accept'.[11] Positivists accept that 'laws' are deterministic, a position that Holmes

---

8   B. Holmes, 'The Problem Approach in Comparative Education: Some Methodological Considerations', *Comparative Education Review*, 2 1 (1958), pp.3–8. B. Holmes, *Problems in Education: A Comparative Approach* (London: Routledge & Kegan Paul, 1965). B. Holmes, 'Comparative Education as a Scientific Study', British *Journal of Educational Studies*, 20 2 (1972), pp.205–219. B. Holmes, 'Paradigm Shifts in Comparative Education', Comparative Education Review, 28 4 (1984), pp.584–604. Holmes, 'Causality, Determinism, and Comparative Education as a Social Science', op. cit. (note 6).

9   Holmes, 'Causality, Determinism, and Comparative Education as a Social Science', op. cit. (note 6), p.116.

10   B. Holmes, *Comparative Education: Some Considerations of Method* (London: George Alien & Unwin, 1981) pp.76–77 and p.53. Holmes, *Problems in Education: A Comparative Approach*, op. cit. (note 8), pp.25–47.

11   Holmes, Comparative Education: Some Considerations of Method, op. cit. (note 10), p.70.

claims to reject. Others have commented critically on Holmes's use of the term 'laws'. In *Comparative Studies and Educational Decision*, Edmund King positions himself against 'Dr. Holmes'. According to King, Holmes's 'writing shows a marked tendency to talk of so called sociological laws not only as if they were physical laws, but also as though they carried the compulsive powers of positive law produced by legislation'.[12]

These perspectives on Holmes ensue according to a misunderstanding of his use of terminology. According to Noah and Eckstein and to King, the argument is that 'laws' are always deterministic and therefore, by using this term, Holmes is a determinist. Where Noah and Eckstein misinterpret Holmes's use of the term 'laws' from the position of determinists, King does the same but this time from the position of an anti-determinist. Yet the fact is, Holmes is surely not an absolute determinist, only a relative-determinist in determinist clothing. His position is actually, I would argue, much closer to King but sounds as if it should be closer to Noah and Eckstein. In an article published in *Comparative Education* in 1977, Holmes even goes as far as to consider King as an intellectual ally with regard to the latter's interpretation of Popper:

> In a number of articles he [King] has claimed Popper's approval... I have no wish to question this. Indeed in so far as King concentrated on Popper's discussion of 'trends' and the 'logic of the situation' I agree with his interpretation. Moreover I welcome an ally in his anti-deterministic stance. He might usefully have criticized those positivists among comparative educationists who have failed to acknowledge the implications of post- relativity science... He is simply mistaken when he tried to make me a determinist by ascribing to me an interpretation of the term 'sociological laws' which I do not hold.[13]

King obviously considered Holmes to be closer to Noah and Eckstein than to himself but, I believe, he was mistaken. Noah and Eckstein obviously understood Holmes as being 'something' like themselves but they were also, it seems, in error.

Prescriptive, Normative and Sociological Laws

It is important to unpack the meaning of Holmes's use of terminology. First, what does he mean when he refers to 'laws'? Holmes makes an important distinction

---

12   E. King, Comparative Studies and Educational Decision (London: Methuen, 1968), p.53.

13   B. Holmes, 'The Positivist Debate in Comparative Education: an Anglo-Saxon Perspective', *Comparative Education*, 13 2 (1977), pp.115–132, in particular p120.

between prescriptive, normative, and sociological laws referring directly to the work of Popper's *The Open Society and its Enemies*.[14]

Prescriptive laws are those assumed to be universal by positivists. They are the rules defining the parameters of J. S. Mill's theory of induction, an approach that Holmes never ceases to critique. Prescriptive laws are assumed to be universal to all times and to all places. For many years Newton's theory of gravity would have been given such a status. Prescriptive laws can be contrasted with normative laws. Normative laws are 'man-made'.[15] Different cultures may develop different normative laws, codes or statements 'representing... beliefs'.[16] Thus, normative laws... can be accepted, rejected, or changed by man. Normative statements are commands – 'Thou shalt not kill' – and can usually be made into an 'ought' state-ment. Examples of normative statements are: 'All persons ought to be treated as equals.' 'All persons ought to be free.'... Noble declarations such as the USA Declaration of Independence or the United Nations Declaration of Human Rights omit the 'ought' but their intentions are plain.[17]

Normative laws express 'what ought to be the case', regardless of whether or not they 'are obeyed'.[18] They are not synonymous with moral laws, since they may be constituted through custom or tradition – e.g., in patriarchal societies it may be assumed that 'men ought to be in control.' Nevertheless, normative laws will exert a strong influence on the order of things within a given educational context. 'They must be known' writes Holmes 'if we hope to understand how schools function.' Indeed, establishing 'an acceptable pattern of normative statements and normative laws for particular nations represents... one of the most important tasks a com-parative educationist should tackle'.[19]

---

14   K. R. Popper, *The Open Society and its Enemies* (London, Routledge & Kegan Paul, 1945).

15   Holmes, 'Causality, Determinism, and Comparative Education as a Social Science', op. cit. (note 6), p.115.

16   Holmes, Comparative Education: Some Considerations of Method, op. cit. (note 10), p.78.

17   Holmes, Comparative Education: Some Considerations of Method, op. cit. (note 10), p.77.

18   Holmes, 'Causality, Determinism, and Comparative Education as a Social Science', op. cit. (note 6), p.116. R. Scruton, *A Dictionary of Political Thought* (New York: Harper & Row, 1982), p.327.

19   Holmes, Comparative Education: Some Considerations of Method, op. cit. (note 10), p.78.

In contrast, 'sociological laws' are 'conjectures from which limited predictions can be deduced under carefully specified conditions'.[20] By sociological laws Holmes is referring to criteria that are neither rigidly prescriptive, in the positivist sense, nor normative, according to the dictates of context. Rather, sociological laws provide the bases for the formulation of meaningful hypotheses within given grounds and parameters. For Holmes, to hypothesise that, say, an increase in private sector educational provision will lead to greater levels of inequity in terms of outcomes exemplifies a sociological law. In the first instance, it is 'tentative', in the second instance, 'not universally valid' but 'contingent' and finally, 'never certain, only probable'.[21] Few concepts are more central to Holmes's enterprise, yet few are more 'misunderstood'.[22] In a paper published in the mid-1980s, Holmes engages emphatically with his critics:

I reject categorically the interpretation placed on my use of the term 'sociological law' by my critics. The determinism associated with sociological laws comes from an aetiology (theory of causation) that I discarded long ago and finds no place in my paradigm...[23]

Only by coming to grips with Holmes's terminology, does the meaning and purpose of 'sociological laws' become apparent. 'Their function' writes Holmes, 'is to permit social regularities of a sequence of social events to be explained'.[24] They are thus conceived as a vital conjectural tool to be used by the researching subject. 'The characteristics' writes Holmes 'of the social scientific laws induced from observations carried out on an international scale', and from a prescriptive positivist perspective, 'are vastly different from the man-made statements I choose to call sociological laws. In failing to recognise these differences critics who have categorised me as a determinist have missed the point'.[25]

Much of Holmes's thinking originates from his reading and adaptation of the ideas of Karl Popper. In particular, Holmes adopts Popper's stance on the need to

20   Holmes, 'Causality, Determinism, and Comparative Education as a Social Science', op. cit. (note 6), p.124.
21   Holmes, 'Causality, Determinism, and Comparative Education as a Social Science', op. cit. (note 6), pp.78–79.
22   Holmes, Comparative Education: Some Considerations of Method, op. cit. (note 10), p.78.
23   Holmes, 'Paradigm Shifts in Comparative Education', op. cit. (note 8), p.593.
24   Holmes, Comparative Education: Some Considerations of Method, op. cit. (note 10), p.78.
25   Holmes, 'Causality, Determinism, and Comparative Education as a Social Science', op. cit. (note 6), p.123.

'refute' rather than 'verify' hypotheses as a basis for evaluating and making decisions. Sociological laws 'are man-made' and 'remain, hypothetical, and if they are to be scientific should be refutable.' Basically, using Popper, Holmes's sociological laws are, therefore, cautious 'prediction statements' concerning 'possible outcomes'.[26] What are the implications of this for methodology in comparative education? Holmes provides the following example:

> In practical terms it means that to make predictions, for example, about the effects of introducing a comprehensive school into a national system... [particular] ... types of statement should be made. 'If comprehensive schools are introduced and become more widespread, social equality will increase' constitutes a general hypothetical statement. The particular socioeconomic conditions of the nation into which this type of school is to be introduced need to be described to predict from... this statement. For example initial conditions in the USA differ from those in England, or in France, or in Sweden. Hence somewhat different outcomes may be anticipated in each of these countries when a similar institution, some sort of comprehensive school, is introduced into the education system.[27]

Essentially, Holmes conceives the researching subject as an agent in time and in space. A given educational context will be characterised by specific normative laws that make it impossible for the subject to make rigidly prescriptive statements, ignoring temporal and spatial variables. To reiterate, Holmes is strongly critical of absolute determinism or reductionism, prescriptive laws, but he is also critical of absolute relativism too. He therefore adopts the 'intermediate position between pure-chance and perfect determinism' that we read about earlier in the chapter.[28] 'Can we predict all the consequences of human action with certainty before they occur?' asks Holmes. 'Certainly not' is the reply. Indeed,

> To believe this would make us perfect social determinists. On the other hand, I do believe that some of the consequences of human activity can with a measure of certainty be anticipated provided the specific conditions under which the predictions are made are adequately taken into account.[29]

---

26 Holmes, Comparative Education: Some Considerations of Method, op. cit. (note 10), p.78.
27 Holmes, Comparative Education: Some Considerations of Method, op. cit. (note 10), pp.78–79.
28 Holmes, 'Causality, Determinism, and Comparative Education as a Social Science', op. cit. (note 6), p.116.
29 Holmes, 'Causality, Determinism, and Comparative Education as a Social Science', op. cit. (note 6), pp.124–125.

For many, Holmes's position has appeared unwieldy and unusable. Writing in the late 1980s, Epstein is doubtful about the viability of Holmes's attempt to reconcile the oppositions:

> Unfortunately, in trying to avoid the disabilities of positivism and relativism the problem approach may satisfy no one... Both relativists and positivists can argue that... [Holmes's] ...attempts to mesh irreconcilable epistemological assumptions, is so unwieldy as to be impractical.[30]

Are the epistemological oppositions irreconcilable? The answer to this would have to be no. The circular and re-generative definition of 'laws' in Holmes's comparative methodology needs simply to be clearly understood. Underpinned by the researching subject's self-acknowledged limits, the only way to move ahead in a meaningful way is to formulate tentative hypotheses, conjectures, 'sociological laws', that are neither purely absolute nor relative. These will be understood, as Holmes writes in an early paper, 'not in any sense as a definitive statement but as a tentative exploratory outline of a theoretical position'[31]. Following Popper, it is the task of the researching subject to attempt to refute or falsify the conjecture in the light of contextual evidence. In turn new conjectures will be formulated, viewed again in the light of contextual evidence, and refuted, and so on. This is a circular and ongoing dynamic – the underpinning law that, according to Holmes, should define the limits and the possibilities of comparative educational research.

Before we interpret other concepts used by Holmes, it would be useful to consider the legacy of Popper. Falsification lies at the heart of Popper's system. It is the permanent critique that enables us to know by knowing what is not. In *The Open Society and its Enemies*, Popper provided a fierce critique of Hegel's totalitarian leanings.[32] Popper's reading of Hegel is an orthodox one, yet the notion of 'refutation' as a kind of ongoing 'negation' brings Popper strangely close to the reading of Hegel that I propose. Moreover, where Hegel focuses on the relationship between 'rational and real', Popper points to the relationship between the theoretical and the observable. Holmes also considers the underpinnings of this relationship. 'The issue is' according to Holmes 'how far can observation

---

30   Epstein, 'The Problematic Meaning of "Comparison" in Comparative Education', op. cit. (note 6), p.22.
31   Holmes, 'The Problem Approach in Comparative Education: Some Methodological Considerations', op. cit. (note 8), p.3.
32   K. R. Popper, *The Open Society and its Enemies* (London, Routledge & Kegan Paul, 1945).

be construed as independent of conceptualisation [?]'[33] In answer to this, he then goes on to state his position: 'the divorce of measurement from conceptualisation is… unacceptable'.[34] Thinking back to the discussions of Chapter Five, reason and empiricism are by no means antithetical.

It is equally interesting, at this point, to consider Popper's location in relation to some of his contemporaries. *The Positivist Dispute in German Sociology* is a collection of papers covering a conference debate – that took place in the early 1960s – between Popper and members of the Frankfurt School. Across the papers it is clear that Popper considers the Frankfurt writers to be Marxists according to his own definition.[35] At the same time, the various members of the Frankfurt School understand Popper to be a positivist. Holmes recognises the misclassification of Popper in the introduction to *Comparative Education: Some Considerations of Method*:

> Popper's critique of Marx in *The Open Society* made him the object of neo-Marxist criticism. The failure of members of the Frankfurt school of sociologists to make him a positivist is plainly shown in the volume *The Positivist Dispute in German Sociology*.[36]

The great irony is that one comes away from reading *The Positivist Dispute* thinking that Popper and are essentially saying similar things. In his 'Remarks on the discussion of the papers by Karl R. Popper and Theodor W. Adorno' Ralf Dahrendorf makes the following comment:

> Several contributors to the discussion regretted the lack of tension between the symposiasts' papers. At times, it could indeed have appeared, astonishingly enough, as if Popper and Adorno were in agreement… The discussion provided a series of amusing instances of similarities in the formulations of the symposiasts.[37]

First, just as Popper clearly is no positivist, as noted by Holmes, Adorno is no Marxist. Second, both are anti-positivist without resorting to an absolute relativism.

---

33   B. Holmes, 'Comparative Education as a Scientific Study', *British Journal of Educational Studies*, 20 2 (1972), p.210.

34   Holmes, 'Comparative Education as a Scientific Study', op. cit. (note 33), p.210.

35   K. R. Popper, 'Reason or Revolution?' in T. W. Adorno (ed.) *The Positivist Dispute in German Sociology* (London: Heinemann, 1976), p.288.

36   Holmes, Comparative Education: Some Considerations of Method, op. cit. (note 10), p.13.

37   R. Dahrendorf, 'Remarks on the discussion of the papers by Karl R. Popper and Theodore W. Adorno', in T. W. Adorno (ed.) *The Positivist Dispute in German Sociology* (London: Heinemann, 1976), p.124.

This feels like familiar terrain. Located in this way it is interesting to consider Popper as the thinker who exerts the biggest influence on Holmes.

Piecemeal Social Engineering

If Holmes's use of the term 'sociological laws' is easily mistaken for being reductionist how about his appropriation of 'Popper's phrase "piecemeal social engineering"'?[38] Here Holmes sounds as if he is literally endorsing some kind of social eugenics programme. What can he mean by social engineering? Again, it is Holmes's cranky terminology that proves to be the greatest barrier to understanding.

Holmes's references to 'engineering' and 'planning' resemble his use of the term 'laws'. At face value his terminology suggests that he is being reductionist when, in fact, he is merely suggesting that some types of social planning, like laws, have more determinist meanings and implications than others. In his writings Holmes makes the important distinction between 'total social planning' and 'piecemeal social engineering' as follows: 'while total long-term social planning is theoretically indefensible and in practice leads to totalitarianism, piecemeal social engineering is within man's power'.[39] 'Piecemeal social engineering' is Holmes's way of saying we can make tentative plans within given grounds and parameters. To return to the oppositions, Holmes wants to avoid 'total planning' without denying 'planning' through the championing of absolute relativism. In his seminal work of the 1960s, *Problems in Education: A Comparative Approach*, Holmes makes it very clear that conceptions of planning are a matter of perspective[40]. 'In the modern world' writes Holmes,

> attitudes towards planning fall on an extended continuum. At one extreme left-wing governments are committed to social and economic development in accordance with overall plans. At the other end of the scale, some governments completely reject the notion of social planning as neither desirable nor possible. Somewhere between these two positions are those who accept the need for some form of piecemeal social engineering.[41]

Looked upon in this way, Holmes's favoured conception of planning sounds reasonable. The form of planning desired by Holmes develops from his notion of

---

38 Holmes, Problems in Education: A Comparative Approach, op. cit. (note 8), p.92.
39 Holmes, Problems in Education: A Comparative Approach, op. cit. (note 8), p.77.
40 Holmes, Problems in Education: A Comparative Approach, op. cit. (note 8).
41 Holmes, Problems in Education: A Comparative Approach, op. cit. (note 8), p.26.

laws. Indeed he considers 'sociological laws… to be of fundamental importance to social planning and to piecemeal social engineering'.[42] For Holmes, the comparative educationist predicts and plans within specified limits towards nothing more than hypothetical solutions. Thus,

> Ultimately, it is probably true to say that the social scientist can offer only a choice of solutions in the light of known outcomes and not the solution. Even then he cannot be sure his policy will succeed. Many conditions and considerations will help to influence the decision taken. Frequently these will be political or based on expediency.[43]

In this way, 'social engineering' refers to an approach by which speculative policies or plans are offered according to 'national and local circumstances'.[44] The comparative researcher is therefore conceived as a contextually located agent motivated by praxis:

> In so far as the comparative educationist hopes as a result of careful problem-analysis to discover novel policies (formulate new hypotheses) or to describe more adequately the national circumstances in which the problem arises and the solution is to be applied, he is involved in planning procedures designed to formulate decisions for future action.[45]

The grounds for planning are pragmatic. After an educational problem has been identified, the researcher must then formulate conjectural hypotheses as a means to act on the problem (sociological laws). This procedure will involve planning; that is, the suggestion of alternative procedures that will enable the potential overcoming of the initial problem. Here it is important to consider the importance of John Dewey on Holmes's thinking. In *Problems in Education* Holmes writes favourably on Dewey as follows:

> According to Dewey the function of reflective thinking is to clear up a confused situation, i.e. to solve a problem… In the face of a perplexing situation possible solutions may immediately spring to mind. Further reflection involves a process of intellectualisation out of which the problem to be solved becomes clearly formulated. This stage directs attention to data of a certain kind, namely those which are relevant to the problem. Out of it emerge refined or new possible solutions which are then put forward as hypotheses.[46]

---

42 Holmes, 'Paradigm Shifts in Comparative Education', op. cit. (note 8), p.593.
43 Holmes, Comparative Education: Some Considerations of Method, op. cit. (note 10), p.47.
44 Holmes, Comparative Education: Some Considerations of Method, op. cit. (note 10), p.52.
45 Holmes, Comparative Education: Some Considerations of Method, op. cit. (note 10), p.52.
46 Holmes, Problems in Education: A Comparative Approach, op. cit. (note 8), pp.32–33.

Holmes's 'problem approach' can be traced back to Dewey. Like many of the thinkers I have explored, including those favoured by Holmes, Dewey is a philosopher who charts a middle way between determinism and relativism. In Dewey, the researching subject is conceived in action and engaged, dealing with problems as and when they arise. Interestingly, unlike Popper, Dewey admitted 'that acquaintance with Hegel... [had] ...left a permanent deposit in my thinking'.[47] As pointed out by Burleigh Taylor Wilkins in 'James, Dewey, and Hegelian Idealism', the relationship between mind and experience – 'rational' and 'real' – is an essential feature of Dewey's philosophical approach.[48]

The Construction of Ideal-typical Models

Having come to grips with the meaning of Holmes's use of terms like 'laws' and 'social engineering', we are brought directly to the question of how we go about approaching, charting and assessing educational contexts in a meaningful way. This is where Holmes's appropriation of Max Weber's methodological concept of the 'ideal-type' comes into play. What did Weber actually mean by 'ideal type'? In *The Methodology of the Social Sciences*, Weber describes the concept in accordance with its function:

> The ideal-typical concept... is no "hypothesis" but it offers guidance to the construction of hypotheses. It is not a description of reality but it aims to give unambiguous means of expression to such a description... An ideal-type is formed by the... accentuation of one or more points of view and by the synthesis of a great many diffuse, discrete, more or less present and occasionally absent concrete individual phenomena, which are arranged... into a unified analytical construct.[49]

Donald MacRae explains that an ideal type does not refer to something 'good or noble', nor to something 'extreme' or 'perfect' or 'typical'.[50] An ideal type is essentially a 'diagnostic device'; it describes 'the pure case... uncluttered by extraneous attributes and ambiguities', enabling us to approach complex social phenomena in a meaningful way.[51]

47   J. Dewey, 'From Absolutism to Experimentalism', *Contemporary American Philosophy*, Vol. II (1930), p.21.
48   B. Taylor Wilkins, 'James, Dewey, and Hegelian Idealism', *Journal of the History of Ideas*, 17 3 (1956), pp.332–346
49   M. Weber, *The Methodology of the Social Sciences* (Illinois: The Free Press, 1949), p.90.
50   D. MacRae, *Max Weber* (London: Fontana Modern Masters, 1987), p.65.
51   MacRae, *Max Weber*, op. cit. (note 50), pp.65–66.

Society to Weber is made up of the interplay of... social acts so numerous, so kalei-doscopic that we can only seize and hold them in the mind by some device such as the ideal type, knowing all the time that the device itself is only a tool.[52]

As tools, ideal types pervade all aspects of social scientific research, providing the necessary fixed moment in time and space from which to describe and make assess-ments. Whimster argues that ideal types are essentially 'rationalistic in inspiration.' They 'are purely mental constructs or imaginative experiments'.[53] Likewise, as a rational construct, the ideal type provides the provisional gauge against which com-parisons become possible. Whimster provides the following example:

In analysing the decisions of opposing generals in a battle, we run a thought experi-ment as if both generals were acting fully rationally, and for this a model of rational battle action would have to be devised [an ideal type]. We then compare how... the generals' strategy and tactics deviated from the rational model.[54]

As MacRae reminds us, there is 'for Weber' an 'ideal type' for all concepts, includ-ing 'any crime, horror or sin.' In essence, whenever 'one uses such concepts as "capitalist", "feudal", "entrepreneur", "romantic", "charismatic" and so on, one is, consciously or not, using ideal types. All such complex descriptive and generalis-ing terms are ideal types in the social sciences'.[55]

In the work of Brian Holmes the ideal-type 'of the kind proposed by Max We-ber' is considered as an important and useful apparatus.[56] Indeed, in trying to chart a course between absolute determinism and absolute relativism, Holmes sug-gests that the ideal-type is fundamental:

It is not easy to see how the technical difficulties faced by Max Weber and modern comparative educationists can be met without resorting to ideal- typical models. Ac-cording to Weber any view of the world must be limited, partial and conditioned by the observer's point of view. To reduce this kind of subjectivity and to make sense of many and complex data Weber proposed that ideal types should be established... Weber proposed that logical, rational, or 'ideal typical' constructs could be employed to examine structures and social relationships.[57]

52 MacRae, *Max Weber*, op. cit. (note 50), p.66.

53 S. Whimster (ed.) *The Essential Weber* (London: Routledge, 2004), p.305.

54 Whimster, *The Essential Weber*, op. cit. (note 53), p.305.

55 MacRae, *Max Weber*, op. cit. (note 50), p.66.

56 Holmes, Comparative Education: Some Considerations of Method, op. cit. (note 10), p.80.

57 Holmes, Comparative Education: Some Considerations of Method, op. cit. (note 10), p.112.

As a fixed point the ideal type is not set in stone, however. It is essentially a construct, pieced together according to the parameters and limits of the subject's 'sphere of liberty', a framework that enables the researcher to proceed in a meaningful way:

Ideal-typical models should not be regarded as providing a comprehensive picture of reality, nor should they be used to stereotype the behaviour of any individual or group of individuals. An ideal-typical model... provides a framework of assumptions within which... research workers pursue their inquiries.[58]

If we are to analyse a syllabus topic across contexts there must be a set of variables that are constant, against which it is possible to make comparisons, 'change can only be measured against something that is fixed'.[59] To reiterate, for Holmes the ideal type, like sociological laws, will be projected according to the limited grounds and parameters of the researching subject, as it is located in time and in space. As the position of the subject changes in relation to contexts, the ideal-typical model is also likely to change. Holmes's conception of the ideal type provides, therefore, an essential guiding instrument.

Is it possible to construct an ideal-typical model consisting of a general set of variables to assess history education across liberal democratic societies? Writing during the Cold War, Holmes designs ideal typical normative models for approaching education systems in the United States, Western Europe and the Soviet Union. With hindsight I believe that aspects of his models do not work. Nevertheless, they offer some interesting pointers.

Echoing the work of Foucault, Holmes argues the case for constructing an ideal typical 'model which will permit research workers to analyse and describe power relationships within a system'.[60] When constructing such models, 'the choice and cross-national meaning of indicators for classifying data' will be fundamental. Yet 'it is clearly impossible fully to describe all' the influencing factors that encircle a given syllabus topic across contexts.[61] The researcher must, therefore, 'establish a taxonomy that has universal applicability' while at the same time being 'useful

---

58 Holmes, Comparative Education: Some Considerations of Method, op. cit. (note 10), p.139.
59 Holmes, Comparative Education: Some Considerations of Method, op. cit. (note 10), p.87.
60 Holmes, 'Causality, Determinism, and Comparative Education as a Social Science', op. cit. (note 6), p.135.
61 Holmes, Comparative Education: Some Considerations of Method, op. cit. (note 10), p.91.

in collecting information about a particular country'.[62] This will require careful consideration on the part of the researcher. The categories that form the constituting parts of the model must be carefully selected in order to give the model meaning across contexts, the '[choice of model… should not be arbitrary'.[63] Indeed, if 'categories… are to be comparable,' writes Holmes 'the indicators used for selecting information must be based on terms which can be given unambiguous cross-cultural meaning'.[64] Crucially, the applicability of the model across contexts will be determined by the number of categories selected as component parts; '[t]he simpler the models used the greater the range of systems which can be incorporated in the scheme'.[65] This being said, a model made up of too few constituting categories may be overly general. The researcher is compelled, therefore, to strike a balance.

HOLMES'S 'IDEAL TYPICAL' MODEL RE-FORMULATED TO GAUGE SYLLABUS TOPIC VARIATIONS ACROSS CONTEXTS

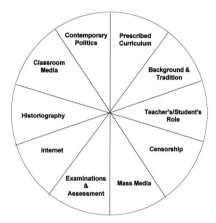

Fig. 6.1:   *Holmes's 'ideal typical' model re-formulated to gauge syllabus topic variations across contexts*

---

62   Holmes, Comparative Education: Some Considerations of Method, op. cit. (note 10), p.92.

63   Holmes, Comparative Education: Some Considerations of Method, op. cit. (note 10), p.131.

64   Holmes, Comparative Education: Some Considerations of Method, op. cit. (note 10), p.93.

65   Holmes, 'Causality, Determinism, and Comparative Education as a Social Science', op. cit. (note 6), p.135.

In the diagram above (Fig. 6.1), an ideal-typical model for syllabus topics in history education in liberal democratic societies is provided. Essentially the ideal type is made up of a cluster of influencing variables, a relationship between whole and parts frozen momentarily in time. To a lesser or greater extent, these variables will be identified as affecting or influencing the constitution of the syllabus topic across the sample of contexts. In some cases, a variable that exerts a strong influence in one context may have little influence in another.

Holmes's use of the ideal type puts into practice that which we encountered in Chapter Four in the discussions on Foucault. In answer to the question 'What are the implications of Foucault's "ontology of the present" for comparing syllabus topics in history education across contexts?' we examined the notion of the syllabus topic as the expression of push and pull variables, a constellation of power/knowledge relations. Likewise, each of the variables identified in the ideal typical model represents a star in the constellation, its brightness determined by the extent to which it influences the overall shape of the syllabus topic. In Chapter Four we established on the abstract level that the task of the researcher would be to understand the relationship between whole and parts from context to context and that some parts, the stars in the constellation, the cluster of influencing variables, would exert more influence than others.

The ideal type provides the fixed point against which to identify variations across contexts. To reiterate, the construction of an ideal-typical model, the type and number of categories incorporated, must be carefully balanced – neither too general nor too specific.

If we return to my own horizon of potential research contexts, discussed in Chapter Five, an ideal-typical model used to compare all of the countries is likely to be different from one constructed to compare, say, the Nordic countries or the English-speaking countries. However, the grounds upon which contexts are clustered will depend on what we are seeking to understand.

Using ideal typical-models the researching subject is able to isolate and approach contexts in a meaningful way. Provisional hypotheses and/or conjectures (sociological laws) will be constructed around a particular issue or problem, based on the perceived contrast between the generic categories of the ideal type and the specifics of a given context. Following this, '[t]entative solutions' to problems may be 'proposed' (piecemeal social engineering). Following Popper, 'conjectures' will be 'eliminated if they fail to survive when they are subjected to critical discussion and put to the test of experience'.[66] It all sounds very reasonable.

---

66   Holmes, 'Causality, Determinism, and Comparative Education as a Social Science', op. cit. (note 6), p.134.

6.2 Isolating and Approaching Educational Contexts in the Work of Edmund King

Compared to the awkward and machine-like delivery offered by Holmes, Edmund King's work is strikingly accessible. A classics specialist and a linguist, King wrote with great clarity in a highly readable and lucid style. Where Holmes's work often appears spiky, bristling and edgy, King's writing has a smooth and well-rounded feel, expressing both confidence and cultural capital and a concern for what is practical. King's work never comes across as haughty or pretentious.

King, like Holmes and Bereday, is one of the great champions of comparative education to have emerged during the middle years of the twentieth century. A prolific writer and long time editor of *Comparative Education*, King offered an essentially liberal-humanist approach that emphasised the importance of society, culture, and context. 'It is impossible' writes King, 'to divorce educational trends and needs from comparative studies of society, economics and technology undergoing rapid change'.[67] For King, education is the expression of a complex mesh of societal and cultural forces. In addition to this, it is King who repeatedly emphasises the necessary location of the subject, and the 'confused tangle of assumptions' that may affect the researching subject's assessment of evidence.[68]

On a personal level King and Holmes disliked each other. Certainly this personal animosity affected the development of their ideas as well as the way that subsequent comparativists have interpreted them. To be sure, King and Holmes arrived at the field of comparative education from vastly different academic backgrounds. For numerous reasons, as alluded to earlier in the chapter, King and Holmes are commonly conceived and used therefore as opposites, beyond reconciliation.

King's Pseudo-hermeneutic Methodology

King presents a distinctive approach to comparative educational research that, I would suggest, is implicitly hermeneutic. Educational objects are conceived as the expression of 'a kind of cultural dynamic… which is hard to measure in plain statistical terms'.[69] Likewise, the researching subject is conceived as formulating perspectives under the influence, at least in part, of emotion, custom, and

---

67   King, Comparative Studies and Educational Decision, op. cit. (note 12), p.1.
68   King, Comparative Studies and Educational Decision, op. cit. (note 12), p.4.
69   King, Comparative Studies and Educational Decision, op. cit. (note 12), p.4.

background: 'Every process of observation has been long rehearsed in accordance with our habits and emotions, not to say the disciplines and habits we have relied on'.[70] King never ceases to recognise the essential relationship between whole and parts, universal and particular. Indeed this dynamic appears to run through his entire enterprise. Writing in 1959 it is King who informs us that:

> Because such an ostensibly uniform body as the Roman Catholic Church is in a different context in Spain, Italy, France, Holland, the United Kingdom, and the United States, one expects and finds that its members and organizations behave somewhat differently from place to place.[71]

King continues with this way of thinking throughout his career. 'We cannot' he tells us, this time in 1980,

> simply talk of countries, cultural contexts, and ideologies in any universalistic way through all time. We have to take account of the precise context of decision, the 'here and now'. That is why perennial philosophies of education… may fail us in practice, if not in quasi- theological discourse. As we have seen, almost all cultures are prepared to accept… universal principles; but what happens in educational actuality is on quite another plane. Such talk arises not from pure relativism but from the realities of place and time.[72]

Universal concepts find expression in particular ways. They are bound to context. Meaning is construed according to the relationship between concept and context, between 'rational and real' in a dynamic and ongoing process. However, this is not to champion 'pure relativism' but simply to recognise the importance of context whenever plans or decisions are formulated. In much the same way King champions neither the quantitative nor the qualitative; scientific and humanistic dimensions of knowledge are considered to be of equal importance – complementary as opposed to conflicting. We must acknowledge both if we wish to 'understand'. As such,

> the increasing specialisation which has accompanied the explosion of knowledge make us forget what a tiny facet of the whole our own "clear view" actually is. Piecing together understanding cannot be done by vacuum-cleaner techniques or simple accountancy. The process of contributing to understanding must be as humanistic as it is scientific, by recognising the complementariness of all related endeavours.[73]

---

70   King, Comparative Studies and Educational Decision, op. cit. (note 12), p.41.

71   E. King, 'Students, Teachers and Researchers in Comparative Education', Comparative Education Review, 3 1 (1959), p.35.

72   E. King, 'Education, Individuality and Community: International Comparisons', *British Journal of Educational Studies*, 28 2 (1980), pp.113–114.

73   King, Comparative Studies and Educational Decision, op. cit. (note 12), p.41.

This pseudo-hermeneutic perspective is not always apparent, it has to be said. In *Comparative Studies and Educational Decision* King appears, at first, to argue the case for the practical over the abstract and the theoretical, '[w]herever possible, let us use plain language and stop theorising about results'.[74] Yet statements like this are deceptive. In the text, it soon becomes apparent that where King is critical of theorising for the sake of theorising, he does not reject theory. Rather, theory is perceived as necessarily entwined in an ongoing and regenerative relationship with method and practice. It must be 'possible', writes King,

> to observe and collect data with discernment, to systematise them further, analyse and penetrate them for their hidden significance, and above all to assess them... for their overall "meaning" in cultural context or in time. Nor can we forget the developmental aspect of any such study – [a] matter which abstract theorists often overlook.[75]

Abstract theorising is out. Theorising in relation to method and practice is in. To exercise 'discernment', to 'systematise', to 'analyse', and to 'assess' requires theoretical grounding while the observation and collection of data are methodical practices. The theoretical, the methodical, and the practical are thus conceived by King in a dynamic relationship; the research process perceived as necessarily 'developmental', within limits imposed by the parameters of 'cultural context' and 'time'. In places, King sounds like Gadamer. The following quotation represents a good case in point:

> Descartes, Locke, and Hume quite unjustifiably presupposed a complete state of detachment in the observer, and a completely external and inert state in whatever was perceived. Whoever observes or experiences some phenomenon outside himself is both involved in his background of experience, and indeed, involved in his relationship to whatever he observes.[76]

The relationship between the observer and the observed, past and present, background and our experience of objects is, claims King, necessarily dynamic, circular and ongoing. In a passage from the chapter 'How do we understand?' that appears in *World Perspectives in Education*, King's conceptualisation of the way that we encounter 'new' objects is implicitly hermeneutic:

> Suppose I set out to look at any problem. I not only bring my whole past and my present involvement along with me but I embark on my studies in a way that is strangely repetitive of the infant's early attempts to see. I pick out points of recognition. There

---

74   King, Comparative Studies and Educational Decision, op. cit. (note 12), p.4.
75   King, Comparative Studies and Educational Decision, op. cit. (note 12), p.20.
76   King, Comparative Studies and Educational Decision, op. cit. (note 12), p.27.

is the recurring phenomenon. Around it are the features often associated with it. They appear and reappear in clusters of impressions. If the clustered impressions always recur together, a definite pattern is presupposed. A rudimentary understanding may crystallize around such recognition.[77]

In King's work, the objective and the subjective are conceptualised as entwined. Indeed, '[t]here is a risk', he tells us

> of thinking that a phenomenon recognized (like a university, a 'comprehensive school', or Latin) has a really classifiable identity with little change in significance from country to country – whereas we know that even if it is 'the same thing' objectively it is put to different subjective use in different contexts.[78]

If King does not sound like Gadamer in these passages, then who does? Like Holmes, whom we investigated above, King charts a pseudo-hermeneutic middle way between the oppositions.

The Construction of Hypotheses and Educational Decision

On the issue of hypothesis development King's position is very clear. Hypotheses enable explanation beyond description. Thus 'phenomena are not merely described, but explained on the basis of some hypothesis. This hypothesis is speculation in the first instance; but it can be tested against observation, and sometimes tested by experiment'.[79] This sounds very much like one of Holmes's sociological laws, speculatively applied and subjected to testing and potential scrutiny following Popper contra induction. 'As Sir Karl Popper has shown in his *Logic of Scientific Discovery*', writes King, 'every scientific observation or discovery is preceded by a hypothesis. This hypothesis is not necessarily formulated; it may be no more than implicit or unspoken'[80]. In some cases, writes King, 'to "identify" the nature and purpose of a particular object, a multitude of hypotheses may be advanced.' However,

> The big question is "Which of them makes sense?" More to the point is the question "Which of them makes the most sense?" Largely as a matter of presumption, the hypotheses click into place almost automatically as though our brain were a computer previously fed and processed... The more familiar our circumstances and the less

77   E. King, *World Perspectives in Education* (London: Methuen, 1962), pp.3–24.
78   E. King, 'Analytical Frameworks in Comparative Education', *Comparative Education*, 11 1 (1975), p.88.
79   King, Comparative Studies and Educational Decision, op. cit. (note 12), p.8.
80   King, Comparative Studies and Educational Decision, op. cit. (note 12), p.44.

changing our environment, the more likely it is that customary patterns of observation and the old rules will seem to give a complete answer for most contingencies.[81]

King's understanding of hypothesis development can be interpreted from a hermeneutic perspective. We develop hypotheses based on our familiarity with circumstances, our own and those that characterise the contexts we aim to research. Deciding on hypotheses that make 'the most sense' as opposed to those that make 'less sense' or even 'the least sense', will require selective criteria. Using reason we must distinguish meaningful from non-meaningful hypotheses. Meaningful hypotheses are, by definition, those most appropriate to the task. For King, the hypotheses that we construct must be worked through, reassessed and re-formulated, both intellectually and in practice:

> By all means we must have hypotheses; but they cannot be formulated in abstraction – only... in concert with other social scientists... Our hypotheses are subjected to their working-over, even intellectually. After any intellectual conclusion there is always the crux of political and social decision.[82]

Educational decision is in many ways King's equivalent to Holmes's social engineering. Educational decision occurs on a piecemeal basis; that is to say neither absolutely nor randomly but rather according to contextual circumstances as they arise, in and across time and space. 'The perceived priorities and (above all) the feasibilities of education', King informs us, 'depend for their expression and implementation upon the context of decision'.[83] Educational decision is a tentative process, a universal conceptual apparatus tied to the particularities of 'the "here and now"':

> After we have collected and collated all data and advice, the various aspects of the discoverers' and the discoveries' social involvement still require exploratory analysis – and require it afresh as each new problem needs clarification and decision. Quite apart from questions of knowledge or understanding, decision depends upon the present context and on the priorities and probabilities to be considered for the future. These all occur in multiple combinations, varying from context to context.[84]

In another passage, educational decision is described as a regenerative process, 'it is clear that major decisions today must represent a kind of "continual creation",

81 King, Comparative Studies and Educational Decision, op. cit. (note 12), 44.
82 King, Comparative Studies and Educational Decision, op. cit. (note 12), pp.49–50.
83 E. King, 'Education, Individuality and Community: International Comparisons', *British Journal of Educational Studies*, 28 2 (1980), p.114.
84 King, Comparative Studies and Educational Decision, op. cit. (note 12), p.46.

no matter what may have happened in the past'.[85] Like Holmes, King takes a position against 'total planning', '[t]here is no question of subsuming everything into one concentric interpretation such as is advanced in totalitarian states'.[86] Since it is impossible to perceive or control the effects of all future variables and circumstances, educational decision may be practised only within the context of self-acknowledged limits. The unexpected' writes King 'is happening all the time. Unexpected factors enter into our wider or long-term calculations. Unforeseen events… are full of human surprises.' In turn, we make decisions based on nothing more certain than 'predictions or probabilities… [the] essential gadgets of modern thought.' Educational decisions are 'statements of probability in certain contingencies… [but] they do not of themselves enable us to control'.[87]

King's Implied 'Ideal-typical' Models

Although King does not refer explicitly to the use of ideal-typical models, in the way that Holmes does, their use is nevertheless implied in his work. 'Detailed comparative analysis of the elements or aspects of a local situation', King tells us, can only be 'clarified by using a constant formula or "model"'.[88] In his conceptualisation of 'the "personality" or preoccupations of a school system', for example, King presents a diagram made up of categories clustered around the central concept.[89] Essentially, the collected categories represent the parts that together make up an 'integrated' whole. In many ways this integrated whole may be identified with Weber's concept of 'ideal' as used in the construction of ideal types. Basically, variations across contexts may be compared against this generic ideal.[90] King speaks of this conceptual construct as an 'ideal type' in all but name. Thus,

> What is represented… is not intended to be appropriate to every single country… But we recognise at once that the notion of school in some countries will inevitably produce an awareness of different provision made for distinct social categories… Furthermore, though the school systems of many countries share these attributes generally, the actual

---

85 King, Comparative Studies and Educational Decision, op. cit. (note 12), p.108.
86 King, Comparative Studies and Educational Decision, op. cit. (note 12), p.36.
87 King, Comparative Studies and Educational Decision, op. cit. (note 12), p.52.
88 E. King, 'Comparative Studies: An Evolving Commitment, a Fresh Realism', *Comparative Education*, 13 2 (1975), p.88.
89 King, Comparative Studies and Educational Decision, op. cit. (note 12), p.31.
90 King, Comparative Studies and Educational Decision, op. cit. (note 12), pp.29–31.

features and the meanings of the various distinctions vary considerably from one cultural context to another.[91]

In his discussion of 'types' and of 'constellations of interest and influence' King echoes Holmes's highly particular appropriation of Weber's concept of the 'ideal type' – as discussed above. 'Part of comparative education's stock-in-trade' writes King 'is to know the well-defined types of context internationally, and the common constellations of interest and influence… to aid dynamic interpretation of what is observed'. Furthermore, we are told, even when 'great educational issues rise up like waves pushed forward by contributory currents into a great climax' their effects are exhibited in particular ways 'in any one social or cultural situation'.[92] King's use of 'ideal-types', although never explicitly acknowledged, provides the 'fixed point' against which variations may be gauged.

KING'S PSEUDO 'IDEAL TYPICAL' MODEL RE-FORMULATED TO GAUGE SYLLABUS TOPIC VARIATIONS ACROSS CONTEXTS

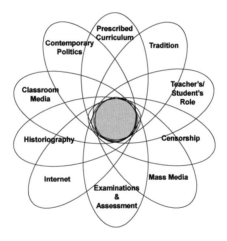

Fig. 6.2:   *King's pseudo 'ideal typical' model re-formulated to gauge syllabus topic variations across contexts*

---

91   King, Comparative Studies and Educational Decision, op. cit. (note 12), p.31.
92   King, Comparative Studies and Educational Decision, op. cit. (note 12), p.18.

The diagram above (Fig. 6.2) illustrates King's pseudo-ideal-typical model reformulated as a fixed point against which to compare, in this case, syllabus topics in history education across contexts. The ideal type is made up of a cluster of generic categories, influencing variables, like those given in the discussion of the work of Holmes. Again we are drawn to the discussions on Foucault in Chapter Four. Using the ideal type, the way that clusters of variables are balanced in and across contexts may be gauged and compared since, for King, 'every topic considered' will derive 'special force and meaning from its dynamic context'.[93] King uses 'ellipses' to define each category but whether he did this to illustrate overlapping inter-relationships between category and concept or between categories is not made clear. Interestingly, King claims, in a rather relativistic way, that 'the various ellipses… will differ greatly for every individual in each case of observation'.[94] I am not sure if I agree with him on his question – 'differ' yes, but 'differ greatly'? King also argues that some variables may be totally absent in certain contexts. This I do agree with. However, if too many of the variables are absent the concept of an ideal type ceases to be valid. To reiterate, the ideal type provides the fixed point against which to identify variations.

King on Holmes

King dedicates several pages to criticising Holmes's concepts. He leaves little room to suggest that a more open interpretation of Holmes's clunky terminology may actually enable a fresh outlook on Holmes's work. King is particularly virulent in his condemnation of Holmes's use of the term 'laws'. The term is overly deterministic, reducing, rationalising, and oversimplifying what are complex social phenomena. While the construction of hypotheses is seen to be totally acceptable, and indeed necessary, 'explanations' of educational situations 'do not merit the distinction of being called "laws"'.[95] At a later point King writes contra Holmes as follows:

> It is worth pointing out the obvious: the answers given for one purpose need not necessarily be the same as those given for another purpose of enquiry… Why then make a naive attempt to oversimplify things forever by talking about "laws" and predictions? For all the reasons already given, such a proceeding is bound to be of dubious value in practice.[96]

---

93   E. King, *Other Schools and Ours: Comparative Studies for Today* (London: Holt, Rinehart & Winston, 1979), p.8.
94   King, Comparative Studies and Educational Decision, op. cit. (note 12), p.30.
95   King, Comparative Studies and Educational Decision, op. cit. (note 12), p.9.
96   King, Comparative Studies and Educational Decision, op. cit. (note 12), p.49.

Writing almost ten years later King reiterates how 'it is difficult to distinguish trends in anything but the short-term view; and in any case "trends are not laws" but explanatory statements in retrospect which "always retain the character of tentative hypotheses" needing many severe tests'.[97] What kind of law is a sociological law? 'A "sociological law" – if it exists' writes King 'is a hypothesis on present evidence and no more'.[98] However, as we know from our earlier discussion, Holmes would undoubtedly agree with King on this. Indeed, the only area of disagreement would in fact be over the use of terminology and not deeper procedural issues. This seems to be a common feature of the King / Holmes debate. King frequently distances his own approach from Holmes's, criticising Holmes's concepts. In response, Holmes spends time in his books and papers clarifying the meaning of his use of concepts, arguing that King has misunderstood them. Finally, we come to understand that, beneath the language of antinomy, there is an implicit and fundamental commonality to each author's intellectual position.

6.3 Holmes and King as Complementary Syntheses

Are Holmes and King really that different? First and foremost it is Holmes who openly recognises that they are not. He even goes as far as to suggest, not immodestly, that, at times, 'the analyses' that 'found favour with King' have been 'based on the problem solving approach which subsequently I developed'.[99] Certainly the two approaches can appear in opposition if you want them to. In his stress on the way that the subject and education in general are embedded in complex social and cultural relationships that change from one context to the next, 'nothing is really static in society', King can appear somewhat more relativist than Holmes, just as, with his pseudo-'scientific' language, Holmes appears less relativist.[100] Yet the fact is that both men are clearly anti-positivist liberals who identified themselves from an early stage with the 'problem approach' to comparative education.[101]

---

97 King, 'Comparative Studies: An Evolving Commitment, a Fresh Realism', op. cit. (note 88).103.

98 King, Comparative Studies and Educational Decision, op. cit. (note 12), p.52.

99 Holmes, 'Causality, Determinism, and Comparative Education as a Social Science', op. cit. (note 6), p.122.

100 King, Comparative Studies and Educational Decision, op. cit. (note 12), p.50.

101 B. Holmes, 'The Problem Approach in Comparative Education: Some Methodological Considerations', op. cit. (note 8), pp.3–8. King, 'Students, Teachers and Researchers in Comparative Education', op. cit. (note 71), pp.33–36.

On a close reading it is possible to interpret the work of both writers as saying essentially the same thing, dressed up in different clothing. Both offer an approach that inspires action in response to problems. Tentative hypotheses are formulated. Ideal types or, at least, pseudo-ideal types, are constructed, implicitly or explicitly, in order to gauge variations across contexts. Data and information are collected. The hypotheses are then subjected to critical scrutiny. Results may then be used as a basis for policy in the form of 'social engineering' or 'educational decision', carried forward on a 'piecemeal' basis. This research process is, for both Holmes and King, essentially regenerative, circular, and ongoing. While there is a more 'empiricist' edge to Holmes's work, he never rules out the role of reason through 'critical discussion', as a basis for scrutiny.[102]

Likewise, King argues that both scientific and humanistic approaches to educational research are complementary, as we just saw. Essentially, both Holmes and King argue the case for developing a methodological approach based in the interplay between 'rational and real' that is neither determinist nor relativist.

For me, Holmes and King offer more together than they do apart. Holmes's awkward language may be softened through the influence of King. Moreover, we gain much from King's critique of Holmes. Even if it is argued that King's interpretation of Holmes's position is somehow incorrect, the critique draws attention to problems of language use. Just as this chapter comes out in favour of Holmes's position, it comes out against his use of terminology. Is it any wonder that academics and students alike have found him impossible to use? Painted up in this pseudo-scientific way, Holmes's blend of science and sociology, located somewhere in the space between absolute determinism and absolute non-determinism, to assist educational policy decisions through a comparative approach, can appear as an awkward fusion. All it takes is one wrong turn for the reader to feel suddenly lost – in the dark, at sea, in translation, all of the above. King's critique of Holmes draws implicit attention, however, to the fact that it is not Holmes's position but his use of language that is the cause of so many misunderstandings.

King's ideas, on the other hand, become somehow more systematic when interpreted under the influence of Holmes. Although King's prose style is very clear, and filled with a never-ending stream of interesting examples, his insistence on the importance of all influencing factors – cultural, social, political, economic, technological etc. – sometimes gives a feeling of not seeing the wood for the trees. What are the stages of a research project? Where do we need to begin? Although

---

102 Holmes, 'Causality, Determinism, and Comparative Education as a Social Science', op. cit. (note 6), p.134.

answers to these questions are given in King's work they are not always immediately apparent. Thus, where Holmes becomes more readable via King, King becomes more systematic via Holmes. Ultimately, it can be argued that the work of both men benefits under the influence of the other, if read in a particular way: 'Action from one side only' could actually come to seem reduced, or diminished, 'because what is to happen can only be brought about by means of both'.[103]

6.4 Concluding Comments

The relationship between Holmes and King is marked with personal antinomy. To be sure, the two thinkers arrived at comparative education from markedly contrasting academic backgrounds, one from the natural sciences the other from the humanities. In addition, the two men write using very different styles. These differences give each writer's work its distinctive tone and colour. Underlying the contrasts, however, there is much to suggest a complementary, although by no means identical, approach. The synthesis of the ideas of Holmes and King may thus be appropriated for the purpose of approaching complex educational contexts in order to gauge variations.

In the following chapter we will focus directly on how it is possible to describe the particularities of a given context, a process that I refer to as constellation mapping. It will be argued that this kind of practical exercise is central to any comparative methodology where researchers are seeking to locate and analyse a given syllabus topic. It is to these concerns that we now turn.

---

103 G. W. F. Hegel, *Phenomenology of Mind* (London: George Alien & Unwin, 1966), p.230.

Chapter Seven
Charting a Syllabus Topic in History Education across Cultures – The Descriptive Exercise of Constellation Mapping

> The objective validity of all empirical knowledge rests exclusively upon the ordering of the given reality according to categories which are subjective.
>
> Max Weber, *The Methodology of the Social Sciences*, 1949, p.110

History education is configured differently in different contexts. This chapter will focus directly on how it is possible to describe the particularities of a given context. Moreover, it will be argued that this essentially practical and descriptive exercise is central to any comparative methodology where researchers are seeking to locate and analyse a given syllabus topic. Syllabus topics cannot be fully understood outside of the context in which they are situated and of which they form a part. To describe a syllabus topic in context is, therefore, an attempt to understand the working parts, the influencing variables; the constituting push and pull factors. How does each part work and with what effects? In what sense do the parts influence the knowledge that constitutes a syllabus topic? What is the relationship between the parts as a whole?

Syllabus themes and topics express their own generality and their own specificity. Some topics, the Second World War, for example, will be recognised 'generally' across contexts, to be taught and examined in contemporary history in many countries. However, the 'specific' push and pull variables that constitute the topic are likely to have different effects in different contexts. In order to describe the precise shape of a topic in a given educational context, therefore, the particularity of influencing factors in given contexts must be acknowledged and understood.

Having defined the Hegelian/hermeneutic approach to making comparisons, and the methodological bases upon which contexts may be determined and approached, I will now demonstrate how it is possible to 'look inside' a particular context. To use pseudo- Holmesian terminology, history education in different systems will be engineered in different ways. Because of this, we need to look at the mechanics of the contexts that we are comparing to see exactly what is influencing what. It is, therefore, in this chapter that we begin to 'get our hands dirty', dismantling contexts in order to investigate parts before putting them back together again. This provides the basis for understanding how the parts work together as a whole as well as the platform from which to proceed towards making meaningful comparisons.

I will only endeavour to demonstrate using those contexts that are located within my own self-imposed research horizon, in acknowledgement of my own limits and in profound awareness of what cannot be done – as described in Chapter Four and Chapter Five. In light of this, I will only describe the cluster of variables as they affect history education in Japan, Sweden and England. From this point onwards these countries will act as exemplars. With regard to the issue of the Second World War, Japan, Sweden, and England are especially fascinating, the affiliations of each nation during the conflict – Axis, Neutral, Ally – contrasting significantly with current affiliations.

ISOLATING CONTEXTS ON THE RESEARCH HORIZON

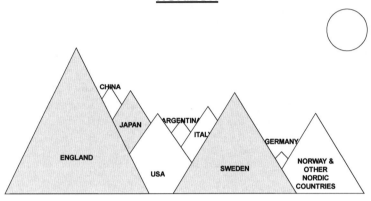

Fig. 7.1:   Isolating contexts on the research horizon

I will seek to demonstrate how the three national contexts can be compared against a provisional 'ideal typical' gauge, according to variables identified in the reformulated Holmes/King models, discussed in Chapter Six. To reiterate, the 'ideal type' will be made up of a cluster of variables against which it will be possible to gauge variations across contexts. In Chapter Six, the variables specific to gauging 'syllabus topic variations' were classified as follows: background and tradition, prescribed curriculum, examinations and assessment, teacher/student role, censorship, mass media, Internet, classroom media, contemporary politics and ideology, historiography. A given syllabus topic such as the Second World War can be understood, therefore, to be constituted via combinations of these variables, each variable conceived as a push and/or pull factor. In this chapter the researcher is thus conceived as immersed in the particularities of each context, one by one. With the 'ideal type' in hand, held like a torch, the researcher is enabled to make sense of the complex particularities that characterise each context, a process that I call 'constellation mapping'. In turn, it is through this approach that we set the groundwork for 'comparative constellation analysis' – as described in Chapter Eight.

7.1 History Education at the Secondary Level in Japan, Sweden and England

We now turn to the particularities of each of the systems, to demonstrate how a given syllabus topic may be located and mapped in relation to and as the expression of the variables identified using the 'ideal-type'. Essentially, each variable beckons a series of questions. These have been listed below as follows:

Background and Tradition

– What significant political and economic changes have occurred to affect history education in each of the three contexts?
– What has been the nature of recent reforms?
– What traditions prevail?
– What is the place of history education in secondary education?

Prescribed Curriculum

– What is the official curriculum for history in each of the three contexts?
– How prescriptive is it?
– How much autonomy will teachers of history have to decide what they teach?

Examinations and Assessment

– In general, how are students of history examined across the three contexts?
– What forms of knowledge are valued and tested?
– Are examinations external or internal?
– How examination-oriented are the three education systems?

Classroom Media

– What forms of educational media are used in history classrooms across the three contexts?

- Is the use of a plurality of classroom media sources encouraged?
- Is the history textbook conceived as the basis of syllabus knowledge or as one source among several others? Neither?
- What types of classroom media are in the ascendant? What types are in decline?

Censorship

- Upon what grounds are various forms of educational media in history education approved across the three contexts?
- Are educational media censored along ideological grounds?
- How controlling is the censorship process?

Contemporary Politics and Ideology

- What is the contemporary political scene in each of the countries?
- How has history education been affected by the contemporary political scene in terms of policy?
- Which national discourses and ideologies prevail?

Internet Access

- To what extent do students have access to the Internet, both at home and at school, in each of the three contexts?
- Are students of history more likely to use Internet sources to complete homework assignments compared to other forms of media?
- Is on-line learning considered to be important?

Mass Media

- How are themes central to syllabus topics in history education portrayed in the mass media of each of the three contexts?
- Are all views catered to? How free is the press? Can students and their parents expect to encounter the full range of views and perspectives through the media?
- Are documentary T.V. programmes subject to forms of censorship?

Teacher/Student Role

- What role does the teacher tend to play in the history classroom, provider of knowledge or facilitator?
- What role do students play?
- To what extent are forms of student-based learning valued across the contexts?

202

- How has the historiography of a given theme or topic changed over the years? Why?
- What is the relationship between historiography and national discourses?

7.2 Japan

Background and Tradition

A wide body of scholarly work exists on various aspects of Japanese education.[1] While historically it was the Japanese who looked to the West for ideas, since the 1980s the Japanese system of education has became a major concern among Western academics and policy-makers.[2] This was due in large part to the rapid growth of the Japanese economy from the 1960s onwards, and the notion that high quality education and economic growth are connected.[3] Japan's school history education, on the other hand, has long been a source of controversy.[4] According to Mayer,

> The Ministry of Education and the Japanese education system have been criticised by some for not incorporating sufficient information about the conduct of the Imperial army... These critics feel that... Japanese people [should] understand the way their army treated such conquered populations as Koreans, Chinese, and Filipinos and the

---

1   B. Duke, 'The Liberalisation of Japanese Education', *Comparative Education*, 22 1 (1986), pp.37–45. E. R. Beauchamp, 'The Development of Japanese Educational Policy, 1945–1985', *History of Education Quarterly*, 27 3 (1987), pp.299–324. T. Horio, *Educational Thought and Ideology in Modern Japan* (Tokyo: University of Tokyo Press, 1988). G. Tsuchimochi, *Education Reform in Post war Japan: The 1946 U.S. Education Mission* (Tokyo: University of Tokyo Press, 1993). L. Schoppa, *Education Reform in Japan: A Case of Immobilist Politics* (London: Routledge, 1993). M. Stephens, *Japan and Education* (London: Macmillan, 1991). L. Hein and M. Seldon (eds.) *Censoring History: Citizenship and Memory in Japan, Germany, and the United States* (Armonk: East Gate, 2000). C. Barnard, *Language, Ideology and Japanese History Textbooks* (New York: Routledge Curzon, 2003).

2   M. White, *The Japanese Educational Challenge: A Commitment to Children* (Tokyo: Kodansha International, 1987).

3   L. W. Beer, 'Japan Turning the Corner', *Asian Survey*, 11 1 (1971), pp.74–85. White, *The Japanese Educational Challenge*, op. cit. (note 2).

4   R. J. B. Bosworth, *Explaining Auschwitz and Hiroshima: History Writing and the Second World War 1945–1990* (London: Routledge, 1994).

way it treated prisoners of war... Failure [to do so]... undermine[s] Japan's credibility when it comes to peace initiatives... and encourages suspicion as Japan develops economic initiatives in Southern Asia.[5]

Hit by recession during the 1990s, Japanese education has come to be viewed in a different light in recent years both internationally and at home. With the rise of grass roots nationalism as well as an increasingly conservative stance from the Liberal Democratic Party (LDP) and the Ministry of Education (*Monbusho*), the controversy over history education in Japan has been exacerbated.[6] Some recent government reforms have been very conservative: making the singing of the national anthem and the raising of the national flag compulsory at school ceremonies and events. The controversy over the coverage of World War II in Japanese history textbooks continues to rage, with pressure coming from domestic and international groups.[7]

History education in Japan is underpinned by conservative conceptions of teaching, learning and of the nature of history itself. Confucian traditions prevail. Since the beginning of the 20th century school history textbooks have been censored by central government, rote learning and the memorisation of knowledge remaining as the central pre-requisites for exam success.[8] Students in Japan take classes in 'social studies' throughout the entire school cycle. By grade five the number of hours spent studying these subjects, including geography and history, increases. Entering secondary education, aged twelve, the number of hours devoted to the study of history comes second only to Japanese. In Senior High Schools, social studies subjects continue to feature strongly. However, the number of classroom hours devoted to the study of history will depend on the type of school attended.[9]

---

5   V. J. Mayer, 'World War II in Social Studies and Science Curricula', *Phi Delta Kappan*, May 2000, pp.705–711.

6   C. Barnard, *Language, Ideology and Japanese History Textbooks* (New York: Routledge Curzon, 2003).

7   Barnard, *Language, Ideology and Japanese History Textbooks,* op. cit. (note 6). M. Ogawa and S. Field, 'Causation, Controversy and Contrition: Recent Developments in the Japanese History Textbook Content and Selection Process', in J. Nicholls (ed.) *School History Textbooks Across Cultures: International Debates and Perspectives* (Oxford: Symposium, 2006).

8   Barnard, *Language, Ideology and Japanese History Textbooks,* op. cit. (note 6).

9   White, *The Japanese Educational Challenge,* op. cit. (note 2). Barnard, *Language, Ideology and Japanese History Textbooks,* op. cit. (note 6).

Prescribed Curriculum

In contemporary Japan there is no fully prescribed 'National Curriculum' for school history, as found in England and Wales, rather a series of curriculum guidelines mandated by the central executive and local governments across the country.[10] Where the centrally designated course of study for history provides 'a basic framework ... at each grade level', Kanaya informs us that it is the 'prefectural and municipal boards of education' that 'prepare guidelines for curriculum development in the schools in their areas'. History teachers at all levels receive curriculum guidebooks, 'prepared by... subject specialists in the Ministry with the assistance of experienced teachers'.[11] The Ministry of Education in Tokyo reviews the curriculum 'approximately every ten years' in order to keep abreast of developments and to update 'courses of study' accordingly.[12]

There are 47 prefectural and 12 municipal boards of education across Japan. While these will receive identical curriculum guidelines for school history from the central Ministry of Education, the interpretation of guidelines will be determined by local factors. It is at this point that we need to acknowledge the place of the Japanese Teachers Union (JTU) within the order of things. Although the JTU should be recognised as an important national force, the Union's power and influence has, historically, been stronger and more influential in some prefectures and municipalities than in others.[13] Sympathetic to communism during the post-war years, locked in conflict with the LDP, the Ministry and local governments, the JTU has fought and struggled over curriculum content in school history education for many decades.[14] Hiroshima has a particularly radical prefectural union, with over 90% membership among teachers. The union has long campaigned against the expression of nationalism in schools. It has also argued – against right wing groups – that the full details of atrocities committed by the Japanese army during World War II should become compulsory features of Japanese history lessons.[15] Exactly how the issue of the Second World War is approached in history lessons in

---

10   T. Kanaya, 'Japan', in N. Postlethwaite (ed.) *International Encyclopaedia of National Systems of Education* (Oxford: Pergamon, 1995), p.486.
11   Kanaya, 'Japan', op. cit. (note 10), p.487.
12   Kanaya, 'Japan', op. cit. (note 10), p.487.
13   H. Ota, 'Political Teacher Unionism in Japan', in J. Shields (ed.) *Japanese Schooling: Patterns of Socialization, Equality and Political Control* (Pennsylvania: Pennsylvania State University Press, 1989).
14   Bosworth, *Explaining Auschwitz and Hiroshima*, op. cit. (note 4).
15   Ota, 'Political Teacher Unionism in Japan', op. cit. (note 13).

a given school will depend, to a significant extent, on local politics. In prefectures with a strong JTU 'peace education' in accordance with Article 9 of the constitution will feature strongly, in those with a weaker union it will not.[16]

Examinations and Assessment

As with many Japanese institutions the origins of the Japanese examination system are Confucian, derived from the system of testing in feudal China used for the selection of bureaucrats.[17] Yet as White points out, it was Japan's distinctive encounter with the West that gave rise to the system of examinations recognisable to this day. Thus,

> external pressure after 1853 created a panicky energy and readiness for change. The vehicle for that change became the human resource developed through education: an elite trained in Western sciences and technology skills through a system of qualifications and credentials.[18]

Examinations in Japan quickly became open to all, regardless of social background, a vital element in the all-out attempt to 'modernise'.

Few elements of the Japanese education system today impose more influence on what is taught and learned in history classes than the high school and university entrance examinations.[19] To proceed from junior to senior high school or from senior high school to an institution of higher education, students must pass an entrance examination – a 'closed paper' set by the schools and universities themselves.[20] Although open to all, pressure to enter the best high schools and universities is extremely intense.[21] Referred to colloquially as examination hell, the experience as a whole, characterised by 'excessive competition in entrance examinations', is considered to be a major national problem.[22] Excessive examination pressure has led to increased demand for additional tuition outside of school hours and the creation of examination preparation schools (the infamous 'cram schools' or *Juku*). Attended during the evenings and on weekends by a large section of the

---

16 Ota, 'Political Teacher Unionism in Japan', op. cit. (note 13). M. Ogawa and S. Field, 'Causation, Controversy and Contrition', op. cit. (note 7).
17 E. O. Reischauer, *The Japanese* (Cambridge: Massachusetts, 1977).
18 White, *The Japanese Educational Challenge,* op. cit. (note 2), p.141.
19 Barnard, *Language, Ideology and Japanese History Textbooks*, op. cit. (note 6).
20 Kanaya, 'Japan', op. cit. (note 10), pp.487–488.
21 Kanaya, 'Japan', op. cit. (note 10), p.484.
22 Kanaya, 'Japan', op. cit. (note 10), p.488.

secondary student population, *Juku* has come to be seen by many as necessary for examination success. The extreme pressure has also forced students to begin preparing for examinations at increasingly younger ages. According to White,

The exam system assumes that distinctions in children's ability to mobilize effort can be measured by a single test; it is further assumed the exams serve the meritocratic, egalitarian ideals of modern Japan. But the existence of the exams, and the increasing number of children who at younger and younger ages sit for them, have produced an explosion of intense anxiety.[23]

History examinations in Japan test the extent to which students are able to memorise the so-called 'facts' rather than reasoning or creative abilities. Students who succeed are, therefore, those with the best memorisation skills and not the creative or 'eccentrically intelligent'.[24] To study history, students are required to memorise enormous quantities of information – names, dates, and words from particular passages – rather than demonstrating their ability to argue using evidence. Multiple choice and 'fill in the blanks' – style questions are common. According to Barnard,

These entrance exams require almost no critical thinking whatsoever; as long as examinees can regurgitate a large number of disconnected facts on demand, they can pass the entrance exam. Pupils are not required to think deeply about the causes for the Pacific War, or the connection between the Japanese education system in the 1930s and the behaviour of Japanese soldiers at Nanking. They are deemed to 'know' history as long as they can remember… the date of the Nanking Massacre Incident.[25]

Writing in the mid-1980s White states prophetically that school and university 'examinations are the most dramatic and visible object of potential reform' in Japan. Veteran comparative educationist, Benjamin Duke, takes a similarly critical position:

If any feature of Japanese education needs reforming, it is the singular emphasis on examination preparation that permeates the classroom from the first grade onward throughout the land, overwhelmingly so in the cities where the majority of Japanese live.[26]

For Duke, the overwhelming pressure to prepare for school and university entrance examinations in history as well as other subjects makes it impossible to

---

23   White, *The Japanese Educational Challenge,* op. cit. (note 2), p.125.
24   White, *The Japanese Educational Challenge,* op. cit. (note x), p.149.
25   Barnard, *Language, Ideology and Japanese History Textbooks,* op. cit. (note 6), p.168.
26   Duke, 'The Liberalisation of Japanese Education', op. cit. (note 1), p.43.

even 'think in terms of individuality, creativity, ingenuity, and all the other grand concepts...[used] ...when describing the purposes of the school'.[27] Accordingly, 'as long as the entrance examination looms... maintaining its overpowering grip', reforms towards developing individualism, creativity and critical thinking among students will be stifled.[28]

Classroom Media

The school history textbook is an essential feature of history classes in Japan.[29] As a teaching resource 'textbooks serve as the main instructional material in the classroom... compiled... by commercial publishing companies on the basis of the courses of study'.[30] The history textbook is central to almost all classroom activities. Textbook content is the central source of curriculum knowledge. Students are required to 'learn' from the textbook, teachers to teach its content. Ultimately, students will be examined based on their knowledge of the textbook.

School history is strictly controlled in Japan, taught at schools using censored textbooks. Bosworth cites the following 'account by an American observer... of history classes' on the causes of the Second World War 'in Japanese high schools':

No hard choices are presented, and failings are ignored. No villains or heroes and no momentous moral or national imperatives emerge. History does not contain good and evil forces... Every textbook I examined offere[d] essentially the same account. It all began with the Great Depression, which destabilised many societies, including Japan. This led to militarism, which led, in turn, to the invasion of China. Japan's 'advance' (not 'imperialism') was not going well.[31]

---

27   Duke, 'The Liberalisation of Japanese Education', op. cit. (note 1), p.43.
28   Duke, 'The Liberalisation of Japanese Education', op. cit. (note 1), p.44.
29   Bosworth, *Explaining Auschwitz and Hiroshima*, op. cit. (note 4). T. Yoshida, 'History Textbooks: For Whom and For What Purpose?', *Asian Studies Newsletter*, 45 4 (2000), pp.13–14. Barnard, *Language, Ideology and Japanese History Textbooks*, op. cit. (note 6). J. Nicholls, 'Are Students Expected to Critically Engage with Textbook Perspectives of the Second World War? A Comparative and International study', *Research in Comparative and International Education*, 1 1 (2006), pp.40–55. Ogawa and Field, 'Causation, Controversy and Contrition', op. cit. (note 7).
30   Kanaya, 'Japan', op. cit. (note 10), p.487.
31   Bosworth, *Explaining Auschwitz and Hiroshima*, op. cit. (note 4), p.182.

In *Language, Ideology and Japanese History Textbooks*, Barnard describes how there is little that is new about the government control of school history textbooks. Thus,

> In Japan, all textbooks used in all schools up to the end of high school have to pass the official screening or authorization procedures of the Japanese Ministry of Education. The state lays down strict auricular guidelines and, by means of the textbook authorization system, maintains control over the content and language of textbooks. This has been the case in Japan for a hundred years, with direct state control of textbooks dating from 1903.[32]

Barnard analyses all high school textbooks currently in use across Japan. There are, Barnard tells us, '55 officially approved history textbooks currently being used in Japanese high schools. Of these books, 29 are world history textbooks and 26... are Japanese history textbooks'.[33] In addition to this,

> The 55 textbooks are published by a total of 11 publishers, with 12 of the textbooks being published by one publisher. The textbooks almost always come in B5 or A5 size, and are about 230 pages in the former [world history] and 350 pages in the latter case [Japanese history]. Textbooks are... rather alike in general design and layout. They have very beautifully designed...colourful soft covers, with several pages of coloured maps, photographs and time charts in the front and back. The body of the book is more austere and business-like, with text and other material on the pages being rather dense and serious looking. Almost every page has one or more footnotes (or marginal notes); maps, photographs and other illustrative material are in black and white.[34]

The use of school history textbooks in Japan must be seen in the context of examinations, both internal and external. 'One of the reasons for studying the textbooks' writes Barnard 'is obviously to successfully finish one's high school education and receive one's diploma. Another important reason is to memorize enough facts to pass university entrance examinations'.[35]

Internet Access

The history curriculum in Japan is driven by the examination system, and by the rote learning of information covered in textbooks.[36] Few alternative forms of classroom

---

32   Barnard, *Language, Ideology and Japanese History Textbooks*, op. cit. (note 6), p.10.
33   Barnard, *Language, Ideology and Japanese History Textbooks*, op. cit. (note 6), p.47.
34   Barnard, *Language, Ideology and Japanese History Textbooks*, op. cit. (note 6), pp.47–48.
35   Barnard, *Language, Ideology and Japanese History Textbooks*, op. cit. (note 6), p.168.
36   Barnard, *Language, Ideology and Japanese History Textbooks*, op. cit. (note 6).

media are used in history classes. The Internet is rarely used as a means to accessing information in Japanese educational contexts. According to *Japan Internet Report* author, Tim Clark, 'Most teens and young adults in Japan rarely use computers to surf the World Wide Web'.[37] The situation '[i]n the United States' writes Clark, where 'the personal computer… is the ultimate media literacy tool' should be contrasted with 'Japan, where few understand the term "media literacy"'. Clark goes on to claim, moreover, that computer illiteracy is particularly prevalent 'among the young'.[38]

The knowledge gained from attending history classes is often insufficient as preparation for the all-important entrance examinations. As identified above, students frequently attend *Juku* after school hours to 'cram more knowledge'. Project work, group activities and independent research are therefore uncommon in the Japanese history classroom. Indeed, there is little or no time to pursue such activities. As such, even though Internet access is relatively high in Japan, motivation to use and navigate the Internet to complete homework assignments is extremely low, especially in the most academic schools.[39]

It should be noted that Japanese is one of the 10 access languages for the Wikipedia free on-line encyclopaedia (http://www.wikipedia.org). At 158,000 the number of entries in Japanese is relatively low, however, when considered in relation to the size of Japan's population (125 million). The German-speaking population of the world is smaller than the Japanese, yet the number of encyclopaedia entries in German is 320,000. Unlike Germany, the number of Japanese secondary school students who are able to speak English competently as a second language is low. Access to on-line information – most of which is in English – is therefore likely to be correspondingly low.

Mass Media (other than the Internet)

With the end of the Cold War and the death of the Showa emperor in 1989, the media in Japan played an important role with regard to 'opening up' over the issue of history and the Imperial past, 'in the 1990s' write Hein and Selden,

37   T. Clark, 'Japan's Generation of Computer Refuseniks'. [Internet] *Japan Media Review*. Available from <http://www.iapanmediareview.com/iapan/wireless/1047257047.php> [Accessed 2nd December 2005], p.1.

38   Clark, 'Japan's Generation of Computer Refuseniks', op. cit. (note 37), p.3.

39   Clark, 'Japan's Generation of Computer Refuseniks', op. cit. (note 37). One quite strongly suspects that the situation being described here has moved on over the subsequent decade. BC

Japan began discussing the war far more frankly than in earlier decades. There was wide media coverage of such Asian grievances as the military comfort women, the Nanjing massacre, Chinese and Korean slave labor, and the grisly experiments of biowar Unit 731.[40]

Yet perspectives on Japan's wartime role would be mixed in the mass media. In fact, by the late 1990s there would be a strong counter-reaction to 'opening up', many factions of the media supporting ultra-conservative agendas. The best-selling books of the nationalist academic Fujioka Nobukatsu, *History Not Taught in Textbooks*, was 'serialized in the business daily Sankei *shinbun*,' that consequently 'sold well'.[41] In addition '[p]opular magazines' would 'regularly feature' Fujioka's analysis.[42]

The Japanese press is free in the sense that it reflects a wide range of viewpoints, from the liberal Asahi Shinbun through to the more centrist Mainichi Shinbun to the conservative Sankai Shinbun. Interestingly, the newspaper consumption rate in Japan is one of the highest in the world.[43] In terms of television there are a range of channels available on the Japanese network. The Japan Broadcasting Corporation (the NHK) provides public television that operates along lines very similar to the BBC in Britain. Yet as Fukuyama points out,

Despite maintaining its claim of independence from public and commercial organizations, the fact that the Diet must approve NHK's budget and management appointees inevitably draws criticism of a pro-government bias. Proving the legitimacy of such concerns, an NHK producer admitted to altering one of a four-part documentary series that aired in 2001 after two Liberal Democratic Party members ordered the producer to incorporate positive viewpoints of the government to balance the coverage on a highly sensitive war-related topic.[44]

There are several commercial TV channels in Japan that compete with each other and with the NHK. Many of 'these broadcasting companies operate…nationally as well as internationally, and many… are affiliates of radio broadcasting companies,

---

40   Hein and Selden (eds.) *Censoring History,* op. cit. (note 1), pp.24–25.

41   Hein and Selden (eds.) *Censoring History:* op. cit. (note 1), p.25.

42   G. McCormack, 'The Japanese Movement to "Correct" History', in Hein and Selden (eds.) *Censoring History,* op. cit. (note 1), p.57.

43   H. H. Lichtenberg, 'Japan's 6 Major Daily Newspapers'. [Internet] *Japan Media Review.* Available at: <http://www.japanniediareview.com/japan/wiki/Shimbunwiki> [Accessed November–December 2005].

44   M. Fukayama, 'Japan's 6 Premier Television Broadcasters'. [Internet] *Japan Media Review.* Available from: <http://www.japanmediareview.com/iapan/wiki/tvwiki/> [Accessed December 2005].

newspapers and professional sports teams'. Fuji TV is affiliated with the conservative Sankei Shinbun while the more liberal TV Asahi Corporation was 'launched as a provider of educational programming'.[45]

It is difficult to ascertain the exact influence of the mass media on the constitution of syllabus topics in history education in Japan. Where in England or Sweden television programmes, newspaper and magazine articles, and various forms of on-line media may be explicitly used as sources for in-class analysis and homework this is far less the case in Japan.[46] Nevertheless, the media play an important role in scrutinising what is taught in schools by taking either a liberal or conservative position on Japan's relationship to Asia, on the events of World War II, and on the content of school history textbooks.[47] In the 'Table of Global Press Freedom Rankings' for 2005 provided by the Freedom House think-tank, Japan is ranked 37, below Sweden and the United Kingdom (http://www.freedomhouse. org/research/pressurvey.htm).

Some commentators suggest that high school students in Japan may actually learn more about the Second World War outside of school than they do in history classes. According to Barnard '[i]f young Japanese are to grow up with a more open minded view of the modern history of their own country, this is something… they are unlikely to learn… at school'.[48] In this sense, national and international media may play an important role.

Teacher/Student Role

Although history classes in Japan are overwhelmingly teacher-centred, the teacher's role is relatively narrow. The teacher must teach from the history textbook. To teach well is to teach the textbook in an interesting and 'memorable' way.[49] History classes often take the form of 'chalk and talk' lectures to support textbook information. In my own three-year work experience in Japanese schools, teachers would almost invariably teach from the front of the class, textbook held in hand,

---

45   Fukayama, 'Japan's 6 Premier Television Broadcasters', op. cit. (note 44).

46   Barnard, *Language, Ideology and Japanese History Textbooks*, op. cit. (note 6).

47   Fukayama, 'Japan's 6 Premier Television Broadcasters', op. cit. (note 44).

48   Barnard, *Language, Ideology and Japanese History Textbooks*, op. cit. (note 6), p.172.

49   Nicholls, 'Are Students Expected to Critically Engage with Textbook Perspectives of the Second World War?', op. cit. (note 29).

chalk in the other.[50] Sitting at individual desks, students would listen to the teacher, copying down what is said as well as what is written on the board.

Although the student's role is passive, the teacher's role, although dominant in the class, is in general far from active. Classes are driven to such an enormous extent by the dictates of the all-important entrance examinations, and by the need to 'get through' the textbook, that the teacher's level of relative-autonomy in relation to these factors is low. Lesson design is determined by the content of the textbook and only very little by the teacher's concept or perception of the topic being taught.[51] According to Barnard,

> There are certainly numbers of teachers who attempt to develop more interesting and critical approaches to history education by, for example, introducing supplementary materials in the classroom. But given the pressures of covering the curriculum in the assigned time and the need to prepare for entrance examinations, this is not an easy task.[52]

As mentioned above, Japanese school students of history require so-called 'factual information', rather than perspectives, to pass exams. History teachers, many of whom are members of the radical JTU, are compelled, therefore, to yield to the authority of the history textbook and to the demands of the entrance examinations. Larsson, Booth and Mathews engage directly with the question of how Japanese students 'experience... history teaching methods in the classroom'.[53]

First, the authors note a tendency in Japanese culture to see history as a linear body of knowledge: 'the history' as opposed to 'a history'.[54] Where 'students and history teachers [in England] see history as a debatable story of the past created from a range of sources of historical evidence' history in Japan is 'a subject to be learned by heart'.[55] Second, the authors conclude that fundamental measures need to be taken if Japanese history education is to become less about learning by rote and more about critical thinking. Thus:

---

50   Nicholls, 'Are Students Expected to Critically Engage with Textbook Perspectives of the Second World War?', op. cit. (note 29).

51   Nicholls, 'Are Students Expected to Critically Engage with Textbook Perspectives of the Second World War?', op. cit. (note 29).

52   Barnard, *Language, Ideology and Japanese History Textbooks*, op. cit. (note 6), pp.171–172.

53   Y. Larsson, M. Booth, and R. Mathews, 'Attitudes to the Teaching of History and the Use of Creative Skills in Japan and England: a Comparative Study', *Compare*, 28 3, 1998, pp.305–314, in particular p.308.

54   Larsson et al, 'Attitudes to the Teaching of History', op. cit. (note 53), p.307.

55   Larsson et al, 'Attitudes to the Teaching of History', op. cit. (note 53), p.310.

If the Japanese seriously wish to reform the teaching and learning of history in their schools, then attitudes and assessment procedures need to alter. That Japanese junior high school students have the capacity to use source material is beyond doubt... Until, however, there is a change of heart about the nature and assessment of history and the critical role that empathy and the creative although critical reconstruction of the past can play, no real progress will be made. Japanese history teaching will remain obsessed with the recall of factual knowledge centred on a mostly male dominated past.[56]

Censorship

It is already clear from the above discussions that the Ministry of Education tightly censors and controls history education in Japan. Students need to pass examinations. Examinations are written based around the content published in school history textbooks. History textbooks are closely scrutinised by authorities at the Ministry of Education before they become available on the market. This is a system involving the strict censorship of knowledge.

In his historical overview, Yamazumi points out how this was not always the case. Prior to 1880, 'the government ... left their [i.e. textbooks] preparation and publication in the hands of private publishers'.[57] Strong nationalist trends within the government after 1880 would lead, however, to a series of 'assaults' on textbook content by the government.

Where Barnard pinpoints 1903 as the starting point of 'full-state control', Yamazumi describes the decisive first wave of government interventions beginning in 1880. Control went hand in hand with the nationalist backlash against the teaching of certain forms of history. In 1880, '[t]he teaching of world history, with which educators had attempted to broaden children's horizons and diffuse modern ideas was banned'. Rather than familiarising students 'with such concepts as freedom, equality, humanism and independence', history education was reduced to Japanese history alone, 'the sole purpose of teaching history... to foster reverence for the emperor'.[58] By the April of 1903 'the preparation and publication of

---

56   Larsson et al, 'Attitudes to the Teaching of History, op. cit. (note 53), p.313.

57   M. Yamazumi, 'State Control and the Evolution of Ultranationalistic Textbooks' in J. Shields (ed.) *Japanese Schooling: Patterns of Socialization, Equality and Political Control* (Pennsylvania, Pennsylvania State University Press, 1989), p.234.

58   Yamazumi, 'State Control and the Evolution of Ultranationalistic Textbooks', op. cit. (note 57), p.234.

textbooks' was firmly in the hands of the State, a situation that remained until the end of the Second World War.[59] The early years of the U.S. Occupation period saw a complete shift in the level of state control due to 'the insistence of the Occupation forces' and the push for 'democratic reform from indigenous groups kept silent during the war'. Textbooks containing messages condoning militarism, nationalism, and imperialism were outlawed and retrieved from circulation and 'the teaching of ethics, Japanese history and geography' were forbidden.[60] The 'new guiding principles for education' were underpinned by a fundamentally liberal and democratic ethos, and a 'resolve… to realize through education the ideals of the [new] Constitution: the sovereignty of the people, the basic rights of the individual and the renunciation of war'.[61] Textbooks became free of charge from 1947, to be selected freely by teachers. With the enactment of the 1947 School Education Law the 'preparation and publication of textbooks' was to be handed back 'to private hands, abolishing after more than forty years the state-run system'.[62]

But there has been a long and drawn-out conservative counter-reaction since the last years of the US occupation.[63] Over the years, the liberal reforms have been dismantled, replaced with, among other things, increasingly strict levels of central government censorial control.[64] The 'official censorship' of Japanese history education has been a source of great controversy, particularly with regard to depictions of the 1931–1945 period. Asian neighbours have long derided the omission of important details in the description of Japan's Imperial campaign in the Pacific.[65] Radical forces within Japan have also been extremely critical.[66] Ienaga

---

59 Yamazumi, 'State Control and the Evolution of Ultranationalistic Textbooks', op. cit. (note 57), pp.235–236.
60 Yamazumi, 'State Control and the Evolution of Ultranationalistic Textbooks', op. cit. (note 57), p.237.
61 Yamazumi, 'State Control and the Evolution of Ultranationalistic Textbooks', op. cit. (note 57), p.237.
62 Yamazumi, 'State Control and the Evolution of Ultranationalistic Textbooks', op. cit. (note 57), p.238.
63 Horio, *Educational Thought and Ideology in Modern Japan*, op. cit. (note 1). Tsuchimochi, *Education Reform in Postwar Japan*, op. cit. (note 1).
64 Yamazumi, 'State Control and the Evolution of Ultranationalistic Textbooks', op. cit. (note 57), pp.239–240.
65 Bosworth, *Explaining Auschwitz and Hiroshima*, op. cit. (note 4).
66 L. Olson, 'Takeuchi Yoshimi and the Vision of a Protest Society in Japan', *Journal of Japanese Studies*, 1 2, 1981, pp.319–348. T. Horio, 'Towards Reform in Japanese Education: a Critique of Privatisation and Proposals for the Re-Creation of Public Education', *Comparative Education*, 22 1, 1986, pp.21–36. Horio, *Educational Thought*

Saburo's court battles with the Japanese government, from the late 1960s through to the 1990s, are one of the most enduring testimonies to this. Yet as Hein and Selden point out, Ienaga is not alone:

> Ienaga Saburo and his three decades of court challenges to Ministry of Education censorship is only the most famous example. Other scholars have painstakingly collected evidence of wartime Japanese crimes, creating a tidal wave of documentation to sweep away claims that Chinese, Koreans, Filipinos, and other victims were inventing tales of Japanese brutality.[67]

Since the mid-1990s, however, there has been a strong ultra-conservative backlash against scholars like Ienaga. This has led to the publication and adoption of several highly conservative textbooks, as well as indignation from neighbouring countries, in particular China and Korea.[68] Barnard suggests that history textbooks in Japan 'encode an ideology of irresponsibility and face-protection'.[69] Rigid censorship and control are fundamental expressions of this process in action.

> The control of the curriculum, including the system of textbook authorization, by the Ministry of Education is a prime example of the way in which the modern Japanese state protects its face. If anyone could write a textbook and, by putting it on the market, make it available to schools, this would infringe on the jealously guarded preserve of the Ministry of Education.[70]

Contemporary Politics and Ideology

In 1993 the LDP suffered an unprecedented election defeat, the conservatives replaced by a Non-LDP coalition government, and losing power for the first time since the 1950s.[71] This led to the fullest official apology to neighbouring Asian

---

and Ideology in Modern Japan, op. cit. (note 1). Y. Noguchi and H. Inokuchi, 'Japanese Education, Nationalism, and Ienaga Subaro's Textbook Lawsuits', in Hein and Selden (eds.) *Censoring History*, op. cit. (note 1).

67 Hein and M. Selden (eds.) *Censoring History*, op. cit. (note 1), p.24.
68 Barnard, *Language, Ideology and Japanese History Textbooks*, op. cit. (note 6). McCormack, 'The Japanese Movement to "Correct" History', op. cit. (note 42). A. Gerow, 'Consuming Asia, Consuming Japan: The New Neonationalist Revisionism in Japan' in Hein and Selden (eds.) *Censoring History* op. cit. (note 1).
69 Barnard, *Language, Ideology and Japanese History Textbooks*, op. cit. (note 6), p.154.
70 Barnard, *Language, Ideology and Japanese History Textbooks*, op. cit. (note 6), p.158.
71 G. W. Noble, 'Japan in 1993: Humpty Dumpty had a Great Fall', *Asian Survey*, 34 1, 1994, pp.19–29.

countries for atrocities committed during the Second World War.[72] Elected in July 1993, the reformist leader of the 'seven-party rainbow coalition' former prefectural governor 'Hosokawa Morihiro' would state openly that the World War had been a 'war of aggression, a mistaken war'.[73]

During this period the official position on the Second World War would be questioned more openly and critically than ever before. Yet the Hosokawa administration would be short lived, lasting a total of 'nine months' and 'ending with his resignation'.[74] A new coalition administration, this time led by Japan's first Socialist Prime Minister, Murayama Tomiichi, would come to replace it. Where Hosokawa had made an official apology his coalition had not passed a resolution. This would change with Murayama. The 'Resolution to Renew the Determination for Peace on the Basis of Lessons Learned from History' would be adopted on the 9th June 1995.[75] It would be 'the first of its kind that explicitly expressed the Japanese Parliament's view of Japan's actions before and during World War Two' and would include 'such words as "colonial rule" and "acts of aggression"'.[76]

Yet by 1996 this brief period of political and ideological reformism would come to a close, as the new-year would see the re-election of the LDP under the leadership of Hashimoto Ryutaro.[77] The coalition governments were too fragile to last or to convince the electorate. The left's brief moment in power did nothing for their future prospects. By the late 1990s they came to appear as a non-option. The right would rule as before but without a credible opposition.

With the end of the Cold War and the economic resurgence of the United States, Japan's relationship to the world has changed. The climate has proved conducive to right wing ideology, populist reassessments of history and, in particular, revisionist positions on the Second World War.[78] By the late 1990s, the largely

---

72   P. C. Jain, 'A New Political Era in Japan: the 1993 Election', *Asian Survey*, 33 11, 1993, pp.1071–1082, in particular p.1071.

73   McCormack, 'The Japanese Movement to "Correct" History', op. cit. (note 42), p.57.

74   M. Blaker, 'Japan in 1994: Out with the Old, in with the New?' *Asian Survey*, 35 1, 1995, pp.1–12, in particular p.2.

75   M. Blaker, 'Japan in 1995: A Year of Natural and Other Disasters', *Asian Survey*, 361, pp.41–52.

76   R. Mukae, 'Japan's Diet Resolution on World War Two: Keeping History at Bay', *Asian Survey*, 36 10, 1996, pp.1011–1030, in particular p.1011.

77   H. Fukui and S. N. Fukai, 'Japan in 1996: Between Hope and Uncertainty', *Asian Survey*, 37 1, 1997, pp.20–28.

78   Ogawa and Field, 'Causation, Controversy and Contrition', op. cit. (note 7), p.54.

conservative Japanese population would be 'depressed' in the wake of economic crises, corruption scandals, and a daily media dosage of Japanese atrocities during World War II, and the Japanese government would pick up on the popular sentiments of the time. Forms of nationalism, consensual and harmonising, came to be welcomed. The government would apply increasing censorship pressures on school textbook publishers and, in spite of protests from the lamenting and now weakened left, this would be accepted without protest.[79]

'In Japan' write Ogawa and Field 'the legacy of World War II seems to continue as a part of everyday reality, directly or indirectly influencing national goals and foreign policies'.[80] Moreover, from the late 1990s and into the 2000s, a more nationalist discourse and ideology has become the standard. Adjustments made by the Ministry of Education to the national course of study in 1998 would include the promotion of 'love of nation' and 'Japanese awareness' in history education. Perhaps more significantly, the raising of the flag and the singing of the national anthem would become 'compulsory' at school ceremonies from the spring of 1999. This would cause tensions across the country but especially in Hiroshima Prefecture. According to Ogawa and Field:

> Perhaps most indicative of a new move toward nationalism in Japan is the government's success at developing and passing a bill concerning the national flag and anthem. The flag, Hinomaru, and song, Kimigayo, were legally designated as the national flag and national anthem in 1999. In response to the law, the Ministry of Education ordered that all schools should fly Hinomaru and perform Kimigayo in school ceremonies. Both have been criticised as symbols of Japanese aggression during World War II and as glorifying the Emperor and have been controversial for over 60 years. Especially vocal in objecting to the ruling were a wide range of Japanese, including leftist politicians, teachers, intellectuals, and every day citizens. Teachers unions in Hiroshima protested loudly, seemingly contributing to the controversial suicide of a high school principal in the prefecture, who was distraught over yielding to pressure from the Board of Education to include Hinomaru and Kimigayo at commencement, the day before graduation, even though teachers were strongly opposed.[81]

---

79   Ogawa and Field, 'Causation, Controversy and Contrition', op. cit. (note 7), pp.54–56.

80   Ogawa and Field, 'Causation, Controversy and Contrition', op. cit. (note 7), p.54.

81   Ogawa and Field, 'Causation, Controversy and Contrition', op. cit. (note 7), pp.55–56.

Popular nationalism has risen, pandered to by politicians, while nationalist intellectuals have fanned the flames. Likewise, Japanese politics and history education has been dominated by the uncertainties of the post-Cold War world.

Historiography

Any researcher comparing a given syllabus topic such as the Second World War will need to focus on the historiography of the topic across contexts. How have 'societies which experienced the great moral crisis of the "long Second World War" historicised and "explained" that experience'?[82] What perspectives have prevailed over time?

History writing on Japan's role during World War II has followed a winding path since 1945. In the 1950s and 1960s the so-called 'modernist' historian, Maruyama Masao, would rise to prominence with 'his celebrated description of Japanese fascism as "dwarfish"'.[83] According to Barshay,

> For postwar modernists such as Maruyama (b. 1914), the entire process leading up to Japan's launching of a total war had already proved the bankruptcy of the "emperor system" (*tennosei*); defeat simply put the period to a demonstrably irrational political and social arrangement. It would be the first – and indispensable – task of intellectuals to subject past institutions and values to scrutiny, destroying those that appeared to be obstacles to democracy.[84]

Other post-war figures engaged with Japan's wartime role. Why had ultra-nationalism occurred? How could it have been avoided? Yoshimoto Takaaki, the poet and polemicist started 'from the fact of total national defeat in 1945' and was 'concerned with what went wrong' and with the '"distortions" and "contradictions"'... [that]... afflicted Japanese history'.[85] Sinologist, Takeuchi Yoshima, would be strongly critical both of Japan's wartime role, and its servility to Western thought and the post-war United States. According 'to Takeuchi', writes Olson

> the past was totally unresolved. The rain of war had settled nothing but had left great pools of guilt all over the landscape, guilt about defeat, about the bankrupt Japanese

---

82   Bosworth, *Explaining Auschwitz and Hiroshima*, op. cit. (note 4), p.30.

83   A. E. Barshay, 'Imagining Democracy in Postwar Japan: Reflections on Maruyama Masao and Modernism', *Journal of Japanese Studies*, 18 2, 1992, pp.365–406, in particular p.390.

84   Barshay, 'Imagining Democracy in Postwar Japan', op. cit. (note 83), p.367.

85   L. Olson, 'Intellectuals and "The People"; On Yoshimoto Takaaki', *Journal of Japanese Studies*, 4 2, 1978, pp.327–357, in particular p.328.

"destiny," guilt about a China misused and little understood. Whatever the merits of the Allied Occupation... Japanese modernization had failed once and for all and should have no second chance. Until the past had been atoned for and Japanese mistakes in China admitted, no post-war leaders could be trusted.[86]

But with no change in the political scene during the post-war years, intellectuals were denied an outlet or platform from which to realise at least part of this agenda. They were preaching to the converted, writing mainly for themselves. There would be no equivalent to Germany's social democrats in the late 1960s and early 1970s; no Willy Brandt figure to bring about a change in the official perspective on the past.[87] More significantly, the Japanese people appeared content with the conservative political atmosphere of the period. As Olson points out, 'most Japanese accepted the necessity for a more conservative political future in close alliance with the United States. Most people deeply wanted to forget the war and to concentrate the blame for defeat on the military'.[88]

Yet by the 1980s Asian neighbours became increasingly vocal, deriding Japan's official line on the past. The JTU sided with the Chinese and the Koreans. And radical forces in the academy continued to critique the LDP and the ministries as well as the official line on World War II.[89] As stated above, Ienaga Saburo's famous court battles with the Japanese government, from the 1960s to the 1990s, are one of the most enduring testimonies to this. One of a group of intellectual 'watchdogs for the whole community', Ienaga was by training an 'historian and political ideologist'.[90] Moreover, to reiterate, Ienaga was not alone, 'his three decades of court challenges to Ministry of Education censorship... only the most famous example'.[91] But in the rising, advancing and prospering Japan of the sixties, seventies and eighties, the position of prominent radicals, their critique of the conservative post-war thesis on the Second World War, 'remained peripheral', Japan's most eminent historians ultimately 'confined in a gilded and permanent opposition'.[92]

---

86 L. Olson, 'Takeuchi Yoshimi and the Vision of a Protest Society in Japan', *Journal of Japanese Studies*, 1 2, 1981, pp.319–348, in particular pp.329–330.

87 Bosworth, *Explaining Auschwitz and Hiroshima*, op. cit. (note 4), p.184.

88 Olson, 'Takeuchi Yoshimi and the Vision of a Protest Society in Japan', op. cit. (note 86), p.329.

89 Horio, *Educational Thought and Ideology in Modern Japan*, op. cit. (note 1). S. Tsurumi, *An Intellectual History of Wartime Japan 1931–1945* (London, KPI, 1986).

90 J. Caiger, 'Ienaga Saburo and the First Postwar Japanese History Textbook', *Modern Asian Studies*, 3 1, 1969, pp.1–16, in particular p.1.

91 Hein and Selden (eds.) *Censoring History*, op. cit. (note 1), p.24.

92 Bosworth, *Explaining Auschwitz and Hiroshima*, op. cit. (note 4), p.189 and p.185.

As outlined in the previous section, the 1990s would be marked by political and economic uncertainty in Japan. Moreover, the nationalist reaction to political reformism would be reflected in the academy. Towards the end of the 1990s, the work of nationalist academic, Nobokatsu Fujioka, would begin to make headway. Fujioka had been educated in Japan and the United States and would be critical of the pacifism espoused by the political and intellectual left. Japan should be proud of its history, argued Fujioka, not least its role during the Second World War, since it was the Japanese Imperial Army that liberated Asia from Western domination. Together with colleagues Kanji Nishio and Ikuhiko Hata, Fujioka would form the 'Association for the Advancement of a Liberalist View of History' in 1996. This represented a revisionist response to the leftist political and intellectual agendas of the preceding years. Likewise, with other nationalist scholars, Fujioka would go on to form the widely supported 'Japanese Society for History Textbook Reform', dedicated to the development of a so-called positive view of Japan, its society, history and culture. This society would aim to publish a decidedly nationalist textbook, free from lamentations concerning the nations wartime past.[93] This nationalist 'history' proved to be exceptionally popular. Four books by members of Fujioka's group, around the collective theme of 'History not taught in Textbooks' would be published in 1997, becoming nationwide best sellers. The popularity of Fujioka and his followers has continued into the 2000s.

The dynamic relationship between historiography and school history is of crucial importance here. McCormack draws attention to the work of Japanese historian Nakamura Masanori, who argues that the Fujioka phenomenon has arisen as a result of 'the desire for a new and positive Japanese identity... especially on the part of the present youth who have been brought up in ignorance of history'.[94] Yet Fujioka's writings are not taught in schools. This being said, in recent years a series of increasingly right-wing textbooks, influenced by Fujioka, have been authored and published. Although these have been adopted by only a handful of municipalities, there can be no doubt that 'the Japanese system... has allowed the (ultra)nationalists to advance their agenda'.[95] To return to Ogawa and Field,

> Historical Revisionism, characterised by Fujioka and other right-wing intellectuals, is but one of the reactionary movements in post-Cold War history education seeking to dominate Japan's consciousness and eventually its school curriculum.[96]

---

93 Ogawa and Field, 'Causation, Controversy and Contrition', op. cit. (note 7).
94 McCormack, 'The Japanese Movement to "correct" History', op. cit. (note 42), p.67.
95 Noguchi and Inokuchi, 'Japanese Education, Nationalism, and Ienaga Subaro's Textbook Lawsuits', op. cit. (note 66), p.121.
96 Ogawa and Field, 'Causation, Controversy and Contrition', op. cit. (note 7), pp.54–55.

7.3 Sweden

Background and Tradition

Pioneering comprehensive schooling during the 1960s the so-called 'Swedish Model' attracted the attention of educationists and educational policy makers from around the world.[97] Along with health, public housing and social security, education formed an integral pillar of Sweden's welfare state, generously funded through taxation and underpinned by a strong commitment to equity. Highly centralised yet comparatively transparent, Sweden offered a socialist model that worked, expensive, yes, but delivering high standards of education acceptable to all.[98]

The contemporary educational scene in Sweden must be understood against the socio-economic and political events and changes of the 1990s, a decade of unprecedented national doubt and self-questioning. Up to the late 1980s Sweden was, along with France, the most centralised state in Western Europe. This was reversed through the 1990s. Along with other public services, education would be radically decentralised. And the history curriculum came to be re-interpreted and re-packaged. With the end of the Cold War, the politics, geography, and historical interpretation of the contemporary world would be rapidly transformed, including Sweden's perception of its place in that world. This would have a direct impact on guidelines for history education.[99]

From the ages of 6 or 7 to 16 the vast majority of children in Sweden will study history at a single state school, the nine-year *grundskola*, with only a small percentage attending private schools. The *grundskola* are fully comprehensive and co-educational. Importantly, elementary and secondary levels of schooling are integrated into the single institution. During the entire 9-year programme, 885 hours will be spent studying social science subjects – history, geography

---

97 S. Ball and S. Larson, 'Education, Politics and Society in Sweden: an Introduction', in S. Ball and S. Larson (eds.) *The Struggle for Democratic Education, Equality and Participation in Sweden* (New York, Palmer Press, 1989).

98 J. Pontusson, 'Sweden: After the Golden Age', in P. Anderson and P. Camiller (eds.) *Mapping the West European Left* (New York, Verso, 1994). S. Marklund, 'Sweden', in N. Postlethwaite (ed.) *International Encyclopaedia of National Systems of Education* (Oxford, Pergamon, 1995). S. Salin and C. Waterman, 'Sweden', in C. Brock and W. Tulusiewicz (eds.) *Education in a Single Europe* (London, Routledge, 2000).

99 A. MacGregor-Thunell, *Teaching History in Sweden, 2003* [Internet]. Available from: <http://www.schoolhistory.co.uk/forum/index.php?showtopic=2218> [Accessed December 2005].

and religious knowledge. This can be compared with 1490 hours for the study of Swedish, 480 hours for the study of English and 900 hours for the study of mathematics.[100]

After attending the compulsory *grundskola* the majority of students go on to attend the non-compulsory *gymnasieskola* where they attend courses for a further three years. Upper secondary education is organised into 'programmes' of which there are 17 in total, and from which students must choose one. The 'social science programme', allows specialisation in history.[101] Yet all upper secondary students will study some '20th Century History' in the compulsory social studies unit 'historical events and personalities of the 20th century'.[102]

Prescribed Curriculum

In Sweden there is no prescriptive curriculum for history, only 'very loose' curriculum guidelines. Salin and Waterman provide an overview of recent developments, both at the compulsory and post-compulsory levels.[103] The delivery of subjects in the 'official curriculum' is characterised by its radically decentralised nature. Thus, the history curriculum at the *grundskola* is based on overarching criteria. These fall under (1) the transmission of 'basic values', (2) 'the tasks of the school', and (3) 'goals and guidelines' to be obtained at the end of the fifth and the ninth years. Essentially, the curriculum guidelines 'do not' prescribe the way that history 'teaching should be planned and organised... nor... its content or teaching methods. This is left entirely to the professionals in the schools – the head teachers and teachers'.[104] There have been decentralised elements in Swedish education since the early 1960s. However, the implementation of reforms through the 1990s gave rise to a much more highly decentralised structure in which teachers, schools, students and their parents, as well as local authorities would receive a much greater say in decisions concerning the history curriculum.[105] Salin and Waterman point out that while students in Sweden have the right to receive a minimum number of hours across the main subject areas, the way that the subjects are taught and subdivided is now an almost entirely local matter.

---

100 Salin and Waterman, 'Sweden', op. cit. (note 98), p.373.
101 Salin and Waterman, 'Sweden', op. cit. (note 98), p.375.
102 MacGregor-Thunell, *Teaching History in Sweden,* op. cit. (note 99), p.1.
103 Salin and Waterman, 'Sweden', op. cit. (note 98).
104 Salin and Waterman, 'Sweden', op. cit. (note 98), p.350.
105 S Salin and Waterman, 'Sweden', op. cit. (note 98), p.356.

Recent curriculum reforms in Sweden express an invigorated concern with identity issues in history education. The minimum number of hours required for the study of 'local issues' has increased since the 1990s. In addition, an international perspective is now considered an essential feature of the Swedish history curriculum. Salin and Waterman quote from the introductory sections of the official curriculum published by the Swedish Ministry of Education:

> An international perspective... is important for making it possible to see one's own reality in a global context, for creating international cohesion and preparing pupils for a society with more and closer contacts with cross national and cultural borders.

The combination of perspectives, local, national, regional and global, should be combined, therefore, to enable every student to develop a positive sense of their place in the world and of their relation to others. Thus:

> A secure identity and consciousness of one's own cultural heritage strengthens the ability to understand and empathise with others and their value systems. The school shall contribute to people developing an identity which can be related to and encompass not just Swedish values but also those that are Nordic, European and global.[106]

Since the official curriculum provides only loose guidelines, teachers of history 'have considerable freedom to decide... the content of their teaching'.[107] In other words, if the stipulated requirements can be covered through the teaching of a single theme or topic then teachers are free to teach a single theme or topic. This is the case for the lower secondary and the upper secondary school. According to Anders MacGregor-Thunell, '[t]here is no formal hindrance for a teacher to focus on one aspect of history... feminism, Gustaphus Adolphus etc... as long as the teacher has made the pupil familiar with the "fundamental features of historical development"'.[108]

Examinations and Assessment

Marklund describes the extremely liberal examination arrangements that existed in Sweden's 'progressive' heyday:

> There are no final examinations in the compulsory comprehensive school (*grundskold*) and the integrated upper-secondary school (*gymnasieskold*). In the compulsory

---

106   Salin and Waterman, 'Sweden', op. cit. (note 98), p.355.
107   Salin and Waterman, 'Sweden', op. cit. (note 98), p.356.
108   MacGregor-Thunell, *Teaching History in Sweden,* op. cit. (note 99), p.1.

school the pass-fail concept was abolished. With few exceptions all students move to the next grade at the end of the year.[109]

With the sweeping reforms of the 1990s this situation changed. Again it is useful to turn to the work of Salin and Waterman. While the National Agency for Education (the mediating body between central government and the municipalities) sets national tests in Swedish, English and mathematics for students in their final year of compulsory education (year 9), local schools are encouraged to examine students in all other disciplines, including history.[110] Essentially, outside of Swedish, English and mathematics, a final test score is not necessary in order to graduate from compulsory school. In history, internal assessment suffices.

Students receive either a pass, credit or distinction grade for history on exiting compulsory education. In order to proceed to the post-compulsory secondary school, students must obtain at least a pass mark in Swedish, English and mathematics, as well as showing an aptitude in subjects relating to the upper-secondary programme they plan to follow.[111]

Classroom Media

Owing to the highly decentralised organisation of school history education in Sweden, the place of the school history textbook in classes – as a learning and teaching tool – is difficult to pin down. If teachers wish to use the textbook as the sole source of information in classes they can, as long as the broad goals outlined in the official curriculum are covered. At the same time, not to use school textbooks during classes is equally permissible.

The Swedish textbook market is historically liberal. However, some commentators suggest that textbook publishing is an unprofitable business in Sweden, increasingly in need of government support. According to MacGregor-Thunell, 'publishing a textbook in Swedish is bound to not be … profitable'. The overall message is that demand for textbooks is declining. '[W]e can see' writes MacGregor-Thunell 'a diminishing market for … writers'.[112] This scenario can be positioned against the development of other types of media – particularly electronic media. Yet it remains extremely difficult to identify national patterns. The decentralisation process

---

109 Marklund, 'Sweden', op. cit. (note 98), p.945.
110 Salin and Waterman, 'Sweden', op. cit. (note 98), p.357.
111 Salin and Waterman, 'Sweden', op. cit. (note 98), p.357.
112 MacGregor-Thunell, *Teaching History in Sweden,* op. cit. (note 99), p.1.

in Sweden witnessed the movement of educational decision making from central government to local municipal bodies, which included the control of educational funding. This had enormous effects in terms of relative equity. In short, the use of information technology in schools is likely to be higher in wealthy urban municipalities than in rural areas where funds are somewhat more limited. Nevertheless, as we shall soon see, the Internet and some electronic media sources appear to be playing an ever-more prominent role in history education across Sweden.[113]

Internet Access

Internet access is higher in Sweden than in almost all other countries. With Sweden's high average standard of living combined with relatively high levels of equity, most families residing in Sweden will possess a computer and be online. In many ways the move to the Internet since the 1990s mirrors the pioneering role Sweden has played in the development of other communication networks, mobile phone technologies for example. Computer literacy in Sweden has long been high relative to other countries.[114]

According to Groth, '[b]etween 1994 and 1998 the use of information technology, especially [the] Internet... rocketed in Swedish K-12 schools'.[115] At this time, the development of The Swedish Schoolnet, a national effort to encourage schools to take advantage of the Internet as a pedagogical tool' in all subjects including history was introduced to foster and support the expansion. Importantly, rather than simply supplying schools with e-learning hardware and software packages for history, the initiative emphasised ways to use the Internet and on-line resources. According to Groth,

> [t]he work is characterised' by a "content driven" approach, i.e., the main role of the project is to increase the amount of... useful content on the Internet and thereby, indirectly, stimulate the use of new tools and media. This is opposed to a "material" approach characterized by government subsidies for hardware, software and Internet access and/ or direct government involvement as an Internet service provider for the educational sector. The work has been most successful. Today a majority of ... Swedish schools regularly use the Internet for communication and to find/or publish information.[116]

---

113   J. Groth, 'Physical or Virtual Networks? Connecting Swedish Schools to the Internet', paper presented at the 1998 Internet Summit, Geneva Switzerland 21st–24th July 1998.
114   Groth, 'Physical or Virtual Networks?', op. cit. (note 113).
115   Groth, 'Physical or Virtual Networks?', op. cit. (note 113).
116   Groth, 'Physical or Virtual Networks?', op. cit. (note 113).

This initiative, supported by the Swedish National Agency for Education, is still going strong, providing Internet links, connections to other schools, sites for multilingual learning, and online data sources for students and teachers of history to interact with. 'Check the Source' constitutes a central 'theme site', accessible from the Schoolnet web page. Here history students are provided with a 'guide for research work', 'tools for examining source material' and a 'Quality Information Checklist' (http://www.skolutveckling.se/skolnet/english/index.html). A downloadable power point presentation on 'Web Evaluation' by Annette Holmqvist is also provided.[117]

It is interesting to note that Swedish is one of the 10 access languages for the Wikipedia free on-line encyclopaedia (http://www.wikipedia.org). The number of entries in Swedish (approximately 115,000) is roughly the same as for those in Italian (approximately 119,000), even though the population of Sweden is over six times smaller than the population of Italy. Likewise, Sweden has more entries than either The Netherlands (approximately 106,000) or Spain (approximately 74,000), both countries that have larger populations than Sweden. Like the other Nordic societies, the number of Swedish secondary school students who are able to speak English as a second language is 'very high' by international standards. Again, this gives young Swedes the chance to access online information – most of which is in English – in a most unprecedented way. Search for 'Andra varldskriget' ('the Second World War' in Swedish) using Google and 658,000 sites are listed.

Mass Media (other than the Internet)

Up until the early 1980s there were only two state TV channels in Sweden. This meant lots of documentaries on social and historical themes as well as drama, no game shows or advertising. From the 1980s this began to change. Now viewers can choose from both public and private television networks. Printed media has a long, liberal and independent history in Sweden, covering a variety of ideological perspectives. In the Freedom House rankings for 'freedom of the press' in 2005, Sweden shared the world's number-one spot with Finland and Iceland (http://www.freedomhouse.org/research/pressurvey.htm). During the Second World War

---

117   A. Holmqvist, *Check the Source: Web Evaluation* [Internet], 2001. Available from: <http://www.skolutveckling.se/skolnet/english/index.html> [Accessed December 2005]

some papers spoke out against the government's 'neutral' policy.[118] There are also several newspapers printed in the language of Sweden's many ethnic minorities, Finnish, for example. On the whole the Swedish media provides an important voice on social, political and cultural issues and events affecting the country. Essentially, students and their parents are as likely to encounter as broad a range of perspectives on current and historical events as in any country.

Teacher/Student Role

The teacher's role in the Swedish history classroom is another factor that is difficult to pin down. Yet again, this is due to the highly decentralised nature of the history curriculum and its assessment in Sweden. To reiterate, history educators may teach as they see fit as long as they meet the loosely conceived curriculum requirements set by the central government. Often teachers will teach a particular topic having consulted their students on the pedagogic methods to be used.[119] In many cases, teachers are likely to use very progressive approaches that are student-based and in which the teacher plays the role of learning facilitator. At the other extreme, some educators, more traditional in outlook, are likely to use teacher-centred approaches. Many teachers will combine several approaches. It has been suggested that history teachers in Sweden experience high levels of 'professional freedom' and autonomy.[120] Yet this is not a clear-cut matter. MacGregor-Thunell tells us, with emphasis, that 'this freedom is also a risk.' Indeed, as discussed above, some teachers may 'focus on a very narrow topic' and, as a result, students in 'this class will not be able to participate in … historical debates'.[121]

Even though it is difficult to determine a didactical approach that typifies the Swedish context, there can be no doubt at all that teachers are key gatekeepers in Sweden.[122] With no prescribed curriculum and no national level examinations it is the teacher and relationships with the teacher that come to be of paramount

---

118 P. Levine, 'Swedish neutrality during the Second World War: tactical success or moral compromise?' in N. Wylie (ed.) *European Neutrals and Non-Belligerents During the Second World War* (Cambridge, Cambridge University Press, 2002).

119 Salin and Waterman, 'Sweden', op. cit. (note 98).

120 A. Walker, *Teaching History in Sweden, 2003.* Available from: <http://www.school history.co.uk/forum/index.php?showtopic=2218> [Accessed December 2005]

121 MacGregor-Thunell, *Teaching History in Sweden,* op. cit. (note 99).

122 S. Thornton, 'What is History in US History Textbooks?' in J. Nicholls (ed.) *School History Textbooks across Cultures: International Debates and Perspectives* (Oxford: Symposium, 2006).

importance in the classroom. Within the context of Sweden's long democratic traditions, inputs by students, school colleagues and local government bodies will be acknowledged and respected. But ultimately, it is the teacher who will define how and especially what history is to be taught and examined.

Censorship

On the issue of censorship the Swedish case is positioned opposite that of Japan outlined above. In other words, the Swedish government does not practise an official censorship policy for history education. History textbooks and educational media exist in an open and completely liberalised market in Sweden. Teachers and students, the schools, and the local municipalities decide, therefore, to make purchases on the 'open market' according to their self-defined needs. There are no lists of government-approved history books from which to choose.

The Swedish government still sees itself as leading by example. Thus, in recent years it is the Swedish government that has supported 'new interpretations' of the national past, in an effort to 'openly' reassess Swedish history, especially the 1939–1945 period and Sweden's compromise with Nazi Germany. The government supported Living History Forum that began its activities in 1997 firmly encourages educational initiatives.[123] As recognised by Julie Henry, recent government-funded initiatives have already affected classroom activities where, within the highly decentralised Swedish curricular structure 'history teachers are incorporating new evidence about the country's neutrality during the war'.[124]

Contemporary Politics and Ideology

Swedish politics and identity are deeply connected to the nation's long history of 'neutrality', so much so that it is even possible to speak of a 'culture of neutrality'. Sweden has not engaged in warfare since 1814, leaving 'a profound mark on the politics and culture of the nation'.[125] Writing in 1960, Ake Sandier

123 H. Loow, 'Programme Declaration' [Internet], Living History Forum, 2003. Available from: <http://www.levandehistoria.org> [Accessed June 2006].
124 J. Henry, 'Europe Declares War on History Books', *The Times Educational Supplement*, 2nd November 2001, p.3.
125 Levine, 'Swedish Neutrality during the Second World War', op. cit. (note 118), p.308.

speaks of 'neutrality' as something fundamental and essential to the Swedish psyche. Thus:

> THE CONCEPT OF NEUTRALITY is so firmly planted in Swedish national consciousness that no Swedish Government could long remain in power which does not unconditionally subscribe to the doctrine that neutrality is the best policy for Sweden. Indeed, a Swedish Government that would oppose this doctrine would be unthinkable. Government and people, regardless of politics, seem to have a secret understanding, or gentlemen's agreement, that anything but strict adherence to this *Weltanschaung* would be intolerable; and they seem to have signed a secret pact to stop anybody with a different concept from getting into a position where he might change the course that was charted almost 150 years ago by the first Bernadotte king.[126]

Neutrality is understood by Sandier to be a 'good thing' and to be an essential feature of Swedish life: a 'good life'. 'Sweden's policy of neutrality' writes Sandier is even 'more than a policy, more than a philosophy; it is almost a natural instinct. The Swedes embrace neutrality with all their hearts and souls, and nothing seems to shake their faith in neutrality as… the only policy they are willing to support'.[127] During World War II, the Swedish Prime Minister, Per Albin Hansson is frequently understood attempting to maintain Sweden's neutrality at any cost. It was the right policy for Sweden and Hansson was determined 'to keep his country at peace'.[128] Neutrality remains on the top of Sweden's political agenda, affected Swedish concerns over history education. Until recently, Sweden continued to be governed by the Social Democrats under Goran Persson. With regard to policy affecting history education the government supported the Forum for Living History.[129] In January 2000, Persson 'became the first [Swedish] head of government to denounce openly, in an official statement, the attitude of the authorities during the Second World War'.[130] Prime Minister Persson would proclaim:

> The Swedish authorities failed both in their actions and in their assumptions of responsibility. It is deeply distressing to have come to that conclusion. The government has done so with the deepest regret. We shall have to bare forever the moral and political responsibility for what happened – or what did not happen.[131]

---

126 A. Sandier, 'Sweden's Postwar Diplomacy: Some Problems, Views, and Issues', *The Western Political Quarterly*, 13 4 (1960), pp.924–933, in particular p.924.
127 Sandier, 'Sweden's Postwar Diplomacy', op. cit. (note 126), p.932.
128 Levine, 'Swedish Neutrality during the Second World War', op. cit. (note 118), p.311.
129 Loow, 'Programme Declaration', op. cit. (note 123).
130 G. Persson, quoted by A. Jacob, 'Persson Turns Spotlight on Sweden's dealings with Hitler', *The Guardian Weekly*, 27th January–2nd February 2000.
131 Persson, op. cit, (note 130).

This represented a reaction from the government to the crisis of the 1990s in which Sweden's neutrality during World War II came to be radically questioned. It was no longer possible to say that Sweden had acted in the right way or to assume that Sweden occupied a position of moral superiority in the world. With the development of new and critical perspectives the government had been forced to take an official position. Yet in the spirit of consensus that has long marked Swedish political and cultural life the government did not venture into a conflict with the new radicals but rather came to support initiatives that would 'make transparent' the realities of Sweden's war time past in all its complexity.[132]

The 'Living History Forum began its work in 1997, with the launch of a major information campaign'. And it would become a government body in 2001 and an official organisation in 2003. In the 'Programme declaration', Director Helen Loow, claims that:

> With the Holocaust as a starting point, the Forum for Living History is to work to strengthen insight on the equal worth of all people and to promote democracy, tolerance and human rights...
>
> There are many instances of genocide and purges during the twentieth century... However, the Holocaust... is the clearest example of an ideology and politics aimed at global, systematic and total extermination. We will always have to live with the consequences of this and other disasters during and after the Second World War. It is vitally important to know about the past to understand our present situation.[133]

The Forum would focus on Sweden, World War II and particularly the Holocaust, and would be structured around a series of closely connected aims. To 'spread knowledge... and contribute to deeper understanding', to 'reach children and young people', to 'achieve the greatest possible geographical spread and support', to 'take initiatives to strengthen knowledge where ... knowledge is lacking or needs to be complemented'.[134] Initiatives developed by the Forum for Living History would reach students in history classrooms. Sweden's role during the war continues to raise a whole series of important moral questions. History needs to be kept 'alive' if we are to avoid past mistakes. The Living History Forum represents a Swedish attempt to move forward by forging a new discourse on neutrality and the Second World War around a new consensus.

---

132 J. Henry, 'Europe Declares War on History Books', *The Times Educational Supplement*, 2nd November 2001, p.3.
133 Loow, 'Programme Declaration', op. cit. (note 123).
134 Living History Forum website, 2005.

Historiography

Post-war historiography on Sweden and World War II has followed an intriguing path. Unlike the case of Japan, history writing during the immediate post-war period does not appear at odds with the official discourse on the war. If anything, historians and politicians occupied a position of consensus over the nature of the war. At this time, the war among the powers was presented as something 'outside' of Sweden's sphere of influence. And there tended to be little discussion as such of the war beyond Europe. The plight of the Scandinavian countries tended to receive the most attention. That 'neutrality' is the natural position of small states and the right choice for Sweden provides the essential underpinning of this early post-war thesis. Sweden is thus understood responding and at times conceding to the political manoeuvres of the great powers – to the east, to the south and to the west. But concessions – particularly to Nazi Germany would be viewed not in moral terms but as matters of practical necessity.

During this period, members of the Swedish academy tended to uphold a so-called 'traditional or standard view of neutrality'. From this perspective, writes Levine,

> the coalition government led by Social Democratic Prime Minister Hansson succeeded in keeping the nation at peace, a political status with a higher moral value than freedom... According to this school, the concessions [to Nazi Germany] were not only necessary, they were (and are) morally defensible. Sweden had limited choices during the war, and made the correct ones.[135]

For Levine post-war Swedes have been 'raised on' this 'myth of neutrality'.[136] Moreover, where 'literature about the Second World War in Swedish' Levine informs us 'is comprehensive', the majority of 'books published give clear evidence of the predominance of... [this] ... standard interpretation'.[137] The war was a catastrophe of the highest order, a cause of the deepest suffering. Sweden was therefore right to have had as little to do with the fighting as possible. Writing as late as 1990, Sundelius argues that at the time of 'World War II, the government's primary objective was' beyond all else 'to keep the nation out of a conflict that caused so much suffering in Europe'.[138] Sweden was fortunate to emerge 'unscathed from the war', writes Sandier, because

---

135 Levine, 'Swedish Neutrality during the Second World War', op. cit. (note 118), pp.305–306.
136 Levine, 'Swedish Neutrality during the Second World War', op. cit. (note 118), p.307.
137 Levine, 'Swedish Neutrality during the Second World War', op. cit. (note 118), p.312.
138 B. Sundelius, 'Sweden: Secure Neutrality', *Annals of the American Academy of Political and Social Science*, 5 12 (199), pp.116–124, in particular p.116.

of 'its policy of neutrality'.[139] This should be celebrated. Since war is unquestionably wrong, Sweden's neutral policy between 1939 and 1945 was right.[140]

Post-war analyses of World War II by Swedish commentators often engage with the question of 'neutrality put to the test'.[141] Invariably, the difficulties of remaining neutral are emphasised over and above the question of scrutinising neutrality as a policy.[142] Gunnar Hagloff brings attention to the fact that Sweden was one of many small states that declared themselves to be neutral at the beginning of the war.[143] Sweden was not alone. 'In September 1939' no less than 'twenty European States declared their neutrality'. Yet 'when the war came to an end in 1945, only five… remained, the other fifteen… dragged into the war, mostly against their own will'. The manner in which a state maintains a policy of neutrality, it is claimed, will depend on its relationship to the great powers. Of the wartime neutrals Sweden is conceived as 'the State which saw its neutrality threatened in the most insistent and varied way'.[144] Sweden is thus portrayed doing what any small state would have done under the circumstances. Moreover, according to Sandier, 'Sweden's policy of neutrality had succeeded, and the conclusion drawn from that fact was elementary and powerful: it pays to be neutral'.[145]

From the 1940s to the 1980s the analysis of new information continued to be interpreted according to the parameters of this post-war thesis.[146] But the

---

139 Sandier, 'Sweden's Postwar Diplomacy', op. cit. (note 126), p.924.

140 A. W. Johansson, 'Neutrality and Modernity: The Second World War and Sweden's National Identity', in S. Ekman and N. Edling (eds.) *War Experience, Self Image and National Identity: The Second World War as Myth and History* (Sodertalje, The Bank of Sweden Tercentenary Foundation and Gidlunds Forlag, 1997), p.178.

141 H. Wigforss, 'Sweden and the Atlantic Pact', *International Organization*, 3 3 (1949), pp.434–443. W. Zartman, 'Neutralism and Neutrality in Scandinavia', *The Western Political Quarterly*, 7 2 (1954), pp.125–160. G. M. Hagloff, 'A Test of Neutrality: Sweden in the Second World War', *International Affairs*, 36 2 (1960), pp.153–167. Sandier, 'Sweden's Postwar Diplomacy', op. cit. (note 126). D. J. Edwards, 'Process of Economic Adaption in a World War II Neutral: A Case Study of Sweden', *The Journal of Finance*, 6 3 (1961), pp.437–438.

142 E. C. Bellquist, 'Maintaining Morale in Sweden', *The Public Opinion Quarterly*, 5 3 (1941), pp.432–447.

143 Hagloff, 'A Test of Neutrality', op. cit. (note 141).

144 Hagloff, 'A Test of Neutrality', op. cit. (note 141).

145 Sandier, 'Sweden's Postwar Diplomacy', op. cit. (note 126), p.927.

146 W. Carlgren, *Swedish Foreign Policy during the Second World War* (New York: St. Martin's Press, 1977). A. W. Johansson, *Per Albin och Kriget* (Stockholm, Tiden, 1984).

1990s would be a time of economic and political uncertainty, identity crisis and re-alignment, anxious Swedes often struggling to find their balance in the new reality. It is in this context that Sweden's role during the Second World War came to be radically re-interpreted.

The publication of *Honour and Conscience: Sweden and the Second World War*, in the early 1990s, would mark a major turning point. With this book, authored by Maria-Pia Boethius, the post-war thesis would be inverted, collapsed, capsized, dismantled and overturned, cosy perspectives on wartime neutrality exposed as a farce, a myth, and 'a conspiracy of silence'.[147] According to Johansson, 'it was written in the white heat of indignation and savaged Sweden's wartime policy'. In the book 'Boethius listed Sweden's concessions and condemned them in unmistakably moral language'.[148] Essentially, 'neutrality' during World War II would be portrayed as an act of national cowardice. How could Sweden justify its concessions to Nazi Germany? How was it possible not to take up arms against such an abhorrent regime? According to Johansson, Boethius's central objective was to show how 'Sweden ought to have entered the war in order to save her soul'.[149]

With the publication of this volume a debate suddenly emerged, forcing people to take a position.[150] If some historians felt that the book was overly sensationalist, using too few sources, they had to justify why this was the case. Different sections of society reacted in different ways. Johansson even speaks of 'a generation gap'

> in the reactions to her book. Older reviewers found the book a "superficial pamphlet" which was perhaps honourable in its intentions but which was also cocksure in tone and based on an insufficient range of sources. There was a much greater willingness to accept her message among the younger generation of reviewers.[151]

Where conservative forces continued to cling to versions of 'small state realism' and 'neutrality', the new generation began to ask new questions. As Levine points out, 'younger Swedes' began 'demanding a more honest and open discussion of this "holy relic" of their country's history'.[152] Following Boethius's book, researchers like Johansson, Levine and others began to reassess Sweden's wartime role from a far more critical perspective.

---

147 Boethius, quoted by Johansson, op. cit. (note x), p.181.
148 Johansson, *Per Albin och Kriget,* op. cit. (note 146), p.182.
149 Johansson, *Per Albin och Kriget*, op. cit. (note 146), pp.182–183.
150 Johansson, *Per Albin och Kriget*, op. cit. (note 146), pp.182–183.
151 Johansson, *Per Albin och Kriget*, op. cit. (note 146), pp.182–183.
152 Levine, 'Swedish Neutrality during the Second World War', op. cit. (note 118), p.307.

Stig Ekman draws attention to the morally questionable position adopted by the Swedish government during the war. According to Ekman 'Sweden fitted well into the German wartime economy: export and import took place to the two countries mutual satisfaction'.[153] Ekman even argues that the extent of the concessions made to the Nazi's, political, commercial, and military, 'begs the question of whether Sweden was, in practice, indirectly belligerent on the German side'.[154] Important elements within Swedish society were, after all, pro-German. 'Rickman von der Lancken' was 'a Swedish general with pro-Nazi sympathies' who, according to Ekman considered that Sweden had a superior secret weapon at its disposal: the warrior spirit of Charles XII. It was as if that monarch had risen from the dead. It should be pointed out that, in military pro-Nazi circles, Adolf Hitler and Charles XII were regarded as kindred spirits.[155]

In spite of the fact that Sweden remained neutral throughout the war Ekman argues that the Swedish 'government's relationship with Nazi Germany ... commanded a humiliating moral price that cannot be disregarded by posterity'.[156] The Swedish government during World War II supported the regime that was responsible for the Holocaust.

As outlined above, it was in the early 2000s that the Swedish government came to support an official re-assessment of the nation's wartime past. In particular, they stressed the need to focus on Sweden's compromise with the Nazis. The Swedish academy was called upon by the national government to conduct a full investigation of Sweden's role during the Second World War for the public good. This has not only changed the direction of contemporary historiography in Sweden but has also had an important knock-on effect with regard to the way that the conflict is taught in schools. Researchers on the University of Uppsala's 'Programme for Holocaust Studies and Genocide Studies' have been requested, with government support, to collaborate. In turn, this has lead to a series of research contributions by scholars on war related issues.[157]

---

153 S. Ekman, 'Skilful Realpolitik or Unprincipled Opportunism? The Swedish Coalition Government's Foreign Policy in Debate and Research', in S. Ekman and N. Edling (eds.) *War Experience, Self Image and National Identity: The Second World War as Myth and History* (Sodertalje, The Bank of Sweden Tercentenary Foundation and Gidlunds Forlag, 1997), p.191.
154 Ekman, 'Skilful Realpolitik or Unprincipled Opportunism?', op, cit. (note 153), p.192.
155 Ekman, 'Skilful Realpolitik or Unprincipled Opportunism?', op, cit. (note 153), p.190.
156 Ekman, 'Skilful Realpolitik or Unprincipled Opportunism?', op, cit. (note 153), p.203.
157 Levine, 'Swedish Neutrality during the Second World War', op. cit. (note 118). D. Gaunt, P. A. Levine and L. Palosuo (eds.) *Collaboration and Resistance during*

7.4 England

Background and Tradition

Education in England has followed a distinctive path since the end of the Second World War. This being said, although curriculum issues have been debated in England for well over a century, a truly national curriculum was not introduced until 1988.[158] Consisting originally of a fixed set often subjects, including history, the National Curriculum was implemented, according to the government rhetoric of the time, to 'raise standards by ensuring a broad and balanced range of subjects for all, and [to] set clear objectives for achievement'.[159] During the tripartite (1944–1964) and comprehensive (1964–1988) eras, history had been an important and popular school subject even if it was not prescribed by law. But debates in education at the time tended to focus on access and equality issues rather than on the curriculum itself. As such, it was the divisive structure of the tripartite system that determined the 'non-prescribed' history curriculum taught and learned in schools. Similarly, it was the plurality of examination boards that determined courses of study in history at comprehensive schools in the 1960s, 1970s and 1980s.[160]

From the 1970s, a series of commentators, particularly those on the conservative right, argued that general curriculum standards were inconsistent across schools in England.[161] Moreover, this was seen to be one of the reasons behind the stagnation of the British economy in comparison with its European competitors. While some students attended schools that offered a broad and 'well-taught' curriculum, all too many, it was argued, experienced the opposite, leaving school with very little to show for it. The implementation of a 'prescribed' national curriculum from 1988 would guarantee standards across all curriculum subjects for

the Holocaust: Belarus, Estonia, Latvia, Lithuania (Bern: Verlag Peter Lang, 2004). H. R. Huttenbach, The Universality of Genocide (Uppsala: The Uppsala Programme for Holocaust and Genocide Studies, 2004).

158 A. Convey and A. Merritt, 'The United Kingdom', in C. Brock and W. Tulusiewicz (eds.) Education in a Single Europe (London, Routledge, 2000).

159 A. Ross, Curriculum: Construction and Critique (New York: Palmer Press, 2000), pp.64–65.

160 J. Nicholls, 'Compulsory Schooling, Curricular Developments and History Education in England', Journal of the Young Historians of Moldova, 6 (2005), pp.289–295.

161 E. Bolton, 'Perspectives on the National Curriculum', in P. O'Hear and J. White (eds.) Assessing the National Curriculum (London: Paul Chapman, 1993).

all students aged 5 to 16. The implications for the teaching and learning of history would be enormous.[162]

At the present time, it is compulsory for students to attend school in England between the ages of five and sixteen.[163] State secondary education is attended for a period of five years beginning at age eleven. Most schools are large and comprehensive, offering a wide range of national curriculum subjects.[164] In primary schools students will cover key stages one and two (KS1, KS2) of the history curriculum. In the first three years of secondary school they will follow the key stage three (KS3) programme, and during the last two/three years, the key stage four (KS4) programme in preparation for the GCSE examinations. All students will study history at KS3 but at KS4 must choose between history and geography. Where prior to the introduction of the National Curriculum it was possible to study both history and geography to examination level at the age of 16/17, this is no longer the case.

Prescribed Curriculum

In England there is a strongly prescriptive and centralised National Curriculum for history that all schools, teachers and students are compelled to follow. However, the curriculum that exists today is very different from the original version. From its initial implementation the history curriculum has been successively 'tweaked'. Where initially it had been received with disdain, history teachers are now familiar with the dictates and expectations that the curriculum demands. Moreover, owing largely to pressure from teaching unions, the National Curriculum has been modified to such an extent that most teachers now feel comfortable working within its parameters.[165]

---

162   J. Slater, 'A National Curriculum: the Place of Humanities', in P. O'Hear and J. White (eds.) *Assessing the National Curriculum* (London, Paul Chapman Publishing, 1993). I. F. Goodson, '"Nations at Risk" and "National Curriculum": Ideology and Identity', in I. F. Goodson, C. J. Anstead and J. M. Mangan (eds.) *Subject Knowledge: Readings for the Study of School Subjects* (London, Palmer, 1998).

163   De facto, English school students are now largely attending school until 17 – with staying on in education (or full-time training) until 18 emerging in education policy debates as the ideal.

164   Convey and Merritt, 'The United Kingdom', op. cit. (note 158)

165   Goodson, '"Nations at Risk" and "National Curriculum"', op. cit. (note 162).

History in the National Curriculum has been a source of much controversy, debate, protest and review. During the late 1980s the conservative Prime Minister, Margaret Thatcher, was unhappy with the way that the Minister of Education, Kenneth Baker, had allegedly been too sympathetic to 'progressive' opinion, as she was to make clear in her memoirs, *The Downing Street Years:*

> Perhaps the hardest battle I fought on the national curriculum was about history. Though not an historian myself, I had a very clear – and I had naively imagined uncontroversial – idea of what history was. History is an account of what happened in the past. Learning history, therefore, requires knowledge of events. It is impossible to make sense of such events without absorbing sufficient factual information and without being able to place matters in a clear chronological framework – which means knowing dates. No amount of imaginative sympathy for historical characters or situations can be a substitute for the initial tedious but ultimately rewarding business of memorising what actually happened.[166]

On the whole, conservatives tended to accept the National Curriculum at face value denying that there was any hidden ideological agenda. As such, the National Curriculum, an openly prescribed set of subjects with 'prescribed content' for 'learning during the years of compulsory education', was justified on practical grounds.[167] But many commentators on the political left criticised what they saw as the National Curriculum's underlying nationalist agenda. Both the prescribed content and the centrally controlled nature of the curriculum were considered to be means for re-establishing the centrality of 'the nation' in all aspects of education. According to Goodson,

> the political project underpinning the National Curriculum... is a reassertion of the power of the state... This project is diametrically opposed to the alternative project of educating pupils... for active citizenship in a democracy. The history of mass mechanical obedience as a bedrock for nation-building is well known, but it leads not to democracy but to totalitarianism.[168]

National Curriculum history was seen to be essentially over-nationalistic, and far too chronological and linear at the expense of concepts and empathy. Dave Hill refers to the curriculum of '1988 ... as an attempt to create a Conservative hegemony of ideas, and remove liberal progressive and socialist ideas from schools'.[169]

---

166 M. Thatcher, *The Downing Street Years* (New York: Harper Collins, 1993), p.595.
167 Thatcher, *The Downing Street Years*, op. cit. (note 166), p.595.
168 Goodson, '"Nations at Risk" and "National Curriculum"', op. cit. (note 162), p.162.
169 D. Hill, 'The Third Way in Britain: New Labour's Neo-liberal Education Policy', paper presented at Congress Marx International III, Universite de Paris-X Nanterre-Sorbonne, 29th September 2001.

Stephen Ball is poetic in his stinging critique of the tendency of National Curriculum prescribed history to valorise the past of dead Englishmen. For Ball it was

a curriculum suspicious of the popular and the immediate, made up of echoes of past voices of a cultural and political elite; a curriculum which ignores the past of women and the working class and the colonised a curriculum of the dead.[170]

Beyond contrasting ideological perspectives it became apparent shortly after implementation that the curriculum suffered from severe practical limitations, especially 'content overload'. Professional dissatisfaction remained very high, reaching its peak in 1993 and expressed in a large-scale teacher-boycott of National Curriculum tests.[171] The government's response was to instigate a major review led by Sir Ron Dealing with recommendations for a more streamlined National Curriculum to be implemented in 1995.[172] On the whole, the revised curriculum was relatively well received by teachers, students and their parents. In addition, the revisions would have major implications for the subject of history.

Sir Ron Dearing's review of the National Curriculum brought significant changes for history. To begin with, the content was to be reduced. In addition, at Key Stage 4 the curriculum was to be abandoned completely in order for students to concentrate solely on their GCSE final examination studies. A number of other important changes were implemented in order to give students and teachers more space and time to concentrate on 'doing their jobs properly'.

In 1997 the Labour Party returned to power with a centrist ideological platform. David Blunkett was appointed Education and Employment Secretary and made some structural adjustments to the National Curriculum. In particular, at the elementary school level, emphases on foundation subjects such as history were relaxed in order for greater focus to be placed on core subjects such as mathematics and English, that Hill refers to as a 'focus on "the basics"'.[173] In addition, the emphasis on cross-curricular themes such as 'citizenship' and the 'European dimension' was intensified for secondary school students at Key Stage 3. Nevertheless, the study units in 2005 for Key Stages 1 to 3 are almost

---

170 A. Ross, *Curriculum: Construction and Critique* (New York, Palmer Press, 2000), p.76.
171 Goodson, '"Nations at Risk" and "National Curriculum"', op. cit. (note 162).
172 Government Document, *National Curriculum*, Department for Education (London, HMSO, 1995). A. Ross, *Curriculum: Construction and Critique* (New York, Palmer Press, 2000).
173 Hill, 'The Third Way in Britain', op. cit. (note 169).

the same as in 1995.[174] At Key Stage 4, students have continued to prepare for their GCSE examinations, the standard school leavers route to 'further education' and, potentially, A-Levels remaining virtually unchanged under the Labour government.

The National Curriculum exerts enormous influence on the type of knowledge that teachers are required to teach, and that students are required to learn. An analysis of the official curriculum web site 'National Curriculum online' demonstrates how popular aspects of the Second World War are as curriculum topics (http://www.nc.uk.net, 2005).

At Key Stages 1 and 2 there are units on 'What was it like for children in the Second World War?' (Unit 9) and on 'What are we remembering on Remembrance Day?' (Unit 17). At Key Stage 3, there are prescribed units on 'Hot war, cold war why did the major twentieth-century conflicts affect so many people?' (Unit 18) and on 'How and why did the Holocaust happen?' (Unit 19). It is important to note that schemes of work for every unit are downloadable directly from the very informative official web site. For Key Stage 4, at the GCSE level, key units for history include 'Germany: 1919 to 1945' and 'International Relations: 1919 to 1945' (http://www.bbc.co.uk/schools2005).

Examinations and Assessment

An important feature of the National Curriculum has been the implementation of standardised assessment. At the end of the first three key stages, at ages 7, 11 and 14 consecutively, students sit a Standard Attainment Test (SAT). However, these tests are in the core curriculum subjects of English, mathematics and science only, not in history. For the subject of history 'Teacher Assessment is used as the process by which levels of attainment are judged'.[175] Only at the end of Key Stage 4, at the age of 16/17, will students sit GCSE examinations across all National Curriculum subjects.

Assessment targets for history have been designed to gauge student progress throughout the first three key stages, based on continuous assessment, while progress at the end of key stage 4 is ultimately gauged by GCSE results. On completing each of the first three key stages students would be expected to have reached a minimum attainment target across all subjects.

---

174 National Curriculum online, 2005.
175 Qualification and Curriculum Authority, 2004.

Assessment targets are used for history in the National Curriculum to register student progress, defining what is and is not taught across the subject. As the Qualifications and Curriculum Authority (QCA) point out, 'by charting broad progression in the subject [,] ... level descriptions ... inform planning, teaching and assessment'.[176] In history it therefore becomes the role of the teacher to carefully consider the plurality of means by which students may be evaluated, assessed and judged. The teacher, according to the QCA, must 'arrive at judgements by taking into account strengths and weaknesses in performance across a range of contexts and over a period of time, rather than focusing on a single piece of work':[177]

> A single piece of work will not cover all the expectations set out in a level description. It will probably provide partial evidence of attainment in one or more aspects of a level description. If you [a teacher] look at it alongside other pieces of work covering a range of contexts you will be able to make a judgement about which level best fits a pupil's overall performance.[178]

In order to make 'a judgement' teachers must 'consider pupils' breadth and depth of 'historical knowledge' as well as 'the amount of support provided across the range of work' and 'the degree of independence shown'. Students 'will need to use a range of forms of communication to show what they can do'. Likewise, the teacher

> [i]n planning units of work and classroom approaches, will need to provide opportunities for pupils to display their achievements in different ways, and to work in a range of situations, for example oral work, drama, written work, work using ICT. To achieve the highest levels, pupils need opportunities to marshal arguments and communicate effectively.[179]

Key Stage assessment is an essential feature of teaching and learning history within the context of the National Curriculum in England. Typically, it involves a variety of forms of assessment, written work, project work, oral presentations as well as formal tests. By the end of each key stage, students will have built up a considerable portfolio of work for final assessment, some of which will be externally assessed.[180]

---

176 Qualification and Curriculum Authority, 2004.
177 Qualification and Curriculum Authority, 2004.
178 Qualification and Curriculum Authority, 2004.
179 Qualification and Curriculum Authority, 2004.
180 Qualification and Curriculum Authority, 2004.

GCSE level work at Key Stage 4 involves continuous assessment as well as preparation for an externally examined 'closed' written paper by one of the major examination boards, e.g. the Assessment and Qualifications Alliance (AQA). Continuous assessment will develop on many of the assessment activities undertaken by students in the earlier key stages. Throughout Key Stage 4, student portfolios will be evaluated internally, with some pieces of work being assessed by external examiners. The continuous assessment of GCSE coursework will usually make up 25% of the final grade for GCSE history (http://www.gcse-coursework.com/exams.html). For this reason, the written examination constitutes the most significant area of assessment on the GCSE programme. Recent initiatives have sought to make GCSE history even more examination oriented (www.jiscpas.ac.uk). Much of Key Stage 4 is dedicated to preparing for the GCSE examinations.

GCSE examinations in England are written and controlled by powerful external examination boards. Many former boards that controlled syllabuses in the days of the GCE ordinary level examinations (O-Levels) have merged into larger consolidated bodies. Thus the Assessment and Qualifications Alliance (AQA) is the result of a merger between 'the Associated Examining Board (AEB) and the Northern Examinations and Assessment Board (NEAB)' in 2000 (at http://www.aqa.org.uk/over/index.html). The other major examination bodies at the present time are Edexcel and OCR (Oxford, Cambridge and RSA Examinations). GCSE examination papers are always 'closed' and externally assessed. At the BBC Schools web site it is possible to browse GCSE past exam questions on the theme 'International relations 1919–1945' (http://www.bbc.co.uk/schools). The questions are listed with tips for students on how they might go about revising to answer similar questions when they sit the 'real' examination. Not surprisingly many of these are related to events in Nazi Germany and World War II, evident in the following examples:

- Describe Hitler's foreign policy from 1933 to 1938
- Why did Neville Chamberlain sign the Munich agreement?
- Why did Britain declare war on Germany on 3 September 1939?
- Why did the German invasion of Poland on 1 September 1939 lead to the outbreak of World War II?
- Why was the German army so successful in 1940?

In England, students must answer questions in long hand; the highest marks awarded to those students who show evidence that they can reason, argue, and assess. Regurgitating names and dates from memory will guarantee only a pass at a lower grade.

Classroom Media

In England teachers have long been encouraged to develop student-centred approaches to learning history using a wide variety of educational media and resources. At the secondary level these will include learning packs, computer software and educational games, video and DVD, as well as Internet resources. Essentially, the history classroom in England is definitively non-textbook-centred. As we have seen, curriculum and assessment in England is not defined by textbook content but rather by the National Curriculum and the powerful examination boards. In contrast to many countries, teachers are actively discouraged to teach from the textbook in England. As Marsden points out, '[t]he received wisdom remains that textbooks... typify an undesirable transmission model' understood to be 'generally incompatible with progressive educational practice'.[181] If textbooks are to be used in classes, it is as a single source among others.[182]

This was not always the case. In the 1950s and 1960s the textbook was a central teaching tool.[183] Yet with the emergence of 'progressive' history in the 1970s, student-centred approaches became the vogue and the textbook became increasing marginal to lessons. Equally, with the arrival of the Internet it is not difficult to see how, in time, the 'vertically oriented', 'start to finish', textbook could come to be replaced by more laterally oriented forms of electronic media.[184] This is not to

181 W. E. Marsden, *The School Textbook: Geography, History and Social Studies* (London: Woburn Press, 2001), p.1.

182 J. Nicholls, 'Beyond the National and the Transnational: Representations of WWII in the School History Textbooks of Five Countries', paper presented at the Comparative and International Education Society (CIES) 48th Annual Conference, Salt Lake City, Utah, USA, 9th–12th March 2004. J. Nicholls, 'Beyond the National and the Transnational: Perspectives of WWII in the School History Textbooks of Three European Countries', paper presented at the Comparative Education Society in Europe (CESE) 2004 Conference, Copenhagen, Denmark, 27th June–1st July 2004. J. Nicholls, 'Student Engagement with Textbook Perspectives of World War II: Summary of an International and Comparative Study', *Research at Oxford by Students of Education (ROSE)*, 1 3 (2005), pp.39–48. J. Nicholls, 'Are Students Expected to Critically Engage with Textbook Perspectives of the Second World War? A Comparative and International study', *Research in Comparative and International Education*, 1 1 (2006), pp.40–55.

183 V. Chancellor, *History for their Masters: Opinion in the 18th Century History Textbook 1800–1914* (New York: Augustus Kelly, 1970).

184 B. Gates, quoted by O. Gibson, 'Gates Unveils his Vision of a Future Made of Silicon', *The Guardian*, 28th October 2005, p.1.

say that there is no textbook market in England at the present time. In particular, large publishers such as Heinemann produce books that correspond with the syllabuses offered by the major examination boards. Technically the market is liberal, teachers are free to select textbooks as and how they see fit. However, if publishers wish to make profits they must conform to the dictates of the National Curriculum and the examination boards. Although the extent to which students use textbooks inside and outside of class is difficult to ascertain, with the increasing integration of the Internet one cannot but surmise that the use and importance of the textbook in history classes will continue to decline.[185]

Internet Access

After coming to power in 1997, the Labour government showed strong support for Information and Communication Technology in schools (ICT). Many classroom resources required to teach National Curriculum history are now available on-line at the official web-site http://www.nc.uk.net. BBC Schools Online also offers a wide range of resources and links for students and teachers of history (http://www.bbc.co.uk/schools). And there are a plethora of alternative sites offering lesson plans, schemes of work, examination tips for GCSE students, model answers for coursework essays, and advice on school trips.

Evidence suggests that the young in England are using the Internet to complete school assignments like never before, a trend found in other predominantly English speaking societies.[186] Indeed, according to the UK's E-Learning Foundation, '[f]or many children ... access to a computer and the Internet is taken for granted'.[187] However, there is a strong socio-economic divide between Internet-savvy students and those with little dexterity. Interviewed by the Guardian Unlimited on the subject of Internet use among secondary school students in the UK, Alison Pickard comments:

Those who have access to the internet at home and have computer literate parents are better at using the internet [at school]. They're also the ones who can use a public

---

185 J. Nicholls, 'School History Textbooks across Cultures from the Perspective of Comparative Education', in J. Nicholls (ed.) *School History Textbooks across Cultures: International Debates and Perspectives* (Oxford: Symposium, 2006).

186 C. Murray, 'Textbooks Dumped in Favour of Laptops'. [Internet] eSCHOOL NEWS. Available from: <http://www.eschoolnews.com/news/showStory.cfm> [Accessed October 2005].

187 Nicholls, 'School History Textbooks across Cultures from the Perspective of Comparative Education', op. cit. (note 185).

library. Those from lower socio-economic backgrounds aren't encouraged to use such resources. It's a case of the information rich and the information poor.[188]

The use of the Internet for completing assignments for history has become a major cause for concern in recent years. In particular, the plagiarism of Internet sources has ushered in a call for less continual assessment and more closed examinations in the assessment of school history.[189] However, some insist that '[t]here are are many tactics for designing [continual] assessments that are difficult... to plagiarise or be written by someone else'.[190]

English is the chief access language for the Wikipedia free on-line encyclopaedia (http://www.wikipedia.org). There are as many entries in English as in all other languages combined. Search for 'World War II' using Google and no fewer than 117,000,000 sites are listed. The sheer breadth of knowledge available on the Internet to those who speak and understand English is mind-boggling.

Mass Media (other than the Internet)

Television media in the UK are mixed between the public and the private sectors. Officially, BBC television is underpinned by an ethos of politically neutral public service. News and current affairs, drama, comedy and documentaries have tended to dominate the BBC's television agenda. Unlike independent television commercials are never shown. With a set quantity of funds the BBC is compelled to attract viewers through the production of interesting and quality programming suitable for the general public in its entirety. Independent television has a 'commercial' and more populist ethos. Programmes are funded through the sale of advertising space. Game shows and soap operas are a common feature, with less time dedicated to documentaries. This being said, Channel 4 has pioneered liberal and alternative programmes since the 1980s, in competition with BBC 2. Satellite television with its highly commercial ethos is popular in the UK.

Printed media have a long, independent and commercial history in England. A relatively wide range of ideological perspectives are offered by the press.

---

188 Quoted by Rachael Liddle in an article for the *Guardian Unlimited*, 29th July 2003, at http://education.guardian.co.uk.
189 B. Johnson, 'The Unbearable Triteness of Cheating', *The Guardian*, 17th October 2006.
190 S. Bostock, 'Simplistic solution to plagiarism crisis', *Education Guardian*, 24th October 2006, p.4.

Essentially, there are more newspapers on the political right than on the left. Moreover, the biggest selling papers tend to be conservative in orientation. Since the middle decades of the 20th century the UK printed media has been owned by four companies. While there has always been a commitment to an independent free press, printed news in England has been dominated by highly commercial interests.

In the tabloid newspapers and in some of the quality newspapers, unabashed sensationalism is common, with rampant xenophobia and anti-Europeanism frequently used to cater to lowest common denominator interests (http://www.cultsock.ndirect.co.uk/MUHome/cshtml/media/mediaown.html). Likewise, as Paul Coman has pointed out, the British press has long been underpinned by a provocative and profoundly anti-German stance, frequently fanning the flames of 'victory over Germany' during World War II.[191] In the Freedom House rankings for 'freedom of the press' in 2005, the United Kingdom as a whole came 30th, below Sweden but above Japan (http://www.freedomhouse.org/research/pressurvey.htm). The perspectives on events encountered by students and their parents in England will therefore depend on the type of media used. Quality documentaries produced by non-commercial organisations such as the BBC will vary greatly from the often xenophobic hysteria and sensationalism of the tabloid press.

Teacher/Student Role

The National Curriculum and the external examination boards determine the content of history classes in England. However, over the years, Britain has led the way in terms of student-centred approaches to teaching history. Indeed, the assessment of history in England means that students need to understand much more than simply names and dates. The highest grades are awarded to those students who demonstrate argumentation and critical thinking based around the investigation of sources and evidence. As mentioned above, examinations in England commonly ask students to answer in essay format. Likewise, continuous assessment, in which students need to demonstrate a wide variety of skills, is important – although there are now plans to move back to examination based forms of assessment.[192]

---

191 P. Coman, 'Reading about the Enemy: School Textbook Representation of Germany's Role in the War with Britain during the Period from April 1940 to May 1941', *British Journal of the Sociology of Education*, 173 (1996), pp.327–340.
192 Nicholls, 'Are Students Expected to Critically Engage with Textbook Perspectives of the Second World War?', op. cit. (note 29).

In order to prepare students, teachers of history in England are very much facilitators. They are encouraged to use pair and group work and to avoid lecturing from the front of the class as much as possible. Teachers must introduce students to sources using a variety of media. Moreover, they must encourage critical discussion, questions and debate. How is it possible to assess sources? What are the different perspectives on a particular issue or event? In England a strong emphasis is placed on empathy in the history classroom. In other words, students will be encouraged to see things from the point of view of those involved in a particular event in history. What was it like to be a child of the Blitz or a victim of the Allied bombings of Hamburg or Dresden or of the atomic bombing of Hiroshima and Nagasaki? How is it possible to understand how ordinary Germans supported a ruthless dictator like Hitler in the 1930s? And so on.[193]

History teachers may choose from a variety of pedagogical methods but there are important limits, particularly those imposed by the central government's Office for Standards in Education (Ofsted). As stated on the first page of the official Ofsted website: 'Ofsted is the inspectorate for children and learners in England. It is our job to contribute to the provision of better education and care through effective inspection and regulation' (at http://www.ofsted.gov.uk 2006). Ofsted inspections take place at schools every four years. As part of the inspection process, classes are observed and assessed based on 'evidence'. In the document 'Framework for the Inspection of schools in England from September 2005' under the sub-heading 'How are judgements secured?' the following is stated: 'Judgements must be convincingly supported by evidence. Emerging findings must be supported by the head teacher, and where appropriate senior managers, at regular intervals' (http://www.ofsted.gov.uk/publications/index.cfm). Like the centrally imposed National Curriculum, this highly conservative form of surveillance sets significant parameters on liberal teaching practices in England. Nevertheless, in an Ofsted subject report for history (2002/2003) it was argued that, in general, students were improving in England owing to 'good' teaching. The following is the Ofsted report for students at year 9 and 11:

> By the end of year 9, pupils' knowledge and understanding of the subject matter are very good and their listening skills are well developed. They have acquired real strengths in handling and interpreting a wide range of historical sources. They have a very good understanding of how past societies functioned and pupils across the full ability range are willing to express their views on a wide variety of historical issues.

---

193 Nicholls, 'Are Students Expected to Critically Engage with Textbook Perspectives of the Second World War?', op. cit. (note 29).

By the end of year 11, pupils can organise and communicate their research findings in a variety of ways and have developed real strengths in the critical analysis and evaluation of historical sources. The regular use of writing frames and an emphasis on learning key words from year 7 onwards contribute to the high standards achieved by all pupils at the end of year 11. They are well versed in the examination skills required to achieve the highest possible grades. This generates increased self-confidence and is reflected in the large numbers of pupils opting for the subject (http://www.ofsted.gov.uk/publications/index.cfm).

Censorship

The British government does not practise an official censorship policy for school history. As mentioned above, history textbooks and educational media exist in an open and completely liberalised market in England and the UK. Teachers decide to make purchases on the 'open market' according to their self-defined needs. There are no lists of government approved textbooks from which to choose. Because of the highly centralised dictates of the National Curriculum, however, it could be said that the government practises a form of unofficial censorship. As noted in the above Ofsted discussion, history teachers are compelled to cover themes and topics in the National Curriculum and to assess student coursework on these themes. In addition, at Key Stage 4, teachers must prepare their students for the externally examined GCSEs. In other words, the type of knowledge deemed relevant in the history classroom is decided on first by the central government and second by the external examination boards.

Contemporary Politics and Ideology

The rise of a new breed of conservatives during the late 1970s represented an explicit and radical reaction to Britain's industrial and political decline in the post-war period. Combining neo-liberalism and nationalism, the socio-economic apparatus constructed by post-war Labour governments was dismantled. The ideas of Smith, Freedman and Hayek ascended to the detriment of Beveridge and Keynes. Where Thatcher and the new right received marginal support from much of the academic community, they would nevertheless come to re-define national discourse and identity.

The Conservative government of the 1980s was tough talking and ambitious. Its rhetoric was warrior like and stern with 'Thatcher... the Iron Lady' as a kind of 'present-day successor to Churchill'.[194] Under Thatcher's command the government went to war, not simply against the by now ill reputed Labour Party, against the unions, against the Argentines, and against the 'Europeans'.[195] 'Throughout the 1980s' says Hedetoft 'the Thatcherites and the New Right tried to keep the people in a state of putative, war-like emergency, by constantly projecting images of enemies'.[196]

The 'New' Labour government's agenda was centrist and pragmatic, and strongly influenced by the legacy of Thatcherism. Education policy often involved the re-adjustment of measures first initiated by the former conservative administration. According to left-wing commentators such as Dave Hill, 'New Labour... accepted the Radical Right revolution in schooling... in terms of the curriculum'.[197] The same can be said of teacher education, where the Blair administration replicated 'former Conservative government plans for an increasingly regulated, technicist and de-theorised teacher training curriculum'.[198] With specific reference to the history curriculum Hill argues that New Labour initiatives have been 'Pro-tradition', 'Pro-Nationalism and "Britishness"', and generally 'Anti-theoretical'. In addition, during the Labour government it was possible to witness the 'intensification of a regime of testing and assessment for school pupils' first initiated by the Conservatives.[199] In the area of 'social studies' compulsory citizenship education in the National Curriculum represented perhaps the most significant policy initiative of the Blair government.[200]

Historiography

World War II would come to have a highly particular meaning in England's post-war national discourse. Britain, but especially England, had defeated the enemy:

---

194 U. Hedetoft, 'National Identities and Mentalities of War in Three EC Countries', *Journal of Peace Research*, 30 3 (1993), pp.281–300, in particular p.286.
195 M. Davis, *Thatcher's Famous Speeches* [Internet] BBC News. Available from: <http://news.bbc.co.uk> [Accessed 16 May 2006]
196 Hedetoft, 'National Identities and Mentalities of War in Three EC Countries', op. cit (note 194), p.286
197 Hill, 'The Third Way in Britain', op. cit. (note 169).
198 Hill, 'The Third Way in Britain', op. cit. (note 169).
199 Hill, 'The Third Way in Britain', op. cit. (note 169).
200 B. Kisby, 'New Labour and Citizenship Education', paper presented at the Political Studies Association Annual Conference, University of Reading, 3rd–6th April 2006.

Germany. Despite differences of approach and perspective early post-war historians appeared in agreement on this issue. That Britain played a major role during World War II is undeniable: alone after the fall of France, enduring the Blitz, the Battle of Britain, the sea battles in the Atlantic, El Alamain, D-Day, and so on. Moreover, having entered the war 'on principle', with the German invasion of Poland in 1939, Britain could, would and did credit itself with a special kind of moral victory.[201]

From the 1940s to the 1970s, World War II was still very much a living memory. Moreover, during the period, British historians cultivated different investigative approaches. In the volumes that make up Churchill's *The Second World War*, the conflict is depicted very much 'as the continuation of the … story of the First World War'.[202] Alan Bullock, famous for his biography *Hitler: A Study in Tyranny*, focused on leadership.[203] Others, such as Hugh Trevor-Roper were conservatives, fervently pro-Churchill and anti-appeasement. The great Sir Lewis Namier was an elitist and an essentialist. Somewhat later A. J. P. Taylor would appear as something of an iconoclastic radical and a man of the people.[204]

Yet despite differences of orientation, it is across the work of these men that National Socialism would be identified as an essentially German phenomenon. To clarify, 'the problem' had not simply been with 'the Nazis' but with 'the Germans'. The Nazis and the Germans were synonymous. Hitler and the Nazis could not have come from Britain. In this sense the Second World War was seen to be very much like the first, since both 'were in fact "German wars"'.[205] Likewise, for many, such as 'Lord Vansittart, former Permanent Under-Secretary at the Foreign Office' there was 'ample ground for locating the origins of the wars not in the supposed structural defects of the international system but in the innate and distressing characteristics of Germans'.[206] For Robbins, even *The German Wars: 1914–1945* by the American historian D. J. Goodspeed 'could… have been manufactured in Britain' because of its 'title'.[207] Ultimately, work on World War II by

---

201 Bosworth, *Explaining Auschwitz and Hiroshima*, op. cit. (note 4).
202 W. Churchill, *The Second World War,* Vol. 1 (London: Cassell & Co, 1948), v.ii.
203 A. Bullock, *Hitler: A Study in Tyranny* (London: Odhams, 1952).
204 Bosworth, *Explaining Auschwitz and Hiroshima*, op. cit. (note 4).
205 K. Robbins, '"This Grubby Wreck of Old Glories": The United Kingdom and the End of the British Empire', *Journal of Contemporary History*, 15 1 (1980), pp.81–95, in particular p.156.
206 Robbins, 'This Grubby Wreck of Old Glories', op. cit. (note 205), p.156.
207 D. J. Goodspeed, *The German Wars: 1914–1945* (Boston: Houghton Mifflin, 1978). Robbins, 'This Grubby Wreck of Old Glories', op. cit. (note 205), p.157.

major English historians of the early post-war period focused not on British activities but on German ones. What happened there and why? Was it inevitable? How are the Germans different to us?

Hugh Trevor-Roper made the case for the essential relationship between Hitler and the German people. National Socialism was not simply a top-down process but bottom-up too. Hitler tapped into something essential and was willingly received.[208] Accordingly, the German dictator is understood

> able to draw around him, as willing accomplices, not only that nucleus of devoted and fanatical revolutionaries who provided him with his elite, but also those millions of ordinary Germans who, recognising in him the prophet and executor of their half-formulated and since disowned ambitions, followed him readily, even gladly, even to the end, in his monstrous attempt to impose upon the world a barbarous German domination.[209]

For conservatives like Trevor-Roper, the British are understood as the definitive guardians of civilisation, while the Germans – rather than simply 'the Nazis' – are the opposite: barbarous, sadistic and nihilistic. Sir Lewis Namier is similarly essentialist in his analysis of the rise of National Socialism, 'the Germans' understood to be nothing less than 'a deadly menace to Europe and to civilization'.[210]

Taylor deals with National Socialism, Hitler and Germany in several of his works. Amidst the light and sometimes-jesting style, however, there is an implicit message that sometimes raises its head for all to see. In *The Course of German History* Taylor states how 'it was no more a mistake for the German people to end up with Hitler than it is an accident when a river flows into the sea'.[211] Moreover, that '[t]he British people resolved to defy Hitler' makes the British cause appear morally superior to the subsequent engagements of the Soviet Union and the United States.[212] This is not to say that the role played by Britain's allies is not acknowledged. Writing in the early 1960s – when the first phase of the Cold War had began noticeably to thaw – Taylor emphasises the important role played by the Soviet Union during World War II. However, just as the roots of belligerency 'lay

---

208 H. T. Roper, *Hitler's Table Talk: His Private Conversations 1941–44* (London: Weidenfeld & Nicholson, 2002). Bosworth, *Explaining Auschwitz and Hiroshima* op. cit. (note 4), p.26.

209 Roper, *Hitler's Table Talk*, op. cit. (note 208), p.xxviii.

210 Namier, L.B., *Conflicts: Studies in Contemporary History* (London, Macmillan, 1942).

211 A. J. P. Taylor, *The Course of German History: A Survey of the Development of German History since 1815* (London: Routledge, 2001), p.vii.

212 A. J. P. Taylor, *The Origins of the Second World War* (London, Penguin, 1963), p.336.

in the remote German past' it is essentially the German's who lose the war rather than the allies who win.[213] Germany defeated itself by invading the Soviet Union and declaring 'war on the United States'.[214] The moral victory belonged to Britain. World War II continued as a popular topic of investigation among historians from England into the 1980s. But by now 'the word "decline"' had 'lodged itself firmly in the British vocabulary and consciousness', a 'preoccupation [that] inevitably affected the selection and interpretation of... new archival riches'.[215] Essentially, decline as a world power would come to lie at the heart of revisionist interpretations of Britain's role during the Second World War, a situation exacerbated by the realisation of the UK's ever-more subservient role in relations with the United States.[216] Where Thatcher insisted that there was a 'relationship' that is necessarily 'special', 'a union of mind and purpose between our peoples which is remarkable' historians of the period agreed to differ.[217]

The idea that Britain, let alone England, had won the war seemed increasingly untenable. Comments made by those who had appeared cynical in 1945 came to appear reasonable. The conferences held at Yalta and at Potsdam, for example, were not in fact meetings between 'the Big Three' but rather, 'according to Sir Alexander Cadogan, the Big "2 W".[218] For Keith Robbins, nations that win wars should not, in theory, lose empires.[219] Yet Britain had lost its empire by the early 1960s. What did that say about Britain's role during the war? According to Robbins,

> insofar as the loss of the British Empire, or at least the speed of the loss, is perceived to be a consequence of the Second World War, then that war now necessarily has a rather different significance from what it was still widely believed to posses in 1945. The loss of empire was undoubtedly traumatic for many, not least for Churchill himself who towards the end of his life could be heard to wonder whether, in long perspective, his career had been a failure. The British Empire was no more. The

---

213 Bosworth, *Explaining Auschwitz and Hiroshima*, op. cit. (note 4), p.23.
214 Taylor, *Origins of the Second World War* , op. cit, (note 212), p.336.
215 D. Reynolds, 'Rethinking Anglo-American Relations', *International Affairs*, 65 1 (1988–89), pp.89–111, in particular p.91.
216 F. S. Northedge, 'Britain as a Second-Rank Power', *International Affairs*, 46 1 (1970), pp.37–47. G. F. Treverton, 'Britain's Role in the 1990s: An American View', *International Affairs*, 66 4 (1990), pp.703–110.
217 M. Thatcher, *The Daily Telegraph*, 22nd February 1985, p.4.
218 D. Reynolds, 'Rethinking Anglo-American Relations', op. cit. (note 215), p.106.
219 Robbins, 'This Grubby Wreck of Old Glories', op. cit. (note 205). B. Collins, and K. Robbins, *British Culture and Economic Decline* (London: Weidenfeld & Nicolson, 1990). K. Robbins, 'Commemorating the Second World War in Britain: Problems of Definition', *The History Teacher*, 29 2 (1996), pp.155–162.

"victory" which he had inspired... seemed hollow: the British state had paid too high a price for it.[220]

Some revisionist historians would question the nature of the Anglo-American alliance. Britain did not win the war. Indeed, World War II should be understood as rather "The War of British Succession" from which the United States emerges as the victor'. From this position, Britain would have fared far better had they remained independent of the Americans both economically and militarily.[221] In the 1980s Corelli Barnett argued that Britain's decision to fight the war was a strategic miscalculation.[222] As pointed out by Howard, 'Barnett was the first scholar to point out the extent to which, by 1945, Britain had become totally dependent on the United States for its economic survival, let alone its military victory – a dependence that reduced it virtually to satellite status'.[223] Some years later, John Charmley would take a similar position. But now it was Chamberlain and appeasement that would be re-evaluated. According to Charmley, the appeasers were aware that Britain did not possess the strength to take on Germany, Italy and Japan and that doing so would lead, ultimately, to dependence on other powers.[224] According to Schoenfeld, '[f]or Charmley, Churchill's leadership was inspiring but barren, and the 1945 victory went to the Russians and Americans, not the British.[225] Churchill failed in his attempt to uphold British independence'.

It is now many years since the end of the Second World War and perspectives on the conflict have changed – the revisionism of the 1980s and the 1990s replaced by a pluralistic synthesis made up of a variety of perspectives. With the end of the Cold War and access to Russian archives understandings of the allied alliance have been transformed. This has led to a great range of studies on the crucial role played by the USSR during the Second World War. No longer are the Soviets depicted

---

220 Robbins, 'Commemorating the Second World War in Britain', op. cit. (note 219), p.158.

221 Robbins, 'Commemorating the Second World War in Britain', op. cit. (note 219), p.160.

222 C. Barnet, *The Audit of War: The Illusion and Reality of Britain as a Great Power* (London: Macmillan, 1986).

223 M. Howard, '1945–1995: Reflections on Half a Century of British Security Policy', *International Affairs*, 71 4 (1995), pp.705–715, in particular p.706.

224 J. Charmley, *Churchill: the End of Glory: A Political Biography* (London: Hodder & Stoughton, 1993).

225 M. Schoenfeld, 'Book review of Churchill: The End of Glory, A Political Biography by John Charmley', *The Journal of Military History*, 60 2 (1996), pp.385–388, in particular p.387.

playing a minor role somewhere in the distant east but rather as the key players in the battle against Germany – the most formidable of the Axis powers. The work of historians such as Richard Overy and Anthony Beevor stands out here.[226] In *Stalingrad*, Beevor details the enormity and brutality of the war on the Eastern Front and the sacrifices involved.[227] The role played by the Soviet Union during World War II is now a common feature of contemporary writing among British historians.

The 'English' are no longer portrayed as universally 'virtuous' in contrast to the 'evil' Germans. Indeed there now appears to be a greater appreciation of the difference between Nazis and Germans. The recent work of A. C. Grayling, on the British bombing of German cities during the war calls the campaign into question.[228] In spite of atrocities committed by the Nazi regime, were the British justified to conduct night bombing missions on cities such as Hamburg and Dresden that, by the end of the war, were inhabited by women, children and the old? Grayling argues that they were not.

Yet some claim, equally, that the English associate Germany with nothing but the Nazis. Journalist, Matthias Matussek, describes how, after 'being dispatched to London', his 'nine-year-old son was chased around Richmond Park by some English teenagers shouting "Nazi, Nazi"'.[229] On living in London he then described how he discovered the 'insatiable appetite' among the English 'for Nazi folklore and German-bashing'. At the same time, under the influence of 'anything goes' postmodernism, right wing historians from England like David Irving have gone as far as to deny the holocaust.[230]

Are the English obsessed with the war? If so, why? It is surely not because of a popular assumption that the 'English army won the war' alone. The 60th Anniversary Commemorations to mark the end of the conflict were very different to those often years earlier, and filled with a sense of the fading significance of the conflict. Most of the wartime generation have died or are very old. Yet where Winston Churchill would lose the national elections in 1945 he would win the accolade of 'Britain's most Important Person' in the 2000s due largely to Britain's 'moral

226 E. Overy, *Russia's War* (London, Penguin, 1999). A. Beevor, *Stalingrad* (London: Penguin, 2000).

227 Beevor, *Stalingrad*, op. cit. (note 226).

228 A. C. Grayling, *Among the Dead Cities: The History and Moral Legacy of the WWII Bombing of Civilians in Germany and Japan* (New York: Walker & Company, 2006).

229 M. Matussek, 'Beethoven, Claudia Schiffer, Willy Brandt? No, the British are Only Interested in Germany when it Involves Nazis'. [Internet] The Guardian Unlimited, 23r May 2006. Available at: http://www.guardian.co.uk.

230 D. Irving, *Hitler's War and the War Path* (New York: Basic Books, 2002).

victory' in the Second World War under his leadership. If anything, current interest in the war in England could be said to reflect the rising phenomenon of popular nationalism that may accompany decline and insecurity; a sentimental yearning for those days when Britain sat at the top table of world affairs. Nevertheless, at the present time there are clearly a plurality of perspectives on the meaning and reality of the war.

The relationship between current historiography and history education in England is of interest to us here. If we look at the National Curriculum for Key Stage 2 and 3, the programme appears only vaguely influenced by contemporary historiography. At Key Stage 2 teachers may 'choose between a study of Victorian Britain or Britain since 1930'. In turn, if the latter is selected this may involve either '[a] study of the impact of the Second World War or social and technological changes that have taken place since 1930, on the lives of men, women and children from different sections of society'. At Key Stage 3 teachers and students must complete, amongst other things, 'A world study after 1900'. This involves investigating 'some of the significant individuals, events and developments from across the twentieth century, including the two World Wars, the holocaust, the Cold War, and their impact on Britain, Europe and the wider world' (at http://www.nc.uk.net). Greatest attention appears to be given to the Second World War as a curriculum topic at Key Stage 4 in preparation for the GCSE examinations. However, themes do not appear to express the findings and perspectives of recent research by historians.

7.5 Constellation Mapping

Constellation mapping is a necessary pre-requisite for constellation analysis, the end point of this methodological system. With constellation analysis we compare variables according to their value; that is, according to the extent to which they exert influence on a given syllabus topic. In other words, we do not compare 'things in themselves' – i.e. textbooks, the official curriculum, examinations – but rather effects. Those variables that exert the greatest influence on the shape and topography of the syllabus topic will be seen to be most worthy of attention.

Constellation mapping and 'comparative constellation analysis' are different to Paulston's postmodern conception of 'social cartography'. With social cartography 'social' relations and discourses are conceptualised in terms of the concept of mapping, according to a scheme in which subject and object are always de-centred. It is in this way that Paulston maps 'comparative education discourse' and the work of various comparative educationists.[231] In Chapters Three to Six various discourses were positioned both conceptually and visually. However, this process was always under-pinned by a neo-Hegelian dynamic in which subjects and objects are perceived neither purely centred nor de-centred. In Chapter Four, conceptual positioning was understood to lead to the visual metaphor of constellation dynamics. Then, in Chapter Six we saw how ideal typical models – made up of a constellation of variables – may provide the basis for gauging syllabus topic variations across contexts. Essentially, constellations are considered to be the expression of dynamic, circular and hermeneutic relationships between power and knowledge. The syllabus topic – in this case the Second World War – finds expression through a plurality of variables; the task of the subject, operating within its 'sphere of liberty', to investigate the variables in depth and to locate the syllabus topic among them. A syllabus topic is a conceptual rather than physical object, its shape and form determined by the constituting parts.

In this chapter we have explored the meaning and significance of various 'parts' across my three-exemplar nations: Japan, Sweden and England. Essentially, history education across the three contexts is shaped according to the ways in which influencing variables are configured. As a purely metaphorical device, the configuration of variables may be mapped in the form of a constellation. Ten component areas have been identified: background and tradition, prescribed curriculum, teacher/student role, censorship, mass media, examinations and assessment, Internet, classroom media, and contemporary politics and ideology, historiography. Likewise, each of these variables in each of the exemplar countries has now been observed with particular attention to history education.

---

231 E. H. Epstein, 'Currents Left and Right: Ideology in Comparative Education' in P. G. Altbach, and G. P. Kelly, *New Approaches to Comparative Education* (Chicago, University of Chicago Press, 1986), p.457. R. G. Paulston, 'Mapping Comparative Education after Postmodernity', *Comparative Education Review*, 43 4 (1999), pp.438–463.

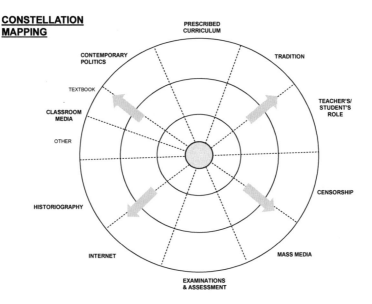

PRESCRIBED
CURRICULUM

CONTEMPORARY
POLITICS

TRADITION

TEXTBOOK

TEACHER'S/
STUDENT'S
ROLE

CLASSROOM
MEDIA

OTHER

CENSORSHIP

HISTORIOGRAPHY

INTERNET

MASS MEDIA

EXAMINATIONS
& ASSESSMENT

Fig. 7.2:   Constellation Mapping

The ten variables – the constellation – are configured around the circumference of Figure 7.2. The outer circle (OC) is used to denote variables that exert the most 'controlling' influence – the 'big' pull factors. The middle circle (MC) denotes variables that have moderate 'controlling' influence. The inner circle (IC) shows variables that exert the least 'controlling' influence. In some contexts a particular variable will have no influence in which case it will be marked by a 'black hole'. This way of gauging influence – power/knowledge relationships – is guided by the following criteria for each variable.

Tradition

OC: Conservative tradition in history education. The memorisation of knowledge is valued. Little or no room for independent assessment or debate. No critical thinking. Nationalistic.

MC: Tradition that values some critical thinking as well as the memorisation of facts. Some room for pluralism. In places nationalist.

IC: Liberal tradition in history education that values critical thinking and the independent assessment of evidence. Pluralism valued. Internationalist in orientation.

Prescribed Curriculum

OC: Highly prescriptive and centralised curriculum
MC: A mixture of guidelines both loose and prescriptive
IC: Loose curriculum guidelines for history education

Examinations and Assessment

OC: External assessment of history with examination requirements for entry into post-compulsory education
MC: Internal assessment of history with examination requirements for entry into post-compulsory education
IC: Internal assessment of history with no examination requirements for entry into post-compulsory education

Classroom Media

– Textbooks
OC: Textbooks are the staple source of information for the purposes of teaching and learning
MC: Textbooks often used in classroom contexts
IC: Textbooks rarely used in classroom contexts, if ever

– Other
OC: Video, DVD, multi-media packages frequently used in the classroom
MC: Video, DVD, multi-media packages sometimes used in the classroom
IC: Video, DVD, multi-media packages rarely used in the classroom, if ever

Censorship

OC: A system in which educational materials and information are strongly controlled
MC: A system with moderate levels of censorship
IC: A system with loose or no censorship guidelines for history education

Contemporary Politics and Ideology

OC: Major policy shift signalling changes for the teaching and learning of history
MC: Some important policy shifts have affected history education
IC: Few if any policy initiatives have affected history education

Internet Access

OC: Internet has become the major source from which students and teachers access information
MC: Some use of the Internet as an educational tool
IC: Little use of the Internet as an educational tool

Mass Media

OC: Press and mass media are not wholly free – conservative editorial control
MC: Free press and media with a tendency to identify with the political and ideological right
IC: Liberal free press and media airing a wide variety of viewpoints and perspectives on historical events

Teacher/Student Role

OC: Teachers and/or students define the nature of classroom knowledge
MC: Teachers and/or students have some control over the definition of classroom information and knowledge
IC: Teachers and/or students play a passive role with little control over the definition of classroom information and knowledge

Historiography

OC: Current historiographical debates have a strong influence over what is taught in history classrooms
MC: Current historiographical debates have some influence over what is taught in history classes
IC: Current historiographical debates have little influence over what is taught in history classes

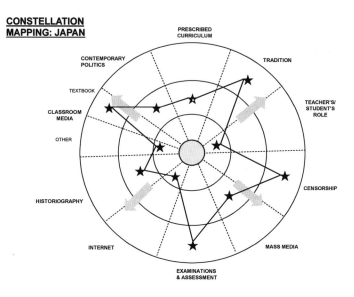

CONSTELLATION MAPPING: JAPAN

PRESCRIBED CURRICULUM

CONTEMPORARY POLITICS

TRADITION

TEXTBOOK

CLASSROOM MEDIA

TEACHER'S/ STUDENT'S ROLE

OTHER

HISTORIOGRAPHY

CENSORSHIP

INTERNET

MASS MEDIA

EXAMINATIONS & ASSESSMENT

Fig. 7.3:   Constellation Mapping: Japan

In the above diagram we observe the constellation of variables as configured in Japan. Essentially, we see what in Chapter Four was described as a frozen constellation. Where the syllabus topic as a whole is understood dynamically constituted in relation to its parts and vice versa, through the process I call constellation dynamics, by momentarily freezing the constellation we are able to detail the various constituting relationships. Constellation mapping is an essentially practical undertaking that involves the detailed description of the constellation of parts in order to begin to assess their relationship to the syllabus topic as a whole. What can be discerned from Figure 7.3? First we can see that a conservative tradition prevails in the teaching and learning of school history in Japan. The memorisation of knowledge is valued where critical thinking is not. Similarly, the curriculum is more explicitly nationalistic than many other countries. Teachers and students play a passive role with little control over the definition of classroom information and knowledge but the curriculum incorporates a mixture of guidelines, both loose and prescriptive, centralised and local. Censored textbooks are the staple source of information for the purposes of teaching and learning. Video, DVD, and multi-media packages and the Internet are rarely used as educational tools. In order to enter post-compulsory education, history will be externally assessed through institutional entrance examinations. Some important policy shifts have affected school history education in recent years, often in a nationalist direction. These issues are likely to have been covered by the free press and media even with its tendency to identify with the political and ideological right. Current 'right wing' historiographical debates have some influence over what is taught in history classes.

Constellation mapping enables the comprehensive description of school history education in Japan. It also enables us to identify those variables that exert the most influence and to discern the topography of the syllabus topic. In the case of Japan the school history textbook, government censorship, and the external 'entrance' examinations are the most important variables influencing history education. In turn, these are the elements most affecting the formation of the Second World War as a syllabus topic in Japanese schools, and any analysis must include these variables.

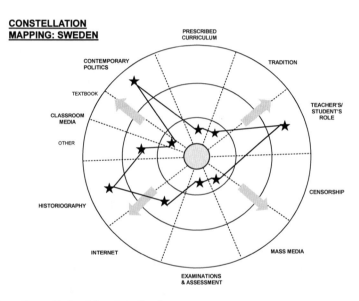

Fig. 7.4:   Constellation Mapping: Sweden

In Sweden we are confronted with a completely different reality. Here we find a liberal tradition in history education that values critical thinking and the independent assessment of evidence. The orientation is both pluralist and internationalist. This is a system with loose curriculum guidelines and no rules of censorship. In addition, video, DVD, multi-media packages and the Internet may tend be used as much as if not more than the textbook. Teachers and students define the nature of classroom knowledge. Indeed it is teachers often in consultation with students who determine what is to be taught. Essentially, history is internally assessed.

Some important policy shifts have affected history education in recent times. And current historiographical debates are likely to have a strong influence over what is taught in school history classrooms. Finally, a wide range of viewpoints and perspectives on historical events are aired in a very liberal free press.

Again by mapping the constellation, we may construct a picture of secondary history education, this time in Sweden, enabling us to identify those variables that exert the greatest influence on the shape of a syllabus topic such as World War II. In the case of Sweden teachers are vital to any understanding of contemporary curriculum knowledge in history education. The government's 'consensual' agenda is also important as is a knowledge of trends in academic historiography. Any analysis of the Second World War as a syllabus topic in Swedish schools will require an investigation of these variables.

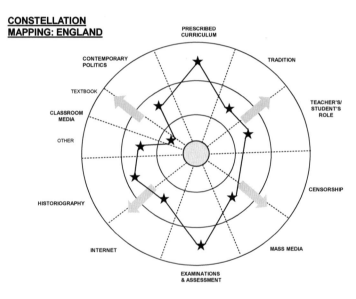

Fig. 7.5: *Constellation Mapping: England*

Finally we arrive at England where the situation appears somewhat between that identified in Japan and Sweden. Here we find a liberal tradition in history education that values critical thinking and the independent assessment of evidence. Yet the orientation is both national and international. Moreover, the curriculum is highly prescriptive and centralised. This being said, teachers and students have some control over the definition of classroom information and knowledge. History is examined externally. Entry into post-compulsory education usually requires the passing of a series of 'closed paper' examinations. And while there is no official censorship of knowledge the National Curriculum acts as a censor. Textbooks are used less and less in classroom contexts while DVD and multi-media packages have become common features. The Internet has become a major source from which students and teachers access information. Some important policy initiatives have directly affected history education in recent years. And current historiographical debates have some influence over what is taught in history classes. A free press exists in England but with a tendency to identify with the political and ideological right. Constellation mapping allows us to look out across the vista of school history education in England, enabling us to identify those variables that exert the greatest influence on the shape of the syllabus topic. In the case of England it is the National Curriculum and the external examination syllabuses that have the greatest effect. For this reason any analysis of World War II as a theme in school history education in England must involve particular investigation of these variables.

7.6 Concluding Comments

We have now become immersed in the particularities of three educational contexts. With the 'ideal type' in hand, held like a torch, the researcher has been conceived making sense of the complexities and variations that characterise school history education in each of the contexts. Accordingly, we discovered that the power/knowledge variables – the push and pull factors – that would define the parameters of a syllabus topic such as the Second World War differed considerably in terms of influence from one context to the next. Although the war is a popular syllabus topic in all of the exemplar countries, the topic is influenced by the ten variables in different ways from context to context. Using what I refer to as constellation mapping we come to understand exactly which factors need to be prioritised for analysis and which do not. Essentially, this process enables the reconstruction of the syllabus topic based on the identification of those factors that exert the greatest influence.

In Japan the university entrance examinations and government-censored textbooks are the prime movers exerting the greatest effects on the parameters and shape of the syllabus topic. What do textbooks and examinations say about the conflict? What perspectives do they enable? In England the official curriculum in conjunction with forms of external assessment exert the greater influence, before any form of intervention from the teacher has even been made. How does this happen? In Sweden, on the other hand, with nothing anywhere near as prescriptive as the official curriculum in England, and no forms of external assessment for history, the role of the teacher in defining what is taught is paramount. The perspectives of teachers will need to be examined before meaningful comparisons of the Second World War as a syllabus topic can ensue. By mapping the constellation of influencing variables the problem of simply comparing, say, school textbooks from each of the countries becomes clear. Where the school textbook plays a central role in defining the history curriculum in Japan, it occupies a negligible place in history education in Sweden and England. The syllabus topic must rather be understood as an output of those 'elements' that exert the most power and influence across contexts. And it is only after these elements have been identified that meaningful comparisons may ensue. This method of comparison I call constellation analysis, and it is to this that we now turn.

Chapter Eight
Comparative Constellation Analysis as Method

> As a constellation, theoretical thought circles the concept it
> would like to unseal, hoping that it may fly open like the lock
> of a well-guarded safe-deposit box: in response, not to a sin-
> gle key or a single number, but to a combination of numbers.

> T. W. Adorno, *Negative Dialectics*, 1973, p.163

In Chapter Seven I demonstrated how the variables influencing the composition of a syllabus topic could be described and charted using constellation mapping. After the more abstract concerns and discussions of the preceding chapters, Chapter Seven appeared as a fundamentally practical and descriptive exercise. Constellation mapping enables the researcher to identify power/knowledge relationships across contexts. Most important of all, it illustrates the fact that variables do not share the same level of influence across contexts. Where a given variable may have enormous influence on the composition of a syllabus topic in one context it may have little or, in some cases, no influence in another. Constellation mapping allows the researcher to gauge the value of a given variable in terms of its effects. In turn, variables that are discovered to exert the most powerful effects are those deemed most worthy of attention.

What can and should we compare to understand the Second World War as a syllabus topic in school history across contemporary contexts? The answer to this question concerns the researching subject as well as the objects being compared. On the level of the subject, the researcher will be confined to the limits set by its own horizon, the parameters of which will be defined by research training, a knowledge of foreign languages and past experiences, as discussed in chapters Four and Five. On the level of objects, I would argue, syllabus topics represent the dynamic expression of clusters of variables, identified according to their influence on the composition of the topic. Essentially, researchers must step beyond comparisons of 'things-in-themselves', e.g. textbooks, towards an investigation of variously configured effects in order to gain the most complete perspective on the syllabus topic. This requires a new mindset, and is embodied in my method: comparative constellation analysis.

Comparative constellation analysis represents the final stage of the methodological system developed in this book. Thus, beyond what 'can' and 'should' be compared, constellation analysis tells us 'how' to make comparisons of syllabus topics. As a method it enables the investigation of clusters of variables according to their effects and level of influence.

8.1 Comparative School Textbook Research and its Discontents

Comparative constellation analysis may be usefully contrasted with comparative textbook research. With comparative textbook research, textbook content is understood to be synonymous with syllabus content. Textbook researchers draw conclusions from the comparison of schoolbooks, therefore, based on the assumption that textbooks are somehow 'universal', the expression of 'official knowledge'.[1] But with constellation analysis, the investigation of schoolbooks requires justification. In other words, textbooks should be analysed only in cases where the researcher can be certain, within reasonable grounds and parameters, that texts significantly influence the composition of a syllabus topic in school history in a given context.

Earlier, I argued that my previous published work in comparative textbook research contained a series of internal contradictions that led not to the consolidation of a thesis but rather to an antithesis. Essentially, my attempt to construct an Hegelian imbibed methodology for researching school textbooks across cultures had the effect of fundamentally 'undermining' the possibility of an Hegelian comparative textbook research. Thus, as I laboured on consecutive papers, refining my approach, I became increasingly conscious of the problems embodied in the approach. The methodological trajectory of these papers led not only to a particular critique of itself or to the general critique of school textbook research as a practice but, also, ultimately, to alternative approaches. Using Hegel, we see that it was 'the contradiction' in the work that pushed it 'beyond itself to a new and potentially more robust perspective.[2]

In my earlier research I compared the content of school history textbooks from England with those from other nations with a specific focus on portrayals and representations of the Second World War. The majority of these works were published in journals or presented at international conferences. While the papers are interesting from the point of view of comparative historiography they appear, with hindsight, seriously flawed from the perspective of comparative education. While textbooks are undoubtedly important educational resources in some contexts they are not important in others. This is not to say that because a thing means different things in different places it cannot be compared. Rather, it is to say that when a thing has no function or

---

1   M. Apple, *Teachers and Texts- A Political Economy of Class and Gender Relations in Education* (New York, Routledge & Kegan Paul, 1986).

2   G. W. F. Hegel, *Science of Logic* (New York, The Macmillan Company, 1929), pp.140–141,

a marginal function in a particular context, its value as a unit against which to make meaningful educational comparisons is greatly if not totally diminished.

The development of comparative constellation analysis as a method owes much to my earlier work in comparative textbook research. As a synthesis comparative constellation analysis arose out of the antithesis that is comparative textbook research; spirit germinating within the parameters of the former endeavour prior to bursting free.

From an educational point of view, how important is comparative textbook research? The answer to this question will depend on the significance of texts for defining curriculum knowledge and teaching practices across contexts. In some cultures the use of textbooks for the teaching and learning of history has long been in decline. And with the Internet and new forms of educational media one can reasonably surmise that this trend will continue. In the post-Gutenberg era, textbook research appears increasingly to 'sink behind the Spirit of the Age'.[3] Textbooks are at most dependent variables, de-centred objects; their educational meaning bound to the ways in which they are used in particular contexts.[4] But in contexts where they are not used, or used only very infrequently, they lose their status as educationally significant variables altogether. They become incomparable.

8.2 Comparative Constellation Analysis

Adorno uses the concept of constellations as a methodological device and as a means to understanding concepts as objects. The 'constellation' Adorno tells us 'circles the concept it would like to unseal, hoping that it may fly open like the lock of a well-guarded safe-deposit box'.[5] I conceive of comparative constellation analysis in much the same way; that is, as a means to illuminate the reality of a syllabus topic in context. Where in comparative textbook research it is presumed that the textbook is an accurate 'reflection' of the syllabus topic, textbooks understood to be the 'single key' to all contexts, constellation analysis requires the use of 'a combination of numbers' that may vary from context to context.[6]

Constellation analysis is thus underpinned by a series of implicit assumptions about history education across cultures. First and foremost, school history

---

3   G. W. F. Hegel, *The Philosophy of History* (New York, Prometheus Books, 1991), p.419.
4   J. Nicholls, 'School History Textbooks across Cultures from the Perspective of Comparative Education', in J. Nicholls (ed.) *School History Textbooks across Cultures – international debates and perspectives* (Oxford, Symposium, 2006).
5   T. W. Adorno, *Negative Dialectics* (London, Routledge, 1973).
6   Adorno, *Negative Dialectics,* op. cit. (note 5), p.163.

education is understood to be 'saturated in cultural particularities' and definitively complex.[7] In addition to this, syllabus topics are understood as being 'locked up' within a context in particular ways. The meaning and reality of the Second World War in contemporary history classes in Japan, Sweden and England is, therefore, likely to be different. Which means that the 'combination of numbers enabling the researcher to 'unlock' the meaning of the conflict as a syllabus topic in each context is also likely to vary.

To ascertain '[h]ow objects can be unlocked by their constellation' Adorno beckons his readers to 'go back... to Max Weber'.[8] It is Weber that gave social science '"ideal types" as aids in approaching the object'.[9] Adorno's references to Weber are highly apt. In Chapter Six we saw how the Brian Holmes/Edmund King dialectic may be interpreted as a means to appropriating Weber's concept of 'ideal types' for use in comparative educational research. In turn, ideal types were understood to be composed of a constellation of variables, enabling researchers to approach complex educational contexts and, as outlined in Chapter Seven, describe variations across contexts. As Adorno points out, 'Weber's... constellations take the place of systematic ... and this is what proves his thinking to be' something of a 'third possibility beyond' the material and the ideal.[10] Once again, Hegel's understanding of the relationship between 'actual' and 'rational' springs to mind.[11]

This connection between Weber and Adorno facilitates an increasingly systematic understanding of the ideas that run through this entire book. Hegel's circular dialectics, Gadamer's concept of horizons, Weber's notion of 'ideal types' and Adorno's 'constellations' are all conceived working together in a hermeneutic space beyond the modernist thesis and its postmodern antithesis. But comparative constellation analysis owes much to Foucault and, in particular, the late-Foucauldian reading of the relationship between power and knowledge that was discussed in Chapter Four. In Adorno, the relationship between the 'stars' in the constellation and the relatively centred concept is defined in largely epistemological terms, on the level of knowledge and reason. Only by incorporating

---

7   Nicholls, 'School History Textbooks across Cultures from the Perspective of Comparative Education', op. cit. (note 4), p.1.

8   Adorno, *Negative Dialectics,* op. cit. (note 5), p.164.

9   Adorno, *Negative Dialectics,* op. cit. (note 5), p.164.

10   Adorno, *Negative Dialectics,* op. cit. (note 5), p.166.

11   G. W. F. Hegel, *Philosophy of Right* (Oxford, Oxford University Press, 1967), p.10.

late-Foucauldian concepts can the points of the constellation be interpreted as relations of the dialectic between power/knowledge and knowledge/power.

Comparative constellation analysis as a method for understanding syllabus topics in context is, most fundamentally, concerned with identifying variables that impact most powerfully on a topic. In turn, the most powerful variables are considered to be the most important and, as a result, the most worthy of attention. The major influencing variables are the stars in the constellation that illuminate the topography of the syllabus topic most brightly.

Constellation analysis represents a new and systematic approach to comparing syllabus topics across cultures. Essentially, it is underpinned by a particular rationality with its own rules and procedures. Constellation analysis must, for example, always be preceded by the descriptive exercise of constellation mapping. In addition to this, it requires the researcher to advance through a series of methodical stages. These stages, six in total, are listed below:

1. Isolating variables for comparison
2. Ranking 'Outer Circle' variables in terms of effects
3. Initial Comparisons – horizontal and vertical
4. Comparing Variable Clusters across Cultures
5. Comparing 'Outer Circle' variables with 'Middle Circle' factors
6. Conclusions and recommendations

The central aim of constellation analysis is to provide an accurate and meaningful picture of syllabus topics in and across settings. Fundamentally, syllabus topics are conceived as the expression of a rich and complex cluster of factors configured differently in terms of relations of power and knowledge from one context to the next. Accepting the intricacy of school history in and across contexts, constellation analysis enables the researcher to identify 'the wood for the trees' in order to proceed forward towards robust and meaningful comparisons.

Stage 1: Isolating Variables for Comparison

Using the constellation mapping technique, outlined in Chapter Seven, we identified the relationship between particular variables and school history in Japan, Sweden and England. First of all, we discovered that the extent to which a given variable exerts influence tends to vary from one context to the next. And second, that the variables exerting the greatest influence in one context were often not the same as those exerting influence in the other two contexts.

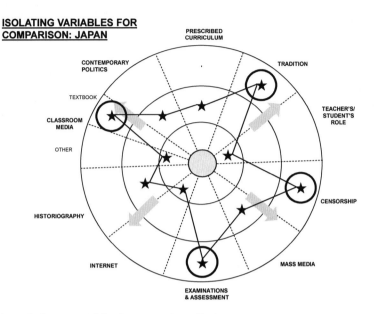

ISOLATING VARIABLES FOR COMPARISON: JAPAN

PRESCRIBED CURRICULUM

CONTEMPORARY POLITICS

TRADITION

TEXTBOOK

CLASSROOM MEDIA

TEACHER'S/ STUDENT'S ROLE

OTHER

HISTORIOGRAPHY

CENSORSHIP

INTERNET

MASS MEDIA

EXAMINATIONS & ASSESSMENT

Fig. 8.1:   Isolating variables for comparison: Japan

To use comparative constellation analysis it is essential to isolate those variables that exert the greatest influence on the syllabus topic in each context. These variables are the 'big' pull factors, identified in Chapter Seven. In the above chart, Figure 8.1, we see the constellation for school history in Japan. In the chart, the variables identified exerting the strongest 'controlling' influence have been isolated: Censorship, Examinations and Assessment, and Textbooks. Japan's notably conservative Tradition is also identified as a powerfully 'controlling' factor. These are in complete contrast with those variables exerting the greatest influence on school history in liberal Sweden, Teacher/ Student Role, Historiography, and Contemporary Politics – identified in Figure 8.2.

The constellation for Japan and the constellation for Sweden are strikingly different. In other words, the 'big' pull factors affecting syllabus topics in school history in each country are profoundly contrasted in terms of effects. Yet this means, at the same time, that the variables identified as having a moderate or lesser impact are also different. Turning to the situation in England, as outlined in Figure 8.3, we find an equally contrasted reality. Now it is the Prescribed Curriculum, Examinations and Assessment that are identified as having the greatest influence. In England it should also be noted that many variables are understood as having a moderate influence.

270

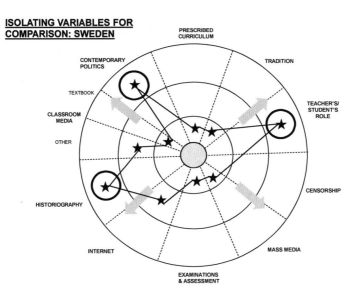

Fig. 8.2:   Isolating variables for comparison: Sweden

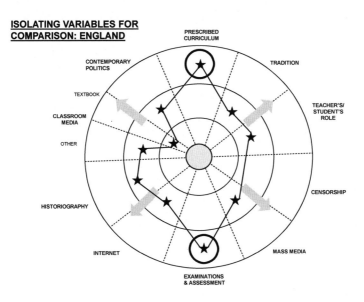

Fig. 8.3:   Isolating variables for comparison: England

Clearly the factors that influence the shape of a syllabus topic in school history in one context may be different to those that shape the same topic in another. Essentially, school history in each of the three countries is a highly complex affair. Unless this fact is acknowledged from the very beginning only superficial comparisons may ensue. In this way, the constellation approach exposes many of the problems intrinsic to comparative textbook research. Textbooks are definitive particularities. The meaning and purpose of the textbook is not universal across contexts but specific to context. Comparing particularities may tell us much about the features of individual texts; that is, of the particularities themselves. But to what extent is textbook content representative of syllabus knowledge in school history as a whole? This will depend on the importance of textbooks as pull factors across the contexts being compared. In contexts where textbooks have been identified as having little impact on the shape of a syllabus topic, 'educational' generalisations based on the content of texts should be avoided.

Stage 2: Ranking 'Outer Circle' Variables in Terms of Effects

Having isolated the most influential variables for comparison – those variables occupying the 'outer circle' of the constellation – it is then necessary to 'rank' these variables in each context. In other words, after identifying and isolating clusters of affecting factors in a context, the researcher must then rank each factor in terms of its level of influence in each context. This is illustrated in the chart below.

	Japan	Sweden	England
First level variables	High school entrance examinations	Teachers	National Curriculum
Second level variables	School history textbooks	Contemporary political initiatives	External examinations
Third level variables	Official censorship policy	Academic historiography	
Fourth level variables	Tradition		

The process of 'ranking' will be guided by reason. In Japan, for example, it can reasonably be argued that high school entrance examinations exert the greatest influence with regard to what is taught and learned in school history classes. As outlined in the previous chapter, school history education in Japan is geared towards passing entrance examinations. In Japan, no factor 'pulls' a syllabus topic in a particular direction like the examinations. For this reason the school entrance examinations are understood as First Level variables in the Japanese context. Next come the school history textbooks that are relied upon as a source of information in history classes (Level 2). Textbooks in Japan are essential for examination preparation. Yet textbooks only become available after they have been 'officially censored' – the third factor among the 'main' variables affecting syllabus topics in Japan (Level 3). Finally, examinations, textbooks, and censorship are located within a highly conservative educational tradition in Japan, in which the memorisation of facts is valued at the expense of critical thinking (Level 4).

In liberal Sweden it is history teachers and in some cases their students who are identified having the greatest effect on the shape and content of a given syllabus topic (Level 1). With very loose curriculum guidelines and the absence of external examinations for history, teachers have enormous freedom to decide on what will and will not be taught in school history classes. Much more than in Japan or England, history teachers in Sweden are key gatekeepers to curriculum knowledge and instruction. In recent years, government initiatives have been very important with regard to questions regarding the teaching of World War II (Level 2). Investigations by historians on Sweden and the Second World War have been similarly important to contemporary debates (Level 3).

In England, it is the National Curriculum (Level 1) that is identified as having the greatest influence on what is taught in school history classes followed by the external examinations (Level 2). Relative to these factors other variables are identified as being of either moderate or minor significance. In England the centralised and prescriptive nature of the National Curriculum cannot be underestimated. In addition to this, in what has become an increasingly examination oriented culture, students are increasingly taught to 'pass examinations'. In other words, classroom instruction in history often takes the form of teaching students the 'tricks of the trade' that will guarantee examination success. Where the National Curriculum pushes the teaching and learning of history in England, the external examinations represent an essential 'pull' factor.

Using comparative constellation analysis variables are ranked and positioned according to their effects or 'magnitude of influence' on the composition of syllabus topics. Viewed in this way, Japanese high school entrance examinations are understood to have more in common with teachers in Sweden, than the internal examination of history in Swedish schools. Similarly, where the school history textbook exerts enormous influence in Japan, its equivalent in England would be the external examinations. Using constellation analysis textbooks in Japan are not comparable with textbooks in England or Sweden. In other words, they are not an equivalent due to the magnitude of their effects. In the same way Sweden's loose curriculum guidelines bare literally no resemblance to the National Curriculum in England. Likewise, any international comparison of school history involving Japan would have to include an analysis of that nation's official censorship policy, even if the other countries in the study have no such policy.

Stage 3: Initial Comparisons

Having 'isolated' and 'ranked' the most influential variables in each context, the researcher then proceeds to the stage of 'initial comparisons'. These take place first horizontally 'across cultures' and second vertically 'within cultures'. The making of initial comparisons represents a preliminary stage, preparatory in nature, providing the basis for deeper more complete comparisons at a later stage.

a. Horizontal Comparisons: First Level Variables 'Across Cultures'

Researchers will begin by making horizontal comparisons of First Level variables across contexts. First Level variables are the 'brightest stars' in the constellation of a given context, illuminating the topography of a given syllabus topic in its context more fully than any other. By investigating First Level variables we make the preliminary step towards understanding the composition and reality of a syllabus topic.

	Japan	Sweden	England
First level variables	High school entrance examinations	Teachers	National Curriculum

In the case of Japan, Sweden and England, the researcher must devise frameworks that will allow for the investigation of the same questions across variables that vary in type. In Japan, for example, we must look to the 'high school entrance examinations'. To investigate the Second World War as a contemporary syllabus topic we would need to research representative samples of high school entrance examinations to discern the questions and issues relating to the conflict that tend to be asked of students. What questions are included? What do they ask of students

274

in terms of knowledge and reasoning? What proportion of questions is related to World War II across examination papers? What other topics are represented? Since Japanese compulsory education is geared towards the passing of examinations, these investigations will enable the researcher to gain important initial insights into the composition of World War II as a syllabus topic in Japan.

In Sweden we would need to approach the teachers themselves. There are a variety of ways to do this, each with its own strengths and weaknesses. A mixed method approach might prove fruitful. This could include sending structured or semi-structured questionnaires to large populations of Swedish school history teachers. A series of unstructured interviews, with a small group of teachers, could be carried out in parallel with the questionnaires. To illuminate the composition of the Second World War as a syllabus topic, researchers would need to ascertain what educators teach and examine in their classes. What is expected from students? What proportion of class time is dedicated to studying World War II in history classes? What other topics are taught? Since Swedish teachers of history are key 'knowledge' gatekeepers, these investigations will facilitate preliminary insights into the composition of World War II as a syllabus topic.

In England we would need to focus on the content of the highly prescribed National Curriculum for history. What are educators obliged to teach with regard to the Second World War? What issues and events are approached? How much space does the study of World War II related issues take up on the curriculum? What other topics must educators cover? Again it is through these investigations that researchers may gain preliminary insights into the composition of World War II as a syllabus topic in England.

By investigating these First Level variables the researcher is likely to gain a firm impression of what is and is not taught on World War II in school history classes in each of the countries. Preliminary differences will become apparent, enabling the researcher to make a series of tentative 'initial comparisons' that should be carefully recorded. However, 'initial' is the key term here. In other words, it should not yet be assumed that the information is 'valid' or 'representative' or 'reliable' or that it is possible to 'generalise' from the data. Rather, these first comparisons across cultures will provide an important 'marked point' from which to move purposively towards vertical comparisons within each context.

b. Vertical Comparisons: 'Outer Circle' Variables 'Within Cultures'

The vertical comparison of 'Outer Circle' variables within a given context is important in several ways. On one level, it broadens the focus of investigation to all of the variables identified as exerting a major influence on the syllabus topic in a given context. On another level, the level of methodological consistency, it facilitates the researcher's sense of the validity and reliability of the first wave of findings. Crucially, the researcher proceeds towards the making of vertical comparisons necessarily conscious of what has already been discovered in each context.

Vertical comparisons will involve the investigation of Second, Third and perhaps Fourth level variables in a given context. Essentially, the findings from research on First Level variables will act as an anchor against which to investigate the other levels. In the case of Japan, for example, the findings from the investigation of high school entrance examinations will, to some extent, guide the next wave of investigations.

	Japan
First level variables	High school entrance examinations
Second level variables	School history textbooks
Third level variables	Official censorship policy
Fourth level variables	Tradition

School history textbooks and Japan's official censorship policy, were ranked as the most important factors influencing the composition of a syllabus topic after the school entrance examinations. Vertical comparisons would involve, therefore, the investigation of representations of World War II in samples of school textbooks. How is the war approached? What content is incorporated in the books? What is omitted? Patterns across the textbook sample would then be compared against findings from the initial investigation of entrance examinations. Do the textbooks include the same stories about the war as were revealed in the investigation of the entrance examinations? Can a core of similarities be identified? This would be followed by an analysis of perspectives on World War II in Japan's official censorship policy. Again the results of this investigation would be compared with those on entrance examinations and textbooks. Can a core of similarities be identified? What are the differences? Finally, the researcher would investigate the conservative traditions that prevail in Japanese history education to identify patterns over time that may explain why World War II is taught and learned in a particular way and why this tends to be accepted practice. How do these traditions relate to what was discovered from the research on examinations, textbooks, and censorship policy?

	Sweden
First level variables	Teachers
Second level variables	Contemporary political initiatives
Third level variables	Academic historiography

In Sweden the results from the investigation of teachers would need to be compared against contemporary political initiatives and academic historiography. What contemporary political initiatives have been instigated to support teaching and learning on World War II? How do they represent attempts to establish a new consensus? What have been the effects of these initiatives? What line is taken on Sweden and the war? Do certain areas of the conflict tend to be omitted? Having probed these questions, comparisons would then be made with the results from the investigation of teachers. Is it possible to observe a core of similarities between the findings on teachers and those on contemporary political initiatives? This would be followed by an investigation of recent historiographical developments. What claims about Sweden and the Second World War are being made by researchers in the academy and how does this compare with the content of government initiatives and the investigation of teachers? Once again researchers will seek to identify a common position on the Second World War and Sweden across the three 'Outer Circle' variables.

	England
First level variables	National Curriculum
Second level variables	External examinations

The situation for making vertical comparisons in England is somewhat different, due to the fact that only two variables affecting the composition of syllabus topics in school history were located in the 'Outer Circle' of the constellation. Essentially, the earlier investigations of World War II in the National Curriculum would be compared and contrasted with representations of the conflict in the external examinations, the GCSEs. What questions on the war are asked? What do students require in terms of knowledge and reasoning skills to answer questions and complete tasks? What proportion of questions is related to the Second World War across the examination papers? What other topics are represented? As in the case of Japan and Sweden, researchers will seek to identify areas of commonality regarding the Second World War as a topic across the two variables.

After conducting vertical comparisons in each of the contexts under investigation, the researcher will ideally have identified a consistent position on World War II across all of the 'Outer Circle' variables in a given context. If this is the case, the dynamic core of the syllabus topic, on World War II, for example, will have been illuminated.

Stage 4: Comparing Variable Clusters across Cultures

Constellation analysis represents a new approach to comparing syllabus topics in school history, requiring a wide range of skills, training, and background knowledge on the part of the researching subject. Essentially, it seeks to provide the basis for robust comparative analyses and, in this way, represents an alternative to comparative textbook research. Comparative constellation analysis is underpinned by the implicit assumption that school history is highly complex and must be researched in depth before any comparisons may take place. If the factors that exert a major influence can be identified in advance the researcher is in a far better position to investigate the variables that 'make a difference'. By researching variables according to their effects, the researcher can be relatively certain of identifying what is 'on the syllabus'.

'OUTER CIRCLE' VARIABLE CLUSTER

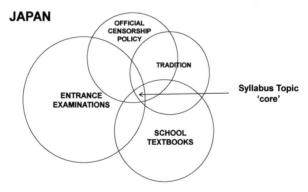

Fig. 8.4:   *'Outer Circle' variable cluster (Japan)*

By conducting vertical comparisons of the 'Outer Circle' variables in each context the researcher looks to consolidate a position or perspective among the variables – the 'core' of the syllabus topic in the school history of the given context. The diagram above, Figure 8.4, offers a way to envision this process in Japan as a cluster in the midst of which is situated a 'core'. The relationship between cluster and core is dynamic. Take away one of the variables and the position and shape of the 'core' changes. Add a new variable and it changes again.

In the diagram below, Figure 8.5, I chart the variable cluster for Sweden. We see here three instead of four interconnected circles, representing the three 'Outer Circle' variables identified as having the greatest impact on syllabus topics in Sweden. Teachers are represented by the largest circle since they have been identified as impacting the most on the shape and composition of syllabus topics in that country.

'OUTER CIRCLE' VARIABLE CLUSTER

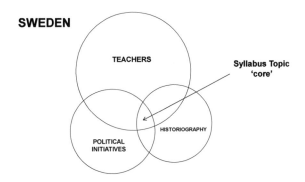

Fig. 8.5:   *'Outer Circle' variable cluster (Sweden)*

In the diagram representing England, Figure 8.6, the cluster is depicted in the form of two large circles with an extensive 'core'. The National Curriculum and the external examination syllabuses exert an enormous 'controlling' influence over what is taught in history classes in schools in England. By investigating the place of the Second World War in the National Curriculum and the examination syllabuses one can be reasonably certain of what will be studied by students in classrooms.

Comparative constellation analysis involves the investigation of clusters of variables that are understood to be important in a given context. It involves the identification of a dynamic essence or syllabus topic 'core' before in-depth comparisons can begin to take place. In this way, it represents an essential alternative to comparative textbook research. This is not to say that textbooks are necessarily unimportant, rather that they are important in only some contexts. Textbooks should be investigated, therefore, in contexts where they are important as a source, but only in those contexts. As an approach, constellation analysis is underpinned by a deeper concern for validity and reliability – concerns that appear largely absent from most textbook research. Although more time consuming as a practice, constellation analysis looks to reveal the dynamic 'essence' of the topic. Only then, it is argued, can generalisations be made.

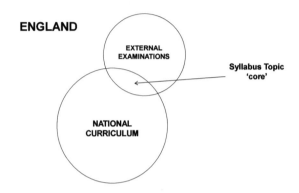

Fig. 8.6:   'Outer Circle' variable cluster (England)

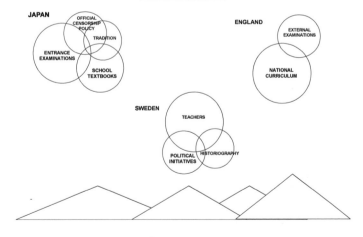

Fig. 8.7:   Comparing variable clusters across cultures

In Figure 8.7 the three clusters are illustrated together in one diagram, appearing as if 'floating' on the research horizon. Essentially, from the position of the Hegelian synthesis the researcher will be understood looking out from the platform of a particular 'sphere of liberty', that space from which it is possible to critically compare and evaluate the clusters under investigation. Hegel's 'sphere of liberty', it should be remembered, closely resembles Foucault's 'zone of de-subjugation'. From this 'zone', moreover, the researcher is positioned neither totally centred, nor totally de-centred, but dynamically located, at a particular point in time and space, from which it becomes possible, within limits, to assess power/knowledge variations. By investigating the most powerfully influencing variables in a context researchers may identify a 'core' of knowledge that can be subjected to critical analysis.

Having completed the stage of initial comparisons, the researcher is now in a position to compare each syllabus 'core', one against the next. This will involve the comparison of dynamic essences. Investigations will likewise be driven by probing questions to illuminate similarities and differences across the target contexts. In the case of the Second World War as a syllabus topic, a series of questions spring to mind. For example,

- Which countries are accredited with winning and losing the war across contexts?
- Which battle arenas receive the most attention?
- How is the plight of civilians presented?
- How is the Holocaust dealt with?
- In what way is the war experience of women and ethnic minority groups presented?
- To what extent is the topic underpinned by nationalism in each of the contexts?
- What are considered to be the major turning points of the conflict?
- What ideological perspectives are covered?
- Do events like the Nanjing Massacre and the atomic bombings of Japan receive special attention? If so how?

The researching subject will also be at liberty to perform critique – within parameters sensitive to cultural difference. Are certain participating countries represented unfairly? How could the situation be changed? How is the under-representation of a particular wartime event or phenomenon unjust and what can be done about it? Why should the victims of a particular episode of the war be remembered? Similarly, why are 'forgotten' in a given context? The researcher must consider 'why' there are differences and similarities across the contexts. To what extent is this a question of, for example, politics and ideology, or tradition? The researcher is thus understood positioned to make qualified yet tentative evaluations. Is the content of the topic in a particular context overly nationalistic or biased? Could a greater variety of perspectives be included? Which important aspects of the war do not appear as an element of the syllabus topic 'core' in each context? And so on.

Stage 5: Comparing 'Outer Circle' Variables with 'Middle Circle' Factors

In constellation analysis 'Outer Circle' variables are understood to exert the greatest influence on the composition of a syllabus topic. Moreover, amidst these variables the researcher may be able to discern a series of 'core' elements – universal to all of the most influential factors. Yet 'Middle Circle' factors are also important and may be fruitfully compared against the syllabus topic 'core'. In Japan, for example, it may be interesting to investigate the presentation of the Second World War in the mass media. In the case of Sweden or England it may be useful to look at Internet sources. Essentially, having identified, analysed and compared the most influential factors, an investigation of 'Middle Circle' factors may enable researchers to discern the pervasiveness of particular perspectives in a given context.

Stage 6: Drawing Conclusions and Making Recommendations

Using constellation analysis the researcher may identify 'what-is-on-the-syllabus' in a given context, making comparisons across contexts and drawing conclusions accordingly. For this reason, results gleaned from conducting constellation analysis are likely to be representative of what is taught in school history in a particular context. Likewise, the results of constellation analysis will allow the researcher to make tentative recommendations. Like Holmes's concept of 'piecemeal social engineering' and King's 'educational decision', the researcher is understood in a position to make recommendations within explicitly specified limits.

8.3 Concluding Comments

In this chapter I have described how to use comparative constellation analysis, presenting it as an alternative to comparative textbook research. Essentially it represents a new approach to comparative enquiries in education. Proceeding through stages the methodology includes its own checks and balances, enabling the researcher to evaluate those variables that are most influential in a given context, and to identify the central elements of a given syllabus topic. As an approach, it is underpinned by the assumption that comparisons may only take place when researchers have already researched the contexts being compared. We cannot assume, therefore, that textbooks or examinations, or the role of teachers and students, have a given meaning across contexts, particularly on the shape and composition of a syllabus topic. Before we even begin to consider comparing 'what-is-on-the-syllabus', we must first identify those factors that impact on the content of the topic and those that do not.

Chapter Nine
Conclusion – Labour, Consciousness and Agency

> ...it is this form of philosophy that, from Hegel, through Nietzsche and Max Weber, to the Frankfurt School, has founded a form of reflection in which I have tried to work.
>
> Michel Foucault, *Politics Philosophy Culture*, 1988, p.95

The relationship between labour and consciousness, class and agency is explored by Hegel in the *Phenomenology*; and by that most famous and radical of all Left Hegelians, Karl Marx.[1] Mind is active, engaging with the task of production. The researcher exercises agency, in the conscious endeavour to contribute to knowledge. Yet the agent – Hegel's bondsman – is constrained by particular material and social relations, as well as rules set by custom and tradition. As the agent struggles with intellectual and material hurdles, periods of doubt and confusion may frequently take hold. But conscious self-realisation on the part of the researcher may come about as their work takes shape as a result of the subject's labours. The self-consciousness and identity of the agent is tied to the work they have created.

This book represents the hermeneutic unfolding of a researcher's self-consciousness as a subject through labour. Indeed, it could even be argued that this development constitutes the book's crux. Essentially, an evolving consciousness of objects by the researching subject consolidates itself, as manifested through its pages. This movement may be understood expressing the dynamic between active mind and this researcher's engagement with objects as an agent through time. Interactions with new objects demand conceptualisation. Yet with each new conceptualisation mind is itself transformed anew, which directly affects future engagements with objects, including those that were experienced or constructed in the researcher's past. With the development of consciousness the researcher arrives at new perspectives that transform understandings of the past and of what it means to exist in the present. In turn, this affects the researcher's plans for future action as an agent and researching subject.

This book, as I have observed, is a synthesis. In it and through it I have charted the components of a methodological system to enable the comparison of a syllabus

---

1   G. W. F. Hegel, *Phenomenology of Mind* (London, George Alien & Unwin, 1966). K. Marx, *Early Writings* (London, Penguin, 1992).

topic in school history across contexts, using the Second World War as an exemplar topic. Essentially, the system is based in the philosophy of Hegel, emerging from a preceding thesis and antithesis. In my work I attempt to chart a distinctive approach to making comparisons; we compare not 'things in themselves' but relationships and effects. Essentially, the book is grounded in the relationship between theory and experience, the ideal and the material, mind and praxis. As a document it brings together the key elements of a journey, from past to present, over a decade of work, suggesting futures, expressed in the initiatives of this researcher as an agent, and interpreted from the conceptual platform of consciousness in the present.

I have been guided by two essential research questions: 1. How is it possible to compare syllabus topics as objects in school history education across cultures? 2. How do the limits of the researching subject affect possibilities for meaningful comparisons? The answers to these questions unfolded with the chapters. History education is complex. To understand it requires an in depth knowledge of contexts and situations. Before the context of a given history education is understood it is not possible to go about comparing. What I hope I have provided is a step by step approach, a methodology for identifying and comparing syllabus topics across cultures in a robust and systematic way.

'Education' writes Broadfoot, 'is a powerful and potentially dangerous tool. We dare not leave its core assumptions unchallenged. As an academic community we have a duty to use our skills, to reveal current realities'.[2] In this spirit, a central aim of my research has been to provide a platform from which it becomes possible to engage critically with the various manifestations of a syllabus topic. To do so requires an in-depth understanding of history education(s) as well as an understanding of our subjective limits. The description of differences across contexts, although necessary, is understood to be little more than a preliminary exercise. Thus, having described and compared differences we contribute to dialogue by forging a critical perspective on the differences. Perspectives will necessarily be open to attack. Yet based in reason, a new perspective will deserve a robust defence. Ultimately, the clash of perspectives has the potential to lead to new syntheses.

The development of a 'critical' or 'left' hermeneutics, it should be noted, is not to identify hermeneutics with critical theory. Critical theory, via Marxism, is grounded in a reading of Enlightenment reason synonymous with faith. All capitalist societies are conceived as the legitimate target of a particular form of

---

2   P. Broadfoot, 'Editorial: structure and agency in education: the role of comparative education', *Comparative Education*, 2002, 38 1, pp.5–6.

critique, the knowing subject understood without limits, positioned to critically engage with all contexts, history education the expression of capitalist ideology in all cases. As we saw in Chapter Four, practitioners of hermeneutics reject this position. Nevertheless, driven by a leftist concern for justice, a critical hermeneutics would stand opposed to the 'unbelieving' nihilism characteristic of post-modernity thinking. Metaphorically speaking, it may be useful to see left hermeneutics positioned somewhere between agnosticism and faith.

Categories used by critical theorists can be embraced within limits. There is a place for exposing the injustices of a particular perspective on a given topic in school history in a context. But critique is only meaningful when the researcher possesses an in depth understanding of the context under scrutiny. Likewise, collective agency may provide an important way forward. A united front composed of researchers or teachers or students from both outside and inside the context under scrutiny may defy nationalist approaches to a given syllabus topic. Yet collective agency, praxis, must be understood as necessarily limited. In other words, by forging a critical perspective on a syllabus topic we cannot decide to speak for everyone. For critical theorists, collective agency assumes the 'limitless' identification of an entire class – the particular will of individual agents significantly reduced. From the position of left hermeneutics, on the other hand, collective agency requires an in depth understanding of subjects. Only by using argument and reason and political will, can agents combine forces in their attack on the injustices identified with a particular perspective, on, for example, World War II, prevalent in the school history of a given context.

The generic dynamic underpinning every element of my work is the philosophy of Hegel. Gadamer's ideas are implicitly Hegelian and may be used to reinterpret Bereday. Foucault's power/knowledge dialectic may be conceptualised anew in the context of a resurrected subject. Holmes and King are usefully understood as the two halves of an Hegelian dynamic that spiral towards Weber's concept of ideal types and Adorno's concept of constellations. Using Hegel, syllabus topics may be located as concepts in the midst of circular and dialectical relationships with influencing variables or parts that together in a given context form a constellation. Even the dynamic underpinning this researcher's intellectual development – from thesis, through antithesis, to synthesis – may be conceptualised along Hegelian lines. Hegel is understood as casting a long shadow over the contemporary age. And it is for this same reason that Foucault becomes the paramount philosopher of the age; his re-engagement with Hegel enabling him to look not just 'between' modernity and post-modernity but to a new space 'beyond' the oppositions.

A Hegelian thesis is never static. It moves. It is dynamic. For the final result is nothing more than the start of something new. In this book, the grounds and procedures for comparative constellation analysis as a method have been explored. On one level, the method is an empirical enterprise requiring experience of contexts. On another level, it is an explicitly rational undertaking in that it attempts to systematically comprehend the relationships that constitute syllabus topics in and across cultures. But essentially, by outlining the parameters of subjective agency, and by providing a robust approach to identifying objects amidst complex contexts, it represents a means to conducting cross-cultural critique that is, at the same time, sensitive to cross-cultural difference.

A new thesis represents only a symbolic beginning, since it is the outcome of prior struggles. A thesis is in fact a synthesis. Yet syntheses are theses just as they arrive on the scene and, in this sense, appear elevated. Syntheses are theses 'flying high' as yet undiminished by antitheses. Rising up to survey new horizons the concept of the old thesis appears small, diminished and insignificant, next to the euphoric glow of spirit in its latest form.

Index

Adorno, Theodor, 27, 37, 50, 122, 126
  and Weber, 268
  constellations, 29, 267, 287
Althusser, Louis, 45, 83
Argentina, 87
Bangladesh, 87
Baudrillard, Jean, 92, 93
Bereday, George, 27, 47, 48, 115, 147,
  148, 149, 152, 156, 164
Bleicher, Josef, 108
Blunkett, David, 239
Bourdieu, Pierre, 86
Carr, Edward H., 100
Central and Eastern Europe, 88
China, 87
Churchill, Winston, 66, 67, 250
comparative education
  and epistemology, 70
  critical theory, 45
comparative educational research, 69
Comte, Auguste, 76, 93. See Positivism
Constellation analysis, 255, 264, 266
  background and tradition, 200
  censorship, 214, 229, 248
  classroom media, 256, 258
  contemporary politics and
    ideology, 216, 259
  England, 262
  examinations and assessment, 200,
    201, 206, 224, 240
  historiography, 140, 186, 219
  horizontal comparisons, 274
  internet access, 209, 226

Japan, 224, 225
  mass media, 202
  middle circle variables, 266
  outer circle variables, 269, 272, 275
  prescribed curriculum, 200, 201,
    205, 223
  Sweden, 224, 225
  syllabus topics, 117
  teacher/student role, 202, 259
  textbooks, 224, 264
  tradition, 224
  vertical comparisons, 275
Constellation dynamics, 138
  and hermeneutic tradition, 108
Constellation mapping, 36, 198, 201,
  255, 265
Cowen, Robert, 98
critical theory, 41, 80
  comparisons from a critical theory
    perspective, 84
  consciousness, 83
  history from a critical theory
    perspective, 88
  implications of critical theory for
    comparing syllabus topics in
    history education, 90
  subjects and objects, 82
  truth, 81
Cuba, 87
Dahrendorf, Ralf, 180
Deleuze, Gilles, 41, 92, 126
Derrida, Jaques, 41, 92
Dewey, John, 173, 182

Dilthey, Wilhelm, 43, 110, 116
Durkheim, Emile. *See* Positivism
educational research
  and philosophical issues, 70
  postmodern perspectives in, 45
empirical social science, 77
Engels, Friedrich, 41, 80, 83
England
  Assessment and Qualifications
    Alliance (AQA), 242
  background and tradition, 236
  Baker, Kenneth, 238
  BBC Schools Online, 244
  Bearing Review, 60
  censorship, 248
  classroom media, 243
  contemporary politics and
    ideology, 248
  digital media, 61
  examinations and assessment, 60,
    62, 240, 263
  Freedom House, 246
  GCE, 242
  historiography, 249
  history textbooks, 26, 61, 135
  internet access, 244
  Margaret Thatcher, 59, 238, 252
  mass media, 63, 245
  National Curriculum, 26, 59, 62, 118,
    135, 236, 255, 263, 273, 275, 277
  Office for Standards in Education
    (Ofsted), 247
  prescribed curriculum, 237
  Qualifications and Curriculum
    Authority (QCA), 60, 241
  socio-economic inequities, 61
  Standard Attainment Test (SAT),
    240
  student-centred approaches, 62
  teacher/student role, 62, 246
  Thatcherism, 62
  World War II as syllabus topic,
    118, 135
Enlightenment, 41, 43, 74, 79, 80, 92,
  103, 105, 109, 111, 119, 120, 122,
  124, 125, 126, 128, 131, 286
Foucault, Michel, 27, 42, 43, 46, 92,
  95, 108, 120, 121, 122, 123, 124,
  125, 126, 128, 136, 143, 171, 185,
  187, 268, 280
  archaeology and genealogy
    periods, 133
  genealogical method, 42
  hermeneutics, 27
  ontology of the present, 130
  power/knowledge, 35, 42, 287
  pseudo-paradigmatic epistemes,
    100
  theory of power, 126
Frankfurt School, 43, 45, 49, 80, 120,
  122, 123, 124, 128, 129, 180
Fukuyama, Francis, 107
Gadamer, Hans-Georg, 108, 115, 116,
  117, 119, 128, 148, 157, 164
  Truth and Method, 110, 117
Gates, Bill, 61
GCSE, 60, 237, 239, 240, 242, 277
Germany, 66, 68, 87, 229, 232
  Brandt, Willy, 220
Giddens, Anthony, 41, 75
Google, 227
Gramsci, Antonio, 86
Habermas, Jurgen, 105, 129
Hegel, Georg Wilhelm Friedrich, 37,
  42, 50, 88, 89, 110, 116, 285, 286
  modernist readings of, 40

Phenomenology, 40
Philosophy of Mind, 40
Heidegger, Martin, 112
hermeneutics, 108, 119
    comparisons from a hermeneutic
        perspective, 113
    conception of the subject, 136
    history from a hermeneutic
        perspective, 116
    implications of hermeneutics for
        comparing syllabus topics, 117
    synthesis, 171
historiography, 63
history textbooks, 33
    as centred objects, 51
    as de-centred objects, 51
    meaning and purpose, 271
Hitler, Adolph, 67, 235
Holmes, Brian, 27, 36, 37, 48, 49, 132,
    150, 169, 172, 181, 187, 287
Holocaust, 33, 68
Horkheimer, Max, 122
Ikuhiko Hata, 221
Japan
    Association for the Advancement of
        a Liberalist View of History, 221
    background and tradition, 203
    censorship, 54, 64, 214, 273
    classroom media, 208
    Confucian traditions, 204
    contemporary politics and
        ideology, 216
    digital media, 54, 135
    education in, 52
    education system and the economy, 53
    examination preparation schools, 206
    examinations and assessment, 26,
        53, 206, 263

fascism, 63
historiography, 219
history curriculum, 53
history textbooks, 26, 31, 32, 53,
    54, 135, 263
internet access, 209
Japan Broadcasting Corporation
    (the NHK), 211
Liberal Democratic Party
    (LDP), 204
mass media, 55, 210
Ministry of Education, 64, 204,
    205, 214
modernist school, 63
nationalism, 56
politics, 55
prescribed curriculum, 205
relationship with Asia and the
    Unites States, 64
rise of nationalist perspectives in
    history writing, 64
role in World War II, 31, 55, 64
rote learning, 53, 62
school history education, 53
teacher/student role, 212
teachers unions, 30, 63, 205
US occupation, 215
World War II, 32, 63
World War II as syllabus topic,
    118, 135
Jay, Martin, 123
journals, 39
Juku. See Japan:examination
    preparation schools
Jullien, Marc-Antoine, 76
Kandel, L., 97
Kanji Nishio, 221
Kant, Immanuel, 30

King, Edmund, 27, 36, 37, 48, 49, 132, 159, 164, 169, 172, 188, 287
Kuhn, Thomas, 99
Ienaga Saburo, 64, 216, 220
Lukacs, Georg, 82, 129
Lyotard, Jean-François, 41, 92
Machiavelli, Niccolo, 107
Mallinson, Vernon, 97
Marcuse, Herbert, 81
Marshall, James, 131
Maruyama Masao, 219
Marx, Karl, 41, 80, 83, 89, 107, 119, 129, 285
Marxism, 80, 98, 107, 129
Merleau-Ponty, Maurice, 40, 105
Michael Sadler, 97
modernism
    thesis, 41
Monbusho. See Japan Ministry of Education
Murayama Masao, 63
Nanjing, 31
National Curriculum. *See* England
Nazism, 66, 68
Netherlands, 227
Nicaragua, 87
Nietzsche, Friedrich, 41, 42, 93, 119, 122
Nobokatsu Fujioka, 221
OECD, 75, 77, 152
Ofsted. *See* England
Parsons, Talcott, 74
Paulston, Rolland, 50, 99
phenomenological approach, 98
PISA, 75
Popper, Karl, 48, 49, 173, 179, 187
Positivism, 41, 74
    comparative education, 79

comparisons from a positivist perspective, 75
history from a positivist perspective, 78
implications for making comparisons, 80
implications of positivism for comparing syllabus topics in history education, 79
relationship between politics and knowledge, 80
relationship between subject and object, 80
theory of knowledge / reality, 80
truth, 79
Postmodernism, 32, 35, 92
anti-thesis, 41
comparisons from a postmodern perspective, 94
history from a postmodern perspective, 99
implications of postmodernist perspectives for comparing syllabus topics in history education, 100
phenomenological approach, 98
power, 126
knowledge/power, 130
power/knowledge, 127
pseudo-hermeneutic readings, 106
Qualification and Curriculum Authority (QCA). *See* England
Rose, Gillian, 42, 110, 119
Russia, 67
Sadler, Michael, 97
Said, Edward, 48, 163
schools
arena for class struggle, 87

Second World War. *See* World War II
Senegal, 87
Singer, Peter, 40, 106
Smith, Steven, 106
Soviet Union, 56, 58, 67, 80, 87, 98,
  107, 147, 185, 251, 254
Spain, 227
Sweden
  background and tradition, 222
  censorship, 229
  classroom media, 225
  contemporary education scene, 222
  contemporary education system, 56
  contemporary politics and ideol-
    ogy, 229
  curriculum, 56, 223, 224
  curriculum reform, 224
  decentralisation, 57, 223
  digital media, 58
  education system, 56
  examinations and assessment, 57, 224
  Freedom House, 227
  Goran Persson, 59, 230
  grundskola, 57, 222, 223
  gymnasieskola, 223
  historiography, 232
  history textbooks, 57, 225
  internet access, 226
  Living History Forum, 59, 66, 229,
    230
  mass media, 58, 227
  Ministry of Education, 224
  National Agency for Education,
    58, 225, 227

neutrality, 56, 58, 65, 230
  Per Albin Hansson, 230
  prescribed curriculum, 223
  role in World War II, 65, 66
  Schoolnet, 226
  Swedish Academy, 232, 235
  teacher/student role, 57, 228, 264
  textbook market, 225
  upper secondary education, 223
  welfare policies, 56
syllabus topic, 47, 264, 271
  and constellation analysis, 269
Takeuchi Yoshimi, 64
textbook research, 51
Thatcher, Margaret. *See* England
TIMSS, 75
UNESCO, 75, 77, 85
United Nations, 32
United States, 147, 251
  World War II as syllabus
    topic, 118
von Ranke, Ludwig, 78
Weber, Max, 27, 36
  ideal types, 27, 36, 37, 50
Wikipedia, 227
Williams, Raymond, 86
World War II, 27, 32, 51, 66
  as exemplar topic, 63
  as research topic, 66
  as syllabus topic, 34, 90, 274
  in history education, 33
  in Japanese education, 53
Yoshimoto Takaaki, 64, 219
Zeitgeist, 107

Annex (Obituary Originally Published in St. Cross College, Oxford, Record)

Jason Nicholls, 1968–2011

I first met Jason Nicholls in 1994, when he began his Postgraduate Certificate in Education (PGCE) course at the Institute of Education, University of London. By the time he completed this, in June of 1995, we had become friends; we remained so for the rest of his life.

During my many years as a teacher trainer I worked with several hundred young people, usually in groups ranging in size from 10–20 students. From all of these individuals it was Jason who truly stood out – not only for his excellent teaching skills and his impressive intellect (attributes which in fact many of my students demonstrated) but for his humanity, vibrancy, sense of humour and humility. He was a beacon within his tutor group, admired without exception by his peers, and by my teaching colleagues.

Jason's energies and his fascination with other peoples and cultures took him to an incredible number and range of places following his PGCE; the 'gallery' of postcards in my study at the Institute expanded steadily the longer he was working and travelling abroad, squeezing into a diminishing space the far less appealing circulars and meeting reminders and the odd cartoon from the education press. Jason was both excited and fulfilled by his time abroad (especially, in my perception at least, when he was teaching in Hiroshima for a three-year period).

It was only logical that when Jason was actually in the UK, we drew on his first-hand perspectives of living and working abroad and regularly (or, rather, as regularly as his schedules permitted!) asked him to come in and talk to our beginning teachers on the satisfactions of the kinds of opportunities that were available to them should they be thinking of deferring taking up UK-based posts. Additionally, over a number of years Jason made incredibly positively evaluated inputs at the Institute as a facilitator of workshops for new teachers of the social sciences. (So modest was he, however, that only by showing him actual originals of student evaluation exercises could I persuade him of the impact his workshops had been having on the developing professional practice of their grateful participants).

Although he was a naturally gifted teacher, it was wholly unsurprising to me that in due course I started to be asked for references in connection with Jason's ambitions to begin working on a doctorate. I was delighted to be able to support his successful applications to the Institute of Education and to Oxford; understandably the latter won the day, hence Jason's time at St. Cross, and his achieving his DPhil under the supervision of Professor David Phillips. The research he conducted was of some true significance, and was given publicity both by BBC Radio 4 and by the educational press, in features highlighting contrasting national perspectives in the depiction of World War II. Jason was enormously proud – though never remotely boastful – of his Oxford doctorate; he loved his time at St. Cross, and when I was his guest for hall nights, as I was on several occasions, I was very proud of him, as I think any former tutor would have been.

It was a very happy day for me when Jason obtained his one-year post-doctoral appointment at the Institute. Not only did I feel that now his academic career would really take off, but I could, quite simply, look forward to seeing a great deal more of him. After a promising start, however, the medical condition that had begun to seriously interfere with Jason's health began to have a seriously detrimental effect on him, and he was forced to withdraw from his work when he was not even a third of the way through the year. As the senior colleague with whom Jason was working most closely, Professor David Scott, expressed matters *'he was a very gifted academic who never fulfilled his undoubted potential'*.

Since Jason's death, the tributes that have been paid to him have been both heartfelt and numerous. Cliched as it may well be to put things in such terms, he truly did touch many people's lives in a wholly positive way. He still had a great deal to offer, not only to teaching and research in academia, but to the wider world. At the time of writing, an editor and potential publisher are being sought for Jason's Oxford thesis. In my view, and that of his family, a book based on his very original, and valuable, work would be a highly suitable memorial; it would also complement his already significant body of published work, including School History Textbooks across Cultures: International debates and perspectives (Symposium), which he edited in 2006.

Bryan Cunningham

KOMPARATISTISCHE BIBLIOTHEK
Comparative Studies Series
Bibliothèque d'Etudes Comparatives

herausgegeben von
edited by / dirigée par
Jürgen Schriewer

Bd. / Vol. 1 Jürgen Schriewer & Brian Holmes (eds.): Theories and Methods in Comparative Education. 1988. 3rd edition 1992.

Bd. / Vol. 2 Achim Leschinsky & Karl Ulrich Mayer (eds.): The Comprehensive School Experiment Revisited: Evidence from Western Europe. 1990. 2nd enlarged and updated edition 1999.

Bd. / Vol. 3 Jürgen Schriewer, Edwin Keiner & Christophe Charle (Herausgeber / Directeurs de la publication): Sozialer Raum und akademische Kulturen / A la recherche de l'espace universitaire européen. Studien zur Europäischen Hochschul- und Wissenschaftsgeschichte im 19. und 20. Jahrhundert / Etudes sur l'enseignement supérieur aux XIXe et XXe siècles. 1993.

Bd. / Vol. 4 Val D. Rust, Peter Knost & Jürgen Wichmann (eds.): Education and the Values Crisis in Central and Eastern Europe. 1994.

Bd. / Vol. 5 S. Karin Amos: Alexis de Tocqueville and the American National Identity. The Reception of *De la Démocratie en Amérique* in the United States in the Nineteenth Century. 1994.

Bd. / Vol. 6 Thyge Winther-Jensen (ed.): Challenges to European Education: Cultural Values, National Identities, and Global Responsibilities. 1996.

Bd. / Vol. 7 Anthony Welch: Class, Culture and the State in Australian Education. Reform or Crisis? 1997.

Bd. / Vol. 8 Noel F. McGinn & Erwin H. Epstein (eds.): Comparative Perspectives on the Role of Education in Democratization. Part I: Transitional States and States of Transition. 1999. Part II: Socialization, Identity, and the Politics of Control. 2000.

Bd. / Vol. 9 Hartmut Kaelble & Jürgen Schriewer (Hrsg.): Gesellschaften im Vergleich. Forschungen aus Sozial- und Geschichtswissenschaften. 1998. 2., durchges. Aufl. 1999.

Bd. / Vol. 10 Jürgen Schriewer (ed.): Discourse Formation in Comparative Education. 2000. Second Edition 2003. Third Revised Edition 2009. Fourth Edition 2012.

Bd. / Vol. 11 Gábor T. Rittersporn, Malte Rolf & Jan C. Behrends (Hrsg. / eds.): Sphären von Öffentlichkeit in Gesellschaften sowjetischen Typs. Zwischen partei-staatlicher Selbstinszenierung und kirchlichen Gegenwelten. Public Spheres in Soviet-Type Societies. Between the Great Show of the Party-State and Religious Counter-Cultures. 2003.

Bd. / Vol. 12 Claude Diebolt, Vivien Guiraud & Marielle Monteils: Education, Knowledge, and Economic Growth. France and Germany in the 19th and 20th Centuries. 2003.

Bd. / Vol. 13 Jonas Sprogøe & Thyge Winther-Jensen (eds.): Identity, Education and Citizenship – Multiple Interrelations. 2006.

Bd. / Vol. 14 Eugenia Roldán Vera & Marcelo Caruso (eds.): Imported Modernity in Post-Colonial State Formation. The Appropriation of Political, Educational, and Cultural Models in Nineteenth-Century Latin America. 2007.

Bd. / Vol. 15 Florian Waldow: Ökonomische Strukturzyklen und internationale Diskurskonjunkturen. Zur Entwicklung der schwedischen Bildungsprogrammatik 1930–2000. 2007.

Bd. / Vol. 16 Hartmut Kaelble & Martin Kirsch (Hrsg.): Selbstverständnis und Gesellschaft der Euro-
             päer. Aspekte der sozialen und kulturellen Europäisierung im späten 19. und 20. Jahr-
             hundert. 2008.

Bd. / Vol. 17 Régis Malet: La formation des enseignants comparée. Identité, apprentissage et
             exercice professionnels en France et en Grande-Bretagne. 2008.

Bd. / Vol. 18 Miguel A. Pereyra (ed.): Changing Knowledge and Education. Communities, Mobilities
             and New Policies in Global Societies. 2008.

Bd. / Vol. 19 Marcelo Caruso: Geist oder Mechanik. Unterrichtsordnungen als kulturelle Konstruktio-
             nen in Preußen, Dänemark (Schleswig-Holstein) und Spanien 1800-1870. 2010.

Bd. / Vol. 20 Patrick Ressler: Nonprofit-Marketing im Schulbereich. Britische Schulgesellschaften und
             der Erfolg des Bell-Lancaster-Systems der Unterrichtsorganisation im 19. Jahrhundert.
             2010.

Bd. / Vol. 21 Markus Maurer: Skill Formation Regimes in South Asia. A Comparative Study on the
             Path-Dependent Development of Technical and Vocational Education and Training for
             the Garment Industry. 2011.

Bd. / Vol. 22 Jason Beech: Global Panaceas, Local Realities. International Agencies and the Future
             of Education. 2011.

Bd. / Vol. 23 Jeremy Rappleye: Educational Policy Transfer in an Era of Globalization: Theory – His-
             tory – Comparison. 2012.

Bd. / Vol. 24 Tavis Deryck Jules: Neither World Polity nor Local or National Societies. Regionalization
             in the Global South – the Carribean Community. 2012.

Bd. / Vol. 25 Cristina Alarcón: Modelltransfer im Schatten des Krieges. „Deutsche" Bildungs- und
             „Preußische" Militärreformen in Chile, 1879-1920. 2014.

Bd. / Vol. 26 Jason Nicholls: Constellation Analysis. A Methodology for Comparing Syllabus Topics
             Across Educational Contexts. Edited by Bryan Cunningham. 2014

www.peterlang.com